GOD IN THEY TRUST?

THE RELIGIOUS BELIEFS
OF AUSTRALIA'S PRIME MINISTERS
1901-2013

GOD IN THEY TRUST?

THE RELIGIOUS BELIEFS
OF AUSTRALIA'S PRIME MINISTERS
1901-2013

ROY WILLIAMS

BIBLE
SOCIETY
Live light

BIBLE
SOCIETY
Live light

In God They Trust?
Published May 2013
Copyright © Roy T Williams

Bible Society Australia
GPO Box 9874
In Your Capital City
Phone: 1300 BIBLES (1300 242 537)
www.biblesociety.org.au

National Library of Australia
ISBN: 978-0-647-51855-7

Designed and typesetting by Lankshear Design.

The king's heart is in the hands of the Lord;
He directs it like a watercourse wherever he pleases.
Proverbs 21:1

For my father, Evan Williams,
the fairest and most eloquent political commentator
I have known.

CONTENTS

FOREWORD

In his autobiography, my father wrote: "In our secular age, biographers rarely give a person's spiritual life the attention it deserves. Usually it is hard to trace. Few Australian politicians flaunt their core beliefs." Roy Williams is filling this void. It is important that he do so. Australians are notoriously uncomfortable with spirituality. However, just as there are few atheists in foxholes in battles, their numbers diminish in politics around election time. More important, not knowing something about what may be held in the deepest corner of a leading politician's mind is to miss a crucial influence on key policy.

My father was fascinated with the spirituality of two politicians, Alfred Deakin and John Curtin. He was interested in Deakin because he was so influential in Australia's federation. More to the point, he was an authentic representative of late 19th century spirituality. He moved from a fascination with theosophy, through a deep Christianity, ultimately to Buddhism. Dad knew little of the latter. He did see Deakin's circumspection as typical of an Australian reticence among politicians to talk about religious convictions. Deakin's private writings are what give us a clue to his convictions.

John Curtin, who was without doubt one of our greatest Prime Ministers, was different. Dad succeeded him in Parliament and was familiar himself with many of the people with whom Curtin engaged on matters spiritual. They were dad's friends too and he consulted them for the published work he did on Curtin.

Curtin's was a journey many Christians make. His Catholicism lapsed in his young years though his wife practised. His press secretary Fred McLaughlin was a member of the Moral Rearmament movement and deeply Christian. He sought spiritual counsel too from Rev. Hec Harrison, who was the minister at St Andrew's Presbyterian Church. At Curtin's request he conducted his funeral – a wish that Curtin made clear was his own to avoid trouble for his wife in her church.

What brought Curtin to a faith was proximity to those with one - and, more important, need. Curtin worried deeply with a sense of helplessness about the fate of Australian soldiers. Overwrought, and in extremity with the seventh division on the high seas, he and McLaughlin went on their knees in prayer with the conviction there was nothing else they could do. My father wrote of Curtin, "Though Curtin never lost his distrust of religious institutions, faith grew within him – faith that he was not alone with the burdens of office, that his job was to do the best he could and to treat everyone as Christ would have treated them."

It is not the Australian style to wear your heart on your sleeve in politics. It is also a secular style. Reticence is a product of factors that come at the issue from opposite directions. On the one hand is a tradition in politics that is secular and is suspicious of religious commitment. We are not a church-going nation. On the other is a concern that as a Christian in politics, one should not claim Jesus as a source for a policy. One fears getting between someone who cannot identify with a policy and therefore may get denied an experience of the cross if he/she feels that seeking one may involve commitments in policy they cannot share. Seeking Christ as a saviour has little to do with planning a health-care policy. It may have something to do with your personal sense of compassion. That, however, is for you, not for flinging in someone's face.

Most of our Prime Ministers would share Churchill's response to a flatterer. The enthusiast called Churchill a "pillar of the Anglican church". Churchill demurred, "A flying buttress perhaps."

In the end, Australian Prime Ministers are much like the people they lead. Were they not, they would not lead them. Unless a Prime Minister has actively rejected the notion of a deity and views their social responsibilities in a humanist context, they like their fellow Australians will retain in a corner of their minds the possibility of a spiritual source of help and possibly a broader point of accounting than an electorate.

My father once wrote, "The thoughts of God, given primacy in the life of a man, bring to the innermost motives the virtue of mercy and with it a cure for hatred that can turn the tide of history. That is the essence of intelligent statesmanship." Roy Williams is examining statesmanship at its most complex but perhaps deepest source.

HE the Honourable Kim Beazley AC
Ambassador to the United States of America
26 April 2013

INTRODUCTION

Australians today exhibit a scant respect for politicians and a slender understanding of Christianity. What on earth does it matter, many might wonder, that "Honest Joe" Lyons believed in God? Or that Edmund Barton (probably) did not? Of what possible relevance are Alfred Deakin's views on the doctrine of the Atonement, or Ben Chifley's about the hierarchy of the Catholic Church? Such scepticism must be anticipated in this age of "potent dualism"[1], in which many people seem eager to consign religion to the strictly private realm. A vocal minority tries to discourage it altogether.

Yet certain facts cannot be disputed. Australia is a splendid country in which to live – democratic, prosperous, and relatively free of violence. The plight of the Indigenous aside, to say that we have been uniquely blessed in human history is scarcely to exaggerate. For this state of affairs our Prime Ministers surely deserve some credit – perhaps a great deal – since under Australia's Westminster system of government the Prime Minister has always wielded huge influence. In today's era of concentrated executive power, his or her personal belief-system matters more than ever.

And consider the psychological factor. A person of active religious faith – in particular, a monotheist who truly believes that they will answer in the afterlife for their conduct on earth – cannot help but be guided by a sense of providence or mission. Their mindset *must* be different from that of a person who is convinced, or assumes, that this world is all that there is. Alfred Deakin was the prime example of the former; Harold Holt of the latter. They are the two extremes, but Holt's languid agnosticism was quite atypical.

Almost all our Prime Ministers thought long and hard about God. A majority attended church schools or had at least one fervently Christian parent. Two were the sons of Protestant clergymen. Four were Sunday school teachers and three others were lay preachers. Several lived in families riven or infected by anti-Catholic prejudice. Many enjoyed close relationships with leading churchmen or theologians of their day – both Australian and foreign. Six married women whom they met at church or through church activities.

The modern tendency has been to downplay or dismiss the faith of our past leaders. Sir Robert Menzies, for example, was categorised recently by one commentator as merely a "nominal" Christian.[2] Billy McMahon was described by another as "at least as disconnected [as Menzies] from any Christian tradition".[3] John Curtin and Gough Whitlam have been labelled as atheists, and Billy Hughes as "a humanist who rejected religious belief".[4] In my judgment, all of those assessments are mistaken. In general, our Prime Ministers have been more spiritually-minded than the people they led. I have come to agree wholeheartedly with an observation of the late Kim Beazley Senior*: "In our secular age, biographers rarely give a person's spiritual life the attention it deserves".[5]

If we accept that religious feeling is a key determinant of personal behaviour, it follows that anyone interested in Australian history or public policy ought to know what our leaders believed about God, particularly during their terms in office. The record shows that their decision-making was often affected by their faith, and not merely as regards matters patently "moral" or "spiritual": abortion, State aid to religious schools, family law, the death penalty, euthanasia and so on. It extended to the perennial issues of practical politics: the distribution of wealth, war and peace, and the recognition and enforcement of human rights.

I will touch on these issues throughout this book. Although my main focus of attention will be each leader's metaphysical worldview, it is hopelessly artificial to try to separate beliefs from conduct – both individual and political. "Faith without deeds is dead" (James 2:26). What people do

---

* Life-long Protestant Christian, Labor MHR for Fremantle (1945-77), and minister for education in the Whitlam government (1972-75).

is a crucial guide to what they truly believe, and Prime Ministers are no different. That said, a person can still have faith even if his or her deeds are open to serious criticism. As the Swiss theologian Karl Barth* insisted, the Bible is not a statute enforceable by human judges. God is the Lord of His Word. The task of each individual is to respond to its "purpose or direction" in accordance with their conscience.[6]

I would argue that Christianity has played a positive role in shaping Australia's broadly egalitarian ethos. Disparities of wealth and income – while significant – have never been as pronounced in Australia as in, say, Britain or the United States. The existence of a strong trade union movement has been a key factor, and the fact that each wave of immigration in the 19th and 20th centuries brought people seeking an escape from poverty and oppression. But it undoubtedly helped that the Labor Prime Ministers were, without exception:

- Protestant Christian socialists or from that tradition – Andrew Fisher, Billy Hughes, Kevin Rudd;
- practising Catholics who had imbibed social justice teachings** as part of their faith – James Scullin, Ben Chifley, Paul Keating;
- sympathisers with Christianity who have been raised in the faith as children or who maintained a keen interest in religion – Chris Watson, John Curtin, Gough Whitlam, Bob Hawke, Julia Gillard. (Some readers may be surprised to see Whitlam and Gillard in this company, but I will seek to support this argument in due course.)

---

* Karl Barth (1886-1968) was one of the finest Protestant theologians of the 20th century. His most famous work, *Church Dogmatics*, was published in 1932. In 1935 Barth was expelled from Germany by the Nazis.
** In very broad terms, the Vatican argued for a compassionate middle ground between the materialist excesses of laissez-faire capitalism on the one hand and of command-and-control totalitarianism (fascism or communism) on the other. The relevant papal encyclicals were Leo XIII's *Rerum Novarum* (1891) and Pius XI's *Quadragesimo Anno* (1931) and *Divini Redemptoris* (1937). In the wake of the Global Financial Crisis, Benedict XVI returned to the same themes in *Caritas in Veritae* (2009). It is noteworthy that B.A. Santamaria (1915-98), Australia's most prominent Catholic intellectual of the 20th century and the founder of the Democratic Labor Party (DLP) in 1956, regarded capitalism and communism as twin enemies – and, of the two, he nominated capitalism as the greater enemy.

One thing may be stated with certainty. With varying degrees of competence and integrity, all of our Labor Prime Ministers *tried* to improve the lot of the less fortunate in society. One is reminded of a wise observation of Franklin D. Roosevelt, made on June 27, 1936 in his speech accepting the Democratic Party's renomination for the American presidency:

> Governments can err, Presidents do make mistakes, but the immortal Dante* tells us that divine justice weighs the sins of the cold-blooded and the sins of the warm-hearted in different scales. Better the occasional faults of a government that lives in a spirit of charity than the consistent omissions of a government frozen in the ice of its own indifference.

The ameliorating influence of Christianity has also been apparent on the Coalition side of politics. Almost all of Australia's non-Labor Prime Ministers were practising, or at least cultural Christians, and the only two lifelong agnostics – Edmund Barton and Harold Holt – had a benevolent side. With the strange exception of Joseph Cook (who defected from Labor before Federation), and the partial exception of S.M. Bruce (who became something of a dreamy idealist after leaving office), none were uncritical worshippers of the market.

Barton and Deakin were progressive protectionists who relied on Labor support. Every member of Australian society, Deakin believed, was "entitled to be considered, not as a cog-wheel in a machine, but as a living human being, endowed with an immortal soul".[7] George Reid believed something similar. Though a fulsome anti-socialist, he led quite an enlightened government in NSW before Federation. As stern a left-wing critic as Manning Clark approved of him as "a liberal with a belief in the use of the state to secure material well-being for all and in a career open to talent".[8] Likewise Billy Hughes. Even after his defection from the ALP in 1916, Hughes never totally forgot his humble origins – he was ousted from

---

* Dante Alighieri (1265-1321) was the author of *The Divine Comedy*, an epic poem about Hell, Purgatory and Paradise. I would point out here that in St Matthew's Gospel the people who suffer in Hell are generally those who enjoyed good fortune on Earth, but who mistreated, exploited or neglected the poor and the weak.

the Nationalist leadership in 1923 and replaced by Bruce for, among other things, the perceived "socialist nature of his policy".[9]

It was only during the mid to late 1920s that capitalism in Australia (and overseas) remained comparatively unrestrained. Disparities of wealth and income rose sharply, as did levels of societal unrest, before the voters stepped in as "avenging angels".[10] Billy Hughes was delighted when the Bruce-Page government of which he had been a member was thrashed at the polls in October 1929 ("a veritable triumph for the people"[11]).

But then came the Great Depression. Labor floundered and for 38 of the next 50 years – until the transformative Hawke-Keating era – Australia was led by a second series of fiscally moderate non-Labor Prime Ministers. All but Harold Holt were deeply influenced by Christianity. Joseph Lyons, another Labor defector, had a sensitive social conscience derived from Catholicism. Robert Menzies, for all his anti-socialist rhetoric, was at heart a puritan: he nursed an old-fashioned barrister's distaste for "money-grubbers" and the big end of town. Policy-wise he was a moderate Keynesian. So, also, were John Gorton, Billy McMahon (if rather less so than the others – he was firmly anti-tariff) and Malcolm Fraser.

John Howard was the outlier in this regard, swayed as he was by the neo-liberal examples of British Prime Minister Margaret Thatcher (1979-90), US President Ronald Reagan (1981-89) and their successors and imitators across the West. Sometime in the 1980s neo-liberalism became conventional wisdom. Even so, at least in government, Howard was less ideologically extreme than some of his Liberal Party colleagues. He once professed to having a "social justice streak" inherited from his childhood Methodism.[12] Indeed, Manning Clark's description of George Reid could equally apply to Howard.

But how, it might justly be asked, can a Prime Minister's religious beliefs be ascertained with confidence? In the case of three of the seven who are still alive – Whitlam, Howard and Rudd – I have had the benefit of one-on-one discussions. Otherwise it has been necessary to scour the public record – speeches, autobiographies, biographies, church and private documents, newspaper articles, obituaries – and to talk with knowledgeable third parties. Menzies' daughter, Heather Henderson, was especially gracious and helpful.

Of course, a degree of caution must be exercised. It is hazardous to be dogmatic about the content and sincerity of anyone else's faith. Ultimately, faith is a personal thing: only *you* know for sure what is in your heart, and only God sees our every step (Job 34:21). But, for an outsider, I suggest a few useful rules of thumb. Actions – church-going, Bible-reading, evangelism, charitable works, peace-making, humility, piety, kindness – speak louder than words. And words written or spoken *in private* are more likely to be reliable than those for public consumption. That said, public professions of faith are far from worthless, provided they are understood in historical context.

For much of the 20th century it was electorally advantageous for a politician in Australia to be associated with Protestantism. For a non-Labor politician of ambition, it was almost essential. Labor's historic relationship with the Catholic Church was more problematic: until the 1970s sectarianism was rife, and Catholics were a distrusted minority. To be labelled a "tyke" or a "mick" or a "papist" was often a barrier to advancement in the professions, and in some government departments as well.

To be clear: there are important theological differences between Catholicism and Protestantism and respectful discussion of those differences is to be encouraged. But hateful bigotry must be deplored. J.D. Pringle, writing in 1958, expressed this view:

> Anti-Catholic feeling is extremely strong in Australia. From time
> to time it bursts like lava from a sleeping volcano, burning and
> destroying everything it touches. The fire is kept alive in the
> Protestant Churches and Masonic Lodges, many of which are
> dominated from men descended from Ulster, but once allowed
> to escape it is inclined to sweep with it a very large proportion of
> the population who have no religious views at all.[13]

It should also be remembered that there was such a thing as *anti-Protestant* sectarianism. B.A. Santamaria was a notable practitioner of this art. He once railed in print against the "bankruptcy of Protestantism", the "herd of bigots in Scotland and Northern Ireland" and "respectable Protestant parsons who had lost any reason they ever had for being anything in particular".[14]

In recent decades the situation has changed – and, as I shall argue, a good deal of the credit must go to our non-sectarian Prime Ministers from

James Scullin onwards. Today, on the Coalition side, Catholicism is fine. But Christian affiliation, while useful, is no longer essential.

On the Labor and Greens side it may now be a handicap. Not so much with the broader citizenry as among many party stalwarts and opinion-makers on the secular Left. By way of example, consider the qualified endorsement of Kevin Rudd in 2007 by an early biographer, Robert Macklin. After lauding Rudd as "the man for our time" he continued:

> Up close, he exudes decency, humour and an unforced charm. Beneath the glitter of high intelligence he has a core of decency and a 'moral compass' that should ensure high standards of probity in any administration that he leads.

But then Macklin felt compelled to add:

> That the [moral] compass is actuated by his religious beliefs remains, in my view, unfortunate. No one should close off an avenue of inquiry, as he did, aged only 17, when he decided he was 'a person of faith'.

Macklin consoled himself with the thought that "[Rudd's] approach to public policy is not motivated by any great attachment to ancient creeds but rather the ideals he learnt at his mother's knee – duty of care for others and hatred of war foremost among them".[15]

This was patronising, to a bizarre degree, and marred an otherwise thoughtful book. It does not seem to have occurred to Macklin that Rudd might have remained open to "inquiry" since the age of 17. Nor that Rudd might have taken a very different view to Macklin of his own motivations. Nor that Rudd's mother's ideals were themselves the product of her staunch Catholicism. Nor – dare I say it – that Rudd's beliefs might be well-founded.

I have conducted my investigations with all these thoughts in mind. Every individual story is of interest. These were 23 eminent and intelligent people, elected by their colleagues and (in most cases) by millions of their fellow citizens. They are a good cross-section of every shade of Christian adherence and existential doubt.

Certain general points emerged. Intriguingly, Australia has never been led by an observant, cradle-to-grave Anglican. Among believers, the ranks have been dominated by Catholics, Presbyterians and Non-Conformists. On the Labor side, Andrew Fisher remains the only lifelong Protestant to have held Prime Ministerial office. And if Tony Abbott reaches the Lodge he will be the first Catholic to do so from the Liberal Party.

Another notable fact: no genuine atheist has ever been Prime Minister. For reasons I will seek to explain, Julia Gillard does not belong in the "atheist" category. Yet in recent decades atheists have come to comprise a not insignificant percentage of the population. Is atheism still a step too far for many Australian voters? Perhaps, though there have been several atheists among Leaders of the Opposition. One of the most vehement – John Latham (Nationalist, 1929-31) – was on the conservative side, and his namesake on the Labor side – Mark Latham (Labor, 2003-05) – has often been categorised as an atheist too. (In fact Mark Latham is an agnostic leaning towards belief, or was in 2004 when he told a biographer that "I think there's something else, a world beyond the material world ... a spiritual dimension which in my life I've not been able to accurately define ... in terms of organised religion."[16])

If atheism has always been exceptional in Australia, the same cannot be said of agnosticism. As the Anglican academic Tom Frame has cogently argued[17], there have always been large numbers of agnostics across the population. Today, it is probably the majority position. It is therefore quite remarkable that there have only been two lifelong agnostics among our 23 Prime Ministers – and arguably only one, Harold Holt, if Edmund Barton is categorised as an Anglican.

One or two out of 23 constitutes a tiny percentage. It becomes even tinier if we count the four "stop-gap" Prime Ministers who served terms measurable in weeks: Earle Page (Country Party, three weeks in 1939), Arthur Fadden (Country Party, five weeks in 1941), Frank Forde (Labor, one week in 1945) and John McEwen (Country Party, three weeks in 1967-68). For the record, Page was a Methodist, Forde a Catholic, and Fadden and McEwen Presbyterians.

Our Prime Ministers can be grouped into eight broad categories. To some extent these are artificial, but they serve to highlight the various religious "types" who have directed the nation's affairs since Federation.

•   •   •

THE GOOD AND FAITHFUL SERVANTS

- Andrew Fisher (1908-09, 1910-13, 1914-15)
- James Scullin (1929-32)
- Joseph Lyons (1932-39)

Each of these thoroughly admirable men was born into the Christian faith and married a woman from the same denomination. None was a theologian of any note, but each adhered assiduously to his church's tenets – or sought to. Only one of them, Fisher, was a Protestant. Scullin and Lyons were Catholics, and, at the height of the Great Depression, they fought the December 1931 election. In retrospect, that election can be seen as marking the beginning of the long and tortuous process whereby religious sectarianism was (more or less) eradicated from Australian society. Fittingly, and not coincidentally, Joseph Lyons was a key figure. His wife Enid (née Burrell) converted from Methodism to Catholicism prior to their marriage, in circumstances to which I will come. On May 8, 1938, both Lyons and Scullin attended the laying of the foundation stone of the new St Christopher's Catholic Church in Canberra, where they both became parishioners.

THE ARDENT SEEKERS

- Alfred Deakin (1903-04, 1905-08, 1909-10)
- Billy McMahon (1971-72)
- Kevin Rudd (2007-10)

All three of these men were university-educated and spoke and wrote extensively about their faith. Each of their spiritual journeys was different, but they had one major trait in common: a genuine passion for theology. Deakin was the most prolific author and the most unorthodox in his beliefs. He was an exceptionally intelligent and well-read man. So is Rudd. McMahon, though not in their league, should not be underestimated in either capacity. Both Rudd and McMahon moved from Catholicism to Anglicanism, and were accused by their opponents – within and outside their own parties – of using "religion" for political advantage. In my judgment the charge was largely unfair in both cases.

THE RIGHTEOUS STRAIGHTENERS

- Joseph Cook (1913-14)
- Billy Hughes (1915-23)
- John Howard (1996-2007)

All three of these men were theologically orthodox. But they held a determinedly Old Testament view of the world. These were tough, resourceful characters who rose from hard-scrabble, lower-middle class origins and expected others to do the same. They did not readily feel pity. Unloved by many of their colleagues and despised by their opponents, they commanded respect and clung doggedly to power. Though mostly upright in their personal conduct, they understood the darker side of the Australian character and were not above exploiting it. They waged war. Both Cook and Howard moved away from the kindly brand of Methodism to which they had been exposed in their youth. Only Hughes had a discernible sense of humour – though of a sardonic, biting sort.

THE MORE-THAN-TRIBAL CATHOLICS

- Ben Chifley (1945-49)
- Paul Keating (1991-96)

The parallels between Chifley and Keating are striking. Both were raised in devout Irish-Catholic families and attended modestly-endowed Catholic schools. Both joined the workforce in their mid-teens. Both advanced by hard work and wide reading, before devoting themselves to the Labor movement. Both served long and distinguished stints as federal Treasurer under a strong Labor leader (Curtin, Hawke), before assuming the top job. Both secured one famous election victory in their own right (1946, 1993) before suffering a heavy and galling defeat the next time around – to a man who would become a Liberal Party icon (Menzies in 1949, Howard in 1996). Both are too frequently dismissed as mere "tribal" or "cultural" Catholics. The weight of the evidence establishes that both of them were deeply religious.

THE ENIGMATIC PRESBYTERIANS

- George Reid (1904-05)
- Robert Menzies (1939-41, 1949-66)
- Malcolm Fraser (1975-83)

Each of these men was born into a proudly Presbyterian family. However, none wore his heart on his sleeve – in public, at least. Down the years questions have been raised as to the nature and sincerity of their personal faith. It has been frequently charged or hinted, especially by critics from the left, that they were mere "formal" Christians and essentially areligious. In Menzies' case, in my view, this notion is quite wrong. Reid and Fraser are more complicated studies. I note here that Fraser's grandfather, Sir Simon Fraser (1832-1919), was Reid's "closest and most reliable personal friend".[18]

LABOR'S LAPSED?

- John Curtin (1941-45)
- Bob Hawke (1983-91)
- Julia Gillard (2010-)

Each of these three Labor Prime Ministers was exposed to extensive Christian teaching in childhood. Hawke's faith lasted until his early twenties and Curtin's until his early teens. It is not clear to me whether Julia Gillard was ever a Christian, but she had certainly renounced any faith by her late teens. All three substituted the Labor movement for the Church. The key questions are: (i) why each of them lost their childhood faith (if any), (ii) whether Curtin regained his faith before he died, and (iii) whether there is any serious prospect of Hawke and/or Gillard regaining theirs. It is interesting that, of the six past Prime Ministers still living, Bob Hawke has been by far the most supportive of Julia Gillard – certainly in public and, one imagines, in private as well.

THE FELLOW-TRAVELLERS

- Chris Watson (1904)
- Stanley Melbourne Bruce (1923-29)
- John Gorton (1968-71)
- Gough Whitlam (1972-75)

The term "fellow-traveller" was coined during the Cold War. It was used by anti-Communist hardliners to describe people who, while not Communists themselves, were broadly in sympathy with the goals (if not the methods) of people who were. In 1973 Gough Whitlam applied the term to himself. He did so tongue-in-cheek in answer to a question about his religion: "Let's say I am a fellow traveller with Christianity".[19] It is a resonant and useful term, in my view, and perfectly captures the state of mind of four of our former leaders. None of them could be classed as a practising Christian. But all four admired Christianity and followed its basic non-theological precepts. It is possible that one or more of them did rather more than that.

THE GENTLEMANLY AGNOSTICS

- Edmund Barton (1901-03)
- Harold Holt (1966-67)

Barton and Holt were both from the upper-middle class. Both belonged on the non-Labor side of politics, but were essentially moderate in their socio-political views. Both were lawyers and capable administrators. Both served less than a full term as Prime Minister. Both were urbane and well-liked, with a hedonistic streak. Both were capable of concentrated spells of work when the inclination took them. Both were nominally of the Church of England. Was either of them anything more than nominal? In Barton's case there is some basis for doubt – but not much. In Holt's case it is virtually certain that he had no religious convictions to speak of.

• • •

Those, then, are my eight categories. Readers might keep them in mind, but I will deal with each Prime Minister *seriatim*, in the order in which he or she first assumed office. The exception is Menzies: he is far better known for his second term (1949-66) than his first (1939-41). In the interests of historical continuity, the chapter on Menzies appears after those on Curtin and Chifley.

Some chapters are rather longer than others. Various factors came into the mix: the amount of material available about a given leader's religious life; the historical importance of that leader's term/s as Prime Minister; and the complexity and modern-day relevance of his or her story. The profiles of John Howard and Kevin Rudd are the longest. Both did me the honour of granting an interview and answering my questions (not all of which were Dorothy Dixers). A comparison of their respective Christian worldviews will, I hope, be of interest to all readers.

My own sympathies will become plain – I saw no easy way of hiding them* – but they are unimportant. I hope I have been fair in representing Christian views that differ from mine, as well as the views of sincere agnostics and non-believers. What matters is that Australians learn and think about religion and its role in the public sphere.

---

* In any event my personal views are on the public record. Chapter 8 of *God, Actually* is devoted to the inter-relationship between Christianity and politics. I should also "disclose" that my father, Evan Williams, worked as Gough Whitlam's press secretary and speechwriter from 1973-77. Though Dad is not a practising Christian, and we sometimes disagree about political issues, his fundamental values shaped many of my own.

EDMUND (TOBY) BARTON (1849-1920)

PROTECTIONIST: 1901-03

Edmund Barton, a key architect of Federation and Australia's first Prime Minister, looms in retrospect as a rather typical Australian male – of the genial, easy-going sort. He was born in Sydney to middle-class parents; enjoyed drinking with the boys; worked only as hard as he needed to; co-existed happily with his wife – and was decidedly lukewarm about religion. Most people liked him because he exhibited "generosity, even temper and ability to keep silent".[1] A more religiously-minded colleague once attributed to him "the Divine gift of sympathy".[2]

In other respects Barton was quite atypical. He remains the only Australian to have served as both Prime Minister (1901-03) and as a justice of the High Court (1903-19). He was also a fine classical scholar and a devotee of Shakespeare ("innumerable passages were stored in his memory"[3]). He co-founded Sydney's Athenaeum Club[4], "a place where a young man could hear first-class minds discussing all things under the sun".[5]

In all, then, Barton was a companionable gentleman of probity and style. Such eclectic achievement is rare today, especially in a man given to frequent periods of lassitude, as Barton was. During these periods he was prone to eating and drinking to excess – he thus attained the unfortunate nickname of "Tosspot Toby".[6] Even his close friend and colleague, "Affable" Alfred Deakin, complained of Barton's "negligences, unpunctualities, etc." It has been suggested by one of his own grandsons that Barton may have suffered from an undiagnosed bi-polar disorder: one common feature is "the capacity to work at ferocious pace with little rest in spasms and appear lazy and indolent at other times".[7]

That exactly describes the pattern of Barton's life. He practised sporadically as a barrister, and had little senior ministerial experience during his career in NSW politics. But he stretched himself to the limit at the Federation conferences of 1891 and 1897-98 ("labours of love", he called them[8]) and during negotiations with British authorities in London in March/April 1900 as to the provisions of the draft Constitution.[9] The Prime Ministership fell into his lap*, because he was the only man personally and politically "acceptable" to all the main players. He coasted in the job for less than three years before gratefully handing over to Deakin.

As I have said, Barton was lukewarm about religious matters. He was a Freemason,[10] but that was commonplace in his era. Importantly, Barton was not anti-Catholic – a fortunate thing for the infant Australian nation. According to one of his biographers, John Reynolds, "his natural tolerance prevented him from holding strong views about people in other spiritual folds".[11] He disliked the warring of the sectarians and – perhaps to pique them? – had an audience at the Vatican in July 1902 with Pope Leo XIII. For this heinous sin he was denounced back in Australia by zealous Protestants, including senior members of clergy. One told an audience at the Sydney Town Hall that "the Pope's existence should be ignored by every Protestant who goes to Italy, and if Mr Barton were only true to his country, he would never have called upon him."[12] No fewer than 30,000 people signed a petition condemning the visit, and, on June 17, 1903, a Protestant MHR named Wilks presented it to Barton in the House.

The Prime Minister replied with dignity (and, surely, a degree of sarcasm):

> The Pope said that he was exceedingly pleased to observe the feeling of tolerance which existed in Australia towards people professing any religious creed, that he had observed with great

---

* The first Commonwealth ministry, which took office on January 1, 1901, was appointed by the Governor-General, Lord Houptoun. The first elections for the House of Representatives and the Senate were held in March 1901. Barton's Protectionist Party won the most seats.

gratification the numerous proofs of the spirit, and hoped that it might long continue.[13]

If Barton had strong feelings about anything, it was "Anglophilic ideals".[14] He gave unquestioning support to the British cause in the Boer War, and his defence of the White Australia Policy was unusually blunt even by the standards of the day: "The doctrine of the equality of man was never intended to apply to the equality of the Englishman and the Chinaman."[15] He believed in slow human progress on the Whig British model. Manning Clark considered him a "Pontius Pilate type of liberal" because "he did not like to face up to big questions".[16] That judgment was harsh as regards politics, but may have been quite acute as regards metaphysics. Barton was a classicist. "He drew his wisdom from the Greeks rather than from the Old Testament or the teachings of Christ."[17] John Reynolds adjudged that Barton "was little influenced by the great battles that raged during his lifetime between the exponents of the Christian faith and scientific materialism".[18]

Manning Clark conjured the following grim image of Barton's meeting with Pope Leo XIII:

> Barton [made] use of the Latin at which he excelled, but never allow[ed] his face to reveal whether what Christ's Vicar on Earth claimed to stand for was true, or intimating to anyone whether he had ever hoped it was true. Four melancholy eyes confronted each other briefly in Rome – the Holy Father's the melancholy of a man of faith in an age of ruins, and Edmund Barton's the melancholy of a man sustained by neither love nor faith.[19]

None of this is to say that Barton was totally irreligious. Arguably, he belongs among the fellow-travellers. He identified with the Church of England, and his remains were buried in the Church of England section of Sydney's South Head cemetery.[20] At least at an intellectual level he must have known something about Christianity, and, probably, other world religions too. As J.A. La Nauze once pointed out, in the second half of the 19th century "it was … impossible for an intelligent and studious youth to avoid thinking about religion".[21]

Matters theological and philosophical must have been discussed in Barton's presence at the Athenaeum Club. On one occasion in 1891 he introduced a public lecture in Sydney by Colonel H.J. Olcott, a world authority on the-then fashionable teachings of Theosophy.[22] He launched the first referendum campaign for unification of the six Australian colonies with a Biblical-sounding pronouncement ("God means to give us Federation"[23]) and the preamble to the Act of July 1900 creating the Commonwealth of Australia – very much Barton's baby – specified that all involved were "humbly relying on the blessing of Almighty God".[24]

Overall, however, Barton exhibited little sign of any passionate faith. In this, it seems, he took after his father. William Barton, an accountant and stockbroker, was only nominally Anglican. His temperament was "rationally benevolent, mildly sceptical, [and of] classically eloquent Georgian ambience".[25] In other words, he was laid back – perhaps too much so. Edmund's brother, George Barton, complained in 1859 that their father had never inculcated in him a proper moral or religious sense. Evidently, as a young man, George had tried to develop one for himself. At all events, he implored his father by letter to "do better" with one of his younger brothers – to "Cultivate his Soul". George believed that "his welfare for time and Eternity entirely depend" upon it.[26]

It seems unlikely that William Barton took these urgings to heart. There is no indication that his youngest son Edmund ever dwelt at length – or at all – upon notions of Eternity. Barton did not leave behind any written record of his innermost beliefs. They remain a matter of speculation.

Another of Barton's biographers, Geoffrey Bolton, attributed to him an "easygoing Anglican conformism".[27] That seems a fair summation; but, if anything, it may be an overstatement. Barton's involvement with his Church was negligible. When he married, in 1877, the ceremony was conducted in the manse attached to his bride's *Presbyterian* church (St Andrew's in Wall Street, Newcastle, at which she played the organ). Jeannie Barton's subsequent decision to join the Church of England was not caused by any insistence on Barton's part. Rather, Jeannie's aunt and childhood guardian – once described as "a very terrifying disciplinarian and unbending Presbyterian"[28] – told her niece that it was her duty to convert to her husband's religion.[29]

As Geoffrey Bolton remarked, Barton would not have cared either way. Indeed, there is discernible in Barton's speeches a certain distaste for (as he saw them), over-zealous religious figures. Barton had been educated in the State school system (Upper Fort Street Primary School) and at the University of Sydney. His mentor as a philosophy student had been Dr Charles Badham, a distinguished Oxford scholar who had taken orders and been a friend of John Henry Newman. As we shall see in the chapter on Alfred Deakin, Newman was one of the great theologians of his day, a famous convert from Anglicanism to Catholicism. But Badham was a free-thinker with some "unorthodox theological views" and he found advancement difficult in England. This brought him to Australia in 1867.[30]

Badham's ambivalence about organised religion seems to have rubbed off on Barton.

In his maiden speech to the NSW Parliament in late 1880, Barton deprecated certain comments about State education which had been made by Sydney's Catholic Archbishop, Roger Bede Vaughan. "I must say," Barton said, "that I do strongly resent the statement that the system under which I have grown up is calculated to produce infidelity, immorality, or lawlessness".[31] It was a spirited and remarkably modern-sounding defence of public education.

In the course of that speech Barton identified himself with the mass of "upright and God-fearing citizens". But this reads like rhetoric. In the end I am compelled to agree with Michael Page's assessment of Barton in the bicentenary year of 1988: our first Prime Minister was "very much a man of the world".[32]

ALFRED DEAKIN (1856-1919)

PROTECTIONIST: 1903-04
PROTECTIONIST: 1905-08
COMMONWEALTH LIBERAL PARTY (FUSION): 1909-10

Researching this book was a challenging investigative exercise. While there is no shortage of information about our former Prime Ministers, religious specifics are another thing again. As John Warhurst has noted, "even ascertaining ... the basic matter of denomination is often no easy task"[1] since few biographers or contemporary commentators focused upon their subjects' inner lives. Pertinent information must be sifted from the general morass like grains of gold from a river bed.

The exception is Deakin. In his case there is an embarrassment of riches. He wrote hundreds of private prayers and many other works of prose and poetry devoted to religious themes. There is even a bizarre work of dramatic fiction (*The New Pilgrim's Progress*) which he wrote in his youth. All of these survive, more or less intact.

Secondary sources also abound. Al Gabay's fine book *The Mystic Life of Alfred Deakin* (1992) covers the ground thoroughly: it is a detailed exegesis of Deakin's "eclectic, almost encyclopaedist search for truth".[2] There is also much to be mined from John Rickard's *A Family Romance: The Deakins at Home* (1996) and from Professor J.A. La Nauze's comprehensive biography, completed in the 1960s. My task has been to digest and condense a plethora of relevant material.

Deakin was the most religiously-minded Prime Minister in Australia's history. Walter Murdoch, his first biographer, remarked in 1923 that religion "lay at the foundation of his being". He was formally of the Church of England, and believed that this great institution was "evidence of the British genius for compromise".[3] But to label Deakin an Anglican would be inaccurate and inadequate. As a young man he practised Spiritualism. He dabbled at various times with Theosophy, the Salvation Army, the Unitarian Church and the Australian Church of Dr Charles Strong. By his twilight years he had developed a complex system of belief. Judith Brett has opined that his "religious imagination remained deeply Protestant"[4], and, albeit guardedly, I would agree. It was a most unorthodox sort of Protestantism. According to Al Gabay, it "could be called Unitarian, and ... had affinities with the Quaker faith". There were also elements of Judaism, Neo-Platonism and Gnosticism.[5]

Alfred Deakin's story should give pause even to hard-core secularists. He was a good and brilliant man, one of the architects of Federation, and the most influential figure during the first decade of the infant Australian nation. He is often referred to as the father of "small-l" liberalism in Australia, though, given his staunch belief in the protective role of the State, and the support that his first two governments received from the Labor Party, "benevolent conservatism" would be a more accurate term.

At all events, what Deakin believed *became* Australia: a lively patriotism, the rule of law, a strong defence, assistance for Australian industry, and a reasonable safety net for the working classes and the elderly. And – the big blot on his record, though even it must be understood in historical context[6] – the White Australia Policy.

Where to begin? With the written word, I think. As Graham Fricke has observed, Deakin "was one of those rare species, an intellectual in active politics."[7] A lawyer by training, there seems little doubt he was the best-read Prime Minister Australia has had. Barton, Menzies and Whitlam might have come close, but, on the evidence I have seen, Deakin surpassed them all. Walter Murdoch once quipped that he "devoured whole libraries".[8]

The breadth of his religious reading was extraordinary. Deakin was steeped in Scripture. He regarded the Bible as "by far the greatest book of religious revelation"[9] and cherished many of its insights, especially those of the Old Testament prophets. But his knowledge extended to all of the world's major faiths and to secular philosophy as well – ancient and modern.

Geoffrey Bolton has suggested that Deakin "might be termed our first post-modernist politician".[10] I would dispute that, because the term "post-modernism" has acquired irreligious and amoral connotations. Deakin was a deist. He believed in God as the Creator of all things and as the ultimate foundation of morality. He believed in an afterlife. He also believed in a *personal* God: "Almost always I realise the existence of God," he once wrote. "Always I believe in Him with my intellect and turn to him with my heart."[11]

But who was this God? How was He revealed? Deakin believed that there was truth to be discovered in most of the world's major religions. He accepted, for example, the reality of Mohammad's experiences at Mount Hira.[12] He studied the Koran and the Hindu *Upanishads*. He admired the Buddha.[13]

Perhaps he was too much of a polymath for his own good. One senses that he never found inner peace. Certainly he was never an orthodox Christian. At the age of 26 he embarked on an extensive study of the life and teachings of Jesus to try to obtain a clearer picture "through the haze of legend". But while Deakin came to extol "the perfect life, love and worship of Christ"[14] and considered Him "the central figure of humanity"[15], he was never convinced that Jesus was the only son of God "in the Trinitarian sense".[16]

Deakin often referred to Jesus as God's son, but he considered that Jesus' deification was mistaken. "[It] disregards the fact," he once wrote, "that while His life is sublime and supreme as that of a man it is insufficient, incomplete and ineffectual if regarded as exhibiting the career of the Deity creating and controlling the Universe."[17]

Deakin struggled most of all with the doctrine of the Atonement, once deprecating "the old theory of proportion between Christ's suffering and the redemption he was supposed to have purchased by it".[18] The notion of a once-and-for-all vicarious sacrifice was, for him, a step too far: it made no sense that an Infinite God would go about things in such a way. Deakin believed in "a Universe based on justice and a Divine will made known to humans in diverse ways".[19]

The example of Jesus was just *one* of those ways – albeit the best. ("The best road to the Father is that of the Son," he wrote in 1901.[20]) Like the

English essayist John Seeley, Deakin much preferred to dwell upon Jesus' gorgeous humanity. In Al Gabay's words, he had "a Gnostic conception of Jesus as the zenith of human development".[21]

Deakin himself once mused:

> Taking thus together Jesus and Buddha, as now interpreted, with Plato and Swendenborg, and with Martineau and Emerson as modern commentaries, I begin to see a religious system of belief and action, of faith and philosophy, which I can not only accept, but act upon and could even preach if necessary.[22]

On a later occasion he extolled "the God of Jesus, of Plato, of Epictetus, of St Francis, of Tauler, of Swedenborg, of St Paul".[23]

For budding theologians there is a lot to consider here. But if some readers' eyes are glazing over, I will stop at this point and make two observations.

First, Deakin's religiosity had earthly consequences. Throughout his career he was driven by a sense of mission. He believed that the chief utility of religion lay in its capacity for motivating individual altruism: a community of saints could work wonders to foster the common good.[24] This was a notion popularised by the philosopher William James, whose most celebrated work, *Varieties of Religious Experience* (1901-02), Deakin read shortly after its publication.[25] Deakin aspired to contribute in such a way; what is more, it is clear from the record that he genuinely strived to do God's will. One of his favourite Bible verses was Psalm 36:9: "By Thy Light shall we see light."[26]

Deakin was convinced that God shared and supported his aspirations. Frequently in his prayers he beseeched God for help, as in this example from 1890:

> I would also crave to do something for my country and my kind, if ever so fractional, and pray to be shattered and crucified, rather than aid anything contrary to thy will and their elevation.[27]

He also regularly thanked God for advancing his career. For instance, after being elected in June 1898 as a member of the Victorian delegation to the Constitutional Convention, he prayed "that it might be the means of creating and fostering throughout all Australia a Christ-like citizenship".[28]

At the same time Deakin felt unworthy. He harboured a conviction that his ample material blessings – position, approbation, comfort, a happy and fruitful marriage – had not been fully earned.[29] In fact Deakin had little to be ashamed of, other than occasional priggishness – he adhered to a code of "fastidious honour"[30] which could puzzle and annoy his lesser contemporaries. The combination in Deakin of a guilty conscience *and* high-minded ambition – and exceptional talent to boot – proved a potent one indeed.

The second observation I would make about Deakin's religious feeling is that it came largely from within. Though he loved them dearly*, neither of his parents was a regular churchgoer. It is true that, from the age of eight, he attended Melbourne Grammar School.[31] But the headmaster in Deakin's day, Dr J.E. Bromby, was a liberal Anglican not given to rigid "indoctrination" of his charges.

For the light it casts upon the nature of religious experience in an informed and cultivated modern man, Deakin's is a fascinating personal story. I will tell a potted version.

It starts with Catherine Deakin, his sister. She was older than him by six years and never married. She and Deakin were close all their lives, no more so than as children, and Catherine was dutiful and pious. She sang hymns to her dear little brother "Alfy"[32], and, when he was old enough, took him to church each Sunday. They walked to the Anglican Christ Church on Toorak Road in South Yarra. Deakin went along obediently and, as a teenager, even taught Sunday school for a while.[33] But he refused to be confirmed: "Christianity as I understood it was wider than any or even all of the churches, and therefore acceptance of any formal limitation [was] impossible," he explained many years later.[34]

J.A. La Nauze doubted that this was really how Deakin reasoned at 15 ("a little pretentious, even for him"[35]) but I am not so sure. There seems no question he was an independent thinker from the start.

It was at the University of Melbourne (where he enrolled in 1873) that Deakin made a decisive break from orthodox religion. He joined the Debating Society on campus and the Eclectic Society off-campus, befriending in the

---

* When his mother Sarah Deakin died in April 1908, Deakin came and knelt by her body. He kissed her and said: "Goodbye, dear" and "God rest her soul." He prayed for her reunion with his father, William Deakin, who had died shortly before Christmas in 1892.

process a number of smart, like-minded young men. Deakin "experienced the liberating excitement of discovering and rehearsing the great intellectual issues of the day".[36] He imbibed the writings of John Stuart Mill, Charles Darwin and T.H. Huxley, among others. Most influential of all was the then-fashionable agnosticism of Herbert Spencer.[37] Once Deakin told a group of students that Spencer had "explained the origins of the universe … and we should start anew from Spencer's theories".[38]

Deakin's Sunday routine changed. Instead of going to church with Catherine, he met at home with two close friends from the Eclectic Society, David Mickle and Arthur Patchett Martin.[39] "Everything in earth and heaven and in space between was with [them] matter for open debate."[40] In his own portentous words, Deakin was consciously seeking "a system of philosophy, an interpretation of the universe, and a key to all the mysteries of life and being".[41] In retrospect it is not surprising that, soon afterwards, he became immersed in Spiritualism.[42]

Spiritualism now has a bad name, and for good reasons, but it had millions of adherents across the West in the second half of the 19th century and well into the 20th. Having first arisen in 1848 in New York State, the movement became associated with the tradition of "free thought". While generally frowned upon by the established churches,[43] its concerns were metaphysical. Adherents acknowledged "the essential verity of all forms of belief"[44] and accepted – or were open to accepting – that the human personality survives beyond the grave.[45] Most adherents were liberal-minded seekers, not charlatans or fruitcakes.

The Victorian Association of Progressive Spiritualists was established in 1870.[46] Deakin subscribed to its monthly journal, *The Harbinger of Light*, as well as *Medium and Daybreak*, the English equivalent.[47] He read the popular writings of Andrew Jackson Davis, a leading American spiritualist of the time, and progressed from there to the much denser work of an 18th century Swedish scientist and Christian mystic, Emanuel Swedenborg.[48]

Although Deakin rejected some of Swedenborg's tenets, and criticised his long-winded style, overall he was much impressed. Swedenborg was rational and practical, yet had a pious regard for the Bible. His core ideas were a tremendous influence on Deakin for the rest of his life. In 1889-90 Deakin would write a lengthy manuscript, "The Gospel According to Swedenborg", which included a survey of beliefs on the afterlife from ancient Egypt to medieval Europe.[49]

Deakin became convinced of the reality of spiritual phenomena and of "out of body" experiences. He moved away from the smug positivism of Herbert Spencer and embraced (or re-embraced) the metaphysical. The episodes related by Swedenborg, he thought, were not only convincingly documented; they resonated in a broader religious way. The existence of the non-corporeal world was necessary in order to make sense of morality. Where, otherwise, do "right" and "wrong" come from?

On this worldview the centre of life's meaning is conscious adherence to the moral law and a person's inner world ("the soul") is the truest reality. These were Kantian ideas, popularised in Deakin's day by John Henry Newman*[50], and, some 70 years later, by C.S. Lewis in *Mere Christianity*.

Of course, there was also a dodgier side to Spiritualism. For a few years Deakin participated in séances, auditions and such. No doubt much of it was contrived tomfoolery[51], but Deakin was too serious and sophisticated a person to be taken in by gimmicks. He was reading widely at this time – Plato, Marcus Aurelius, Whittier, Bacon, Schiller, Dante, Carlyle, Spinoza, to name a few – and was well aware of the emerging "conflict" between religion and science.[52] Deakin was president of the VAPS in 1878 but he always preferred the term "spiritism" to "Spiritualism".[53] It is worth recalling that Jesus Himself said: "God is spirit" (John 4:24). The official aims of the VAPS were as follows: "To extend the domain of science to the realms of the invisible, the impalpable, and the imponderable, and to supersede the supernatural by proving that the occult mysteries of human nature hereforeto deemed beyond the reach of human intellect, are destined to be revealed to the truth-seeker, to the unspeakable advantage of humanity."[54]

---

* Cardinal John Henry Newman (1801-90) was a famous 19th-century convert from Anglicanism to Catholicism and an important influence on Deakin. In one of his best-known sermons, 'The Greatness and Littleness of Human Life', Newman cited Colossians 3:3 as authority for the proposition that the soul's life is "hid with Christ in God". He argued that life on Earth is a kind of "stage", upon which a person decides whether or not to serve God for eternity. Accordingly, any and all thoughts of personal aggrandisement must be put aside. Al Gabay has argued that these ideas were in Deakin's mind when he declined the knighthood offered to him during his visit to England in 1887.

The young Deakin was neither gullible nor closed-minded. Rather, he adhered to Hamlet's worldview: There are more things in heaven and earth, Horatio, than are dreamt of in your philosophy. According to John Rickard, Deakin "was always to believe in the existence of spirits, and he remained convinced that some of the things he had witnessed were otherwise unexplainable."[55] Later in life he began to record his own transcendent experiences – encounters with what he termed "the Invisible". These were comparatively rare, but nonetheless extraordinary.[56]

As I have said, Deakin's religiosity had been reignited. But he soon tired of the sillier aspects of Spiritualism. In early 1879 he sought out Martha Turner, the minister of Melbourne's Unitarian Church in Eastern Hill, to raise the possibility of his succeeding her when she retired. (For an overview of the Unitarian Church, see the next chapter on Deakin's Labor contemporary, Chris Watson.) Miss Turner discouraged him[57] – and this was exceedingly fortunate for Australia. Yet a wistful Deakin would write many years later that, had he "followed his heart", he would have taken the plunge into a life of religious service.[58] In the event he entered Victorian politics soon afterwards and quickly excelled. He became the champion of some notably progressive causes, including factories legislation and irrigation of the Murray-Darling basin.

Deakin's parliamentary duties did not distract him from his spiritual quest. By the early 1880s he was beginning to "weave an idea of Deity".[59] He wrote in his journal:

> 'A wicked and adulterous generation seeketh after a sign'* but so also do the souls of those who aspire to do right and who believe that the universe is full of great but invisible beings sympathising with them and governed by an Almighty Spirit whom they are anxious to obey if only these finite and infinite forms of good could manifest themselves.[60]

By January 1882 Deakin was convinced that God could be found by ardent searching – and, still more crucially, that this God *was interested in him*. Gabay

---

* Matthew 12:39, 16:4.

identified this moment as a vital "turning" in the future Prime Minister's life.[61]

Another vital turning came in April 1883, when Deakin got married. His bride, Pattie Browne, was 19. As a girl in the late 1870s she had been his pupil at the VAPS's version of Sunday school, the "Progressive Lyceum"; she had since acquired a reputation in her own right as a talented medium. Their wedding ceremony did not take place in a church – it was conducted by the Registrar-General of the Colony of Victoria at the home of Pattie's parents* – but this was not Deakin's choice.[62] His religious zeal was very much in evidence. On their honeymoon in Tasmania he twice took Pattie to Salvation Army meetings: "They would go anywhere to get nearer God," he explained to her solemnly.[63]

Throughout the 1880s – even as Deakin built a successful career in Victorian politics, acquired considerable wealth, and became ensconced in his domestic life – he continued his search for God. Perhaps the closest he ever went to distilling his belief system was in September 1890. He wrote a "Personal Testament", in which he argued:

> Three things are certain –
> 1. God is love – Infinite, all-embracing, eternal
> 2. God is a Spirit, though manifest in all nature and humanity, and specially in all life and mind.
> 3. God is our Father and our Mother, including all that in us is various or contradictory, or imperfect, complete and perfect to his perfection.[64]

The 1890s began badly for Deakin when the value of his investments slumped during the Depression.[65] But he recovered his losses at the Bar, and, in the public sphere, devoted his efforts to the cause of Federation. Religiously his search continued too. Around 1894-95 he flirted with Theosophy[66]; then, in May 1896, he joined the recently-formed Australian Church of the Reverend Charles Strong.[67]

Strong was a modernist with progressive tendencies who had been expelled from the Presbyterian Church in 1883 for "promulgating unsound

---

* Pattie's father, Hugh Junor Browne, had been an associate of Deakin's at the VAPS. Both Browne and his wife Elizabeth were the children of clergymen, lapsed in their faith. Hugh Browne became increasingly obsessed with Spiritualism just as Alfred and Pattie Deakin's enthusiasm for it waned.

and heretical doctrine". The tenets of the Australian Church were sufficiently liberal to accommodate Deakin.[68] Members believed that "theology is a progressive science, [and] that genuine religion is confined to no one form of belief". They professed "The Worship of God in Spirit and in Truth; The preaching of the Gospel of Jesus Christ; and the Promotion and Practice of the Religious Life of Faith, Hope and Love."[69] For the next five years Deakin worshipped within the Australian Church's walls. According to Gabay, Deakin's attendance was "more or less weekly" – he went with his daughters and/or his sister Catherine. Sometimes he wrote articles for the church's organ, *Australian Herald*.[70]

Then came Federation. Deakin served for two years as Edmund Barton's Attorney-General before assuming the Prime Ministership in September 1903. But his first term in the job proved frustrating. The Protectionists lacked an absolute majority, and, in April 1904, after an important bill was rejected in the House, Deakin resigned his commission.

There followed another of the "vital turnings" in Deakin's career. Early in 1905 he had "glimpses of the new path, the new duty, the new message" – the pulpit. His (future) son-in-law Herbert Brookes* had long been urging him in that direction.

Brookes wanted Deakin to devote his life to religion, as a sort of roving preacher in the free-thinking style of the Australian Church.[71]

It was not to be. Deakin mulled over his future and opted for politics. He decided – surely correctly – that this was where he could make the biggest difference. In this regard he was inspired by the example of William Booth,

---

* Herbert Robinson Brookes (1867-1963) married Alfred Deakin's eldest daughter, Ivy Deakin Brookes (1883-1970), on July 3, 1905. Brookes' first wife Jennie (who had died in 1899) was the daughter of Dr Charles Strong, founder of the Australian Church at which both Deakin and Brookes worshipped in the 1890s. Neither stayed in the Australian Church in the 1900s – Dr Strong became an outspoken critic of militarism, whereas the Deakins and the Brookeses were firm supporters of both the Boer War and World War I. The respectable Anglican Church at South Yarra became their spiritual home, and Brookes was an early backer of the fiercely Protestant newspaper, *Vigilant*. He was also a "kingmaker" on the conservative side of politics – he played a key role in enticing Billy Hughes away from Labor in 1916-17, and was a confidante of both S.M. Bruce and Robert Menzies. Brookes' anti-Labor (and anti-Catholic) credentials were impeccable. In the early 1880s his father William had been the business partner of Sir Simon Fraser, grandfather of Malcolm Fraser and best friend of George Reid. In 1929, Bruce appointed Brookes as commissioner-general to the United States.

the founder of the Salvation Army, who was touring Australia in the early months of 1905. Deakin sought out Booth and spoke to him at length.[72]

In the end Deakin came to see "the futility of merely intellectual religion, of religion 'not finding constant expression in works'".[73] His own beliefs were, to say the least, of an elevated kind – not easily preachable to the average man or woman. Deakin reconciled himself to the view that sermons were only good "as dragnets and advertisements for the multitude". What the people really wanted from exceptional men was no less than "yourself your heart and life torn out of your self and given them in love in sincerity".[74]

The timing was propitious. Just a few months later George Reid's (minority) Free Trade Government persisted with a piece of industrial legislation that Deakin could not in conscience agree to; he withdrew the Protectionists' support for Reid and soon afterwards became Prime Minister again, with Labor's backing. Dreams of the pulpit at an end, and with appearances to keep up, "his soul came to rest in the capacious bosom of the Church of England in Melbourne, an institution with an infinity of promise and a minimum of demands on its members."[75] On Sunday nights he enjoyed going to evensong in the chapel of Melbourne Grammar School.[76]

Deakin's second term was undoubtedly his most distinguished. It was during those years, 1905-08, that the "Australian settlement" (Paul Kelly's term) was bedded down. Deakin basked in these achievements as the fulfilment of his, and Australia's, divine Destiny – the practical implementation of the Lord's Prayer, the coming of the Kingdom on earth. All this sounds grandiloquent, certainly. But that is what Deakin wrote in his journal in January 1908.[77]

His third and final term, from 1909-10, was a different story. Deakin was in failing health and had become the leader of the Commonwealth Liberal Party (also called "the Fusion") – an uneasy alliance of the Protectionists and the Anti-Socialist Party (formerly the Free Traders) led by Joseph Cook. It was cobbled together to resist Labor. Al Gabay has speculated that Deakin "may well have rationalised the Fusion as being the (Divine?) instrument for forcing that political cleavage into two parties crucial for the effective working of the Westminster system".[78] If so, his plan ultimately worked – but at the expense of Deakin's own ethos. The last government he led was "hardly a liberal administration in anything but name".[79]

Labor under Andrew Fisher won outright victory at the election of April 1910. Initially Deakin was shattered. He told Catherine that it was "the Waterloo of the Liberal Party"[80] – and he was right. But within a few weeks he had come round privately to thinking it a "merciful deliverance".[81]

Deakin stayed on for a while as Opposition Leader, but was now in terminal decline. His last energies were devoted to defeating Labor's referendum proposals of April 1911 (to increase Commonwealth powers over trade and commerce and monopolies). Again, Deakin saw his task as a mission. Rightly or wrongly, he feared that Labor's proposals, if adopted, would "[change] the precarious balance demanded by a true federalism". His duty, hence, was to secure their defeat – and he did. Deluded or not, "it can still be argued that this monition experience had an inordinate influence on Australia's federal history".[82]

The rest of Deakin's story is very sad. In September 1912 he experienced his "first decisive breakdown in faculty and in health, in brain and digestion, in mental and physical energy, all at the same time".[83] He retired in early 1913 but his remaining years were wretched. In 1917 he stopped writing. He died on October 7, 1919, surrounded by his ever-loving family.

JOHN CHRISTIAN (CHRIS) WATSON (1867-1941)
LABOR: 1904

Chris Watson has been dubbed the "forgotten man" of Australian politics, but his story is distinctive and important on several levels. Bede Nairn has written that "none more so than Watson" assisted in the birth of the Federal branch of the Australian Labor Party.[1] He was Prime Minister for only a few months, but led the ALP for seven critical years after Federation (1901-07), and many of the policies he formulated in opposition were later enacted by Andrew Fisher during his terms as Prime Minister. No less towering a figure than Billy Hughes regarded Watson as his "political master".[2]

Watson also remains the youngest Prime Minister Australia has ever had (he turned 37 a few weeks before taking office, in April 1904). He was the first to come from the ALP. Indeed, he was the first Labor Prime Minister anywhere in the world.

These were enormous achievements for a self-taught working-class man from New Zealand who left school at ten. His first job was as a "nipper" on railway construction works[3]; later he joined the *Oamaru Mail* newspaper office and worked his way up in the printing trade. His first job in Australia was as a stable hand at Government House in Sydney, shovelling horse manure.

Watson's career was also notable for the fact he "defected" to the conservative side of politics during World War I over the issue of conscription. It is true that, by the time of the conscription furore in 1916-17, he was no longer in parliament. Even so he was expelled from the party, in which he was still an active member. As recently as 1913 he had declared publicly that "the Labor Party has continued to grow because of the intrinsic justice of its cause."[4]

Watson's expulsion must have caused some rancour, but did not harm his reputation. By almost all accounts he continued to be regarded as a fine man – "genuine and humane, patient and reliable", in the words of one commentator.[5] In later life he was a President of the National Roads and Motorists' Association, a trustee of the Sydney Cricket Ground, and a founding director of the service station chain Ampol, among other substantial achievements in business.[6]

On matters of religion, Watson was unique. He was the product of an oddly cosmopolitan genetic and cultural mix. His biological father, Johan Cristian Tanck, was a German-Lutheran* sailor, resident in Chile when not at sea. His mother, Martha Minchin, was an Irish-Catholic teenager from Port Chalmers in New Zealand, whose family had emigrated from County Tipperary. Tanck and Martha met and married in Port Chalmers in early 1866, but soon afterwards departed for Chile, where their union was registered at the Matriz Catholic Church in the port town of Valparaiso. Their only son was born 15 months later, probably aboard Tanck's ship *La Joven Julia* (*Young Julia*) while it was in port at Valparaiso. (The only record of the birth is held at the Mormon Church in Santiago.)[7]

A year or so later, Tanck and Martha separated. Martha returned to New Zealand with her baby and quickly remarried – a miner this time, George Thomas Watson, who had emigrated from Falkirk in Scotland. Watson was (at least formally) a Presbyterian. He and Martha settled in the small town of Weston, near the port of Oamaru on the South Island, and eventually had nine children of their own.[8] Young Chris assumed his stepfather's surname, his given names were anglicised, and he was passed off thereafter as one of the Watson family. He grew up in New Zealand and seems to have been politicised while working at the *Oamaru Mail*: the proprietor was George Jones, "one of the most advanced, forceful and enlightened politicians of that period".[9]

Watson emigrated to Australia in 1888, a few months after his mother's early death.[10] It appears that he arrived in his new country with no firm

---

* Tanck's own parents had emigrated from Hanover to Chile on "religio-political grounds".

religious affiliation – and never acquired one. His biographers, Al Grassby and Silvia Ordonez, concluded after thorough investigation that Watson "left no explicit record of his personal beliefs".[11] What is known for certain is that when Watson got married – in November 1889, to an English dressmaker named Ada Jane Low – the ceremony took place at the Sydney Unitarian Church in Liverpool Street.[12] So did his second wedding, 26 years later.

There are several indications that Watson cannot have been a fervently religious man. He was never remotely sectarian, for the simple reason he never felt strongly about any branch of Christianity. He was a firm advocate of the "Solidarity Pledge"[13] (see the following chapters on Fisher and Cook), which vexed some in the early Labor Party on the grounds of freedom of religious conscience. He was also a firm advocate of the White Australia Policy. On his watch the Federal Labor Party Platform included this plank: "Total exclusion of coloured and undesirable races."[14]

Nevertheless, Watson is best classified as a "fellow-traveller" rather than an agnostic. He had, after all, a Lutheran father, a Catholic mother and a Presbyterian stepfather. And that middle name.

Only a man of some religious sensibility could have held together the fledgling ALP, as Watson did. "Among the assortment were Fabians, barely literate workers, radical Irish Catholics and Protestant moderates".[15] Watson charmed them all. "At times," observed Manning Clark, "he spoke like a man who believed that salvation for humanity would come from a marriage of the teaching of the Galilean fisherman to the ideas of the enlightenment." [16]

We know for certain that Watson delivered a speech on Christian socialism in 1904 (the year he was Prime Minister).[17] We also know that the firebrand Catholic Archbishop of Sydney, Cardinal Patrick Moran, supported Watson in 1905 during a heated public debate over Labor's socialist objective.[18] When Watson stood down as Labor leader in 1907, exhausted and impecunious, the well-respected Archbishop of Adelaide (John O'Reily) was one of many who wrote to him. Another saddened Irish-Catholic lamented that Watson was "leaving … almost within sight of the Promised Land".[19]

Also to be taken into account are Watson's two marriages at the Unitarian Church in Sydney. In his era Unitarianism was an attractive quasi-Christian option for those of idealistic bent. As we have seen, Deakin flirted with it.

The movement grew out of the Congregational Church in Boston in the early 19th century in reaction against the fiercer strictures of Calvinism and the notion of Original Sin. Unitarians rejected the doctrine of the Trinity and believed in the essential goodness of humanity - "This [made] Jesus not an incarnate God sent to redeem a sin-ridden mankind but a great moral teacher filled with God."[20]

There is no solid evidence that Watson ever worshipped regularly at the Unitarian Church. It was a "tenuous connection".[21] However, Grassby and Ordonez did find (in a box of Watson's papers held at the National Library of Australia), a secretary's report of the proceedings of the "Sydney Troward Society" in an unspecified year. In their judgment, "it seems to be [a record] of a Unitarian study group though no explicit definition or aim is given ... [and] its presence is suggestive rather than conclusive".[22]

A little bit more can be said. The society in question was undoubtedly of a religious character. Judge Thomas Troward (1847-1916) was an English jurist and scholar whose special interest was comparative religion. He devoted the last 20 years of his life to metaphysics and philosophy and was a one-time president of the International New Thought Alliance. His Edinburgh Lectures on Mental Science, delivered in 1904, were widely lauded. Troward's writings were exactly the sort which would have interested members of the Unitarian church. The question in Watson's case is the extent to which, if at all, he actively participated in this society. It seems safe to assume he was at least in broad sympathy with its ethos.

The last fact of note is that Watson, at the age of 58, formally converted to Catholicism! He did so in deference to his second wife, a young woman from Western Australia named Antonia Dowlan. Prior to their marriage in 1925 (Ada had died four years earlier), Watson undertook instruction at Sydney's St Mary's Cathedral.[23] Nothing seems to have come of this, however. His state funeral in 1941 was held at St Andrew's (Anglican) Cathedral in Sydney.

GEORGE HOUSTOUN* REID (1845-1918)

FREE TRADE 1904-05

George Reid was the first of Australia's leaders to be born into the world, and the first to leave it. His term as Prime Minister was short – he resigned after only ten months in the job, after losing the confidence of a finely-balanced House of Representatives[1] – but his significance in Australian history was considerable.

Reid was the Premier of NSW from August 1894 to September 1899, a position he occupied with worldly distinction. He was a superbly entertaining orator and an influential if cynical player in the movement towards Federation. Had he still been the NSW Premier in December 1900, he might well have been invited by the Governor-General to form the first Commonwealth ministry.[2] In the event that honour was bestowed upon Edmund Barton, and Reid became the Leader of the Opposition. For the next ten years he was a dominant figure on the non-Labor side of national politics.

Reid was born in 1845 at Johnstone Manse in Renfrewshire, Scotland. His father, the Reverend John Reid, was a Presbyterian minister of some eminence – his postings in Britain included the Oldham Street Church in Liverpool, where "many of the leading Scottish shipowners attended".[3] But John Reid suffered frequently from bronchitis. In 1852, on medical advice, he emigrated to Australia and brought his wife and children with him.

---

* Reid took his middle name "Houstoun" from his godfather, a local Member of Parliament in Renfrewshire.

Theirs was a close family. Late in life, George Reid lovingly described his parents as "Christians whose outward professions were transcended by the nobility and beauty of their conduct in the family circle. They tempered the standards of principle and conduct by which their own lives were governed with boundless reserves of charity and compassion for those who fell short of their high ideals."[4]

After a stint at Moonee Ponds church in Victoria, John Reid moved to Sydney in 1856 and soon became a close colleague of John Dunmore Lang.[5] Lang's is a truly legendary name in the history of NSW. He was Sydney's first Presbyterian minister (ordained in 1823), a sometime member of parliament, militantly anti-Catholic, and a fiery and talented iconoclast of wide renown and controversy. He and John Reid were colleagues at Scots Church in the city from 1858-62, and shared a love of scholarship.

When they parted company in 1862 Lang gave Reid an affectionate send-off from the pulpit:

> In these friendly and difficult circumstances I left my dear friend and brother to the freedom of his own will – as God did Adam in the Garden of Eden![6]

Thereafter, until his death, Rev Reid presided at the interdenominational Mariners' Church in Lower George Street.[7]

George Reid was the Reverend's seventh child. Like all his siblings he was schooled in the history of the faith and its doctrine, but from an early age he seems to have been a rebel. At the Melbourne Academy (later Scotch College) where he boarded as a teenager, he "had no sort of appetite for that wide range of metaphysical propositions which juveniles were expected to comprehend".[8] Even so, he became an active member (sometime secretary) of the Presbyterian Young Men's Union. At the age of 30 he took a course of instruction from the Rev Barzaillai Quaife, the author of one of the first serious philosophical works published in Australia. The subjects that Quaife covered with Reid included metaphysics, logic and moral philosophy.[9]

Reid's grounding in Christianity was, then, impeccable. What is more, he was proud of his "Puritan ancestors"[10] and his father's "pulpit gifts".[11] Yet W.G. Minn, his biographer, described him as "never notably religious".[12]

John Warhurst has expressed the view that, for the best part of his adult life, Reid was no more than "nominal" in his adherence to the Christian faith.[13]

In 1898 the visiting British socialist Beatrice Webb made this assertion:

[Reid] has never felt a religious aspiration or puzzled over an intellectual problem ... philosophy [is] completely closed to him.[14]

Webb exaggerated, but the overall picture seems clear. By middle age Reid was no longer seriously practising his faith.

How did this come about? The answer is fairly straightforward. Reid's beloved father had died in 1867 and, after 1880, his life was consumed by politics. Socially he was a freewheeling *bon vivant* and man-about-town until his marriage, in 1891, at the age of 46. (His bride, Flora Ann Brumby, a Tasmanian farmer's daughter*, was less than half his age.[15]). After that he settled into comfortable secular domesticity and grew very fat.

To many people of his day Reid appeared a coarse and materialistic man. He was disdained for that reason by the fastidious Alfred Deakin. And yet, of all Australia's early Prime Ministers, Reid was the least racist. In 1908, when a bill was introduced for the payment of old age pensions, it was he who suggested that its provisions might be extended to "decent and reputable naturalised coloured persons". He asked his colleagues to "recognise the common humanity of all members of the human race", but the suggestion fell on deaf ears.[16]

What were Reid's core beliefs? Beyond economic liberalism, it is hard to be sure. In public he displayed "an insatiable hunger for excitement and applause"[17] while revealing little of his private self. His wedding ceremony took place at a Presbyterian manse (in Wangaratta, Victoria) and his funeral service at St Columba's Church of Scotland in London.[18] But not much should be read into that. Nor his forced association with the Rev. Dill Macky of Scots Church in Sydney (a rabid anti-Catholic like John

---

* As W.G. McMinn once noted, Reid claimed to at least one friend that Flora was related to the Anglican Bishop of Tasmania, Charles Henry Bromby (1814-1907), and to his older brother John Edward Bromby (1809-89), the first headmaster of Melbourne Grammar. This was not so, as Reid must surely have known, and his motives for making the claim remain obscure. At all events it seems clear that he had no qualms about being openly associated with Protestant clergymen.

Dunmore Lang), and his frequent hobnobbing with other high clerics, including, on one notable occasion, the Archbishop of Canterbury.

At a sumptuous official dinner in London in June 1897, Reid was seated between the Prince of Wales (later Edward VII) and the then-Archbishop of Canterbury, Dr. Frederick Temple. Reid was exhausted by travel and knew he had a propensity to nod off on such occasions by virtue of his great bulk. He turned to Dr Temple and asked if he would be good enough to keep him awake. In Reid's sardonic words, "I cannot forget the first terrible glance, but it was swiftly succeeded by friendly smiles and a gracious assent when I explained the fearful danger of my position. The Archbishop afterwards expressed a doubt to me whether any one of his 92 predecessors had been asked to undertake a similar mission."[19]

What did Reid say on the record about religion? A couple of snippets are worth noting from his political years. In 1894 he stated that free trade policies were "magnificent practical Christianity … doing what ye would that others should do unto you".[20] During the federal election campaign of 1906, he identified as one of Australia's greatest evils "a socialist movement that aims at the regeneration of humanity, *not by Christian methods of love and self-sacrifice,* but by the dismal sway of State compulsion, preceded by a war of classes, and the destruction of private enterprise and industrial liberty."[21]

It appears that, after his retirement from politics, Reid turned his mind again to matters metaphysical. On February 22, 1912 he read a paper to the Scottish Geographical Society at Edinburgh entitled "The World of Matter and the World of Mind". The *Sydney Morning Herald* reported that "he urged the introduction of simple psychological teaching in schools to enable the masses to grasp the fundamentals of history and religion, and assist in solving the great problems of life".[22]

In December 1914 Reid visited the Anzac troops in Egypt in his capacity as High Commissioner in London. The men were encamped near the Pyramids. Reid delivered a short address and referred to the fact that "the youngest of these august Pyramids was built 2,000 years before our Saviour was born".[23]

But what of Reid's inner life? Manning Clark, though admiring his generosity of heart, considered him "a stranger to religious faith, utterly unresponsive to any promise of the life of the world to come".[24] Yet there is decent evidence – whatever outward appearances to the contrary – that Reid believed in God. As to what sort of God the record is unclear.

Manning Clark was closer to the mark in his observation that Reid "had a faith in the goodness and dignity of mankind".[25] His sentiments often seem to have been far removed from cagy Presbyterianism. Once, in 1913, he expressed himself in a public speech in curiously idealistic terms:

I am … confident in the future happiness of all mankind. The mind may have been kept in darkness for many ages, but it will not end there, because it is the crown of all the life of all the worlds in the whole universe.[26]

In Reid's 1917 memoir *My Reminiscences* he alluded in similarly lofty vein to the nature of the soul:

The soul – or mind – or life – call the sovereign lord of animated function what you will – when it points to the cellular substance within a man as the medium, for who can believe it to be the origin, of thought, feeling and volition.[27]

In Reid's view, the human mind was "the only link which mankind has with the Supreme Mind". He added sagely that "the mind is the most elusive and unseeable of all existences … like the Divine Mind, it can be seen by mortal eyes never for what it is, only for what it does."[28]

My best guess is that, by the end of life, Reid was a believer of a sort. Certainly he was unashamed to express fondness for Christians and Christianity. He recalled in his memoirs a conference in the United States which had closed with the communal singing of a hymn – 'God Be With You Till We Meet Again'. According to Reid, it "was sung with a fervour of deep religious feeling which made upon my mind an impression I shall never forget".[29] Likewise, Reid treasured a memory of having once met British Prime Minister William Gladstone, then aged 87. As they parted, the great old man took Reid by the hand and said: "May the Lord cause His face to shine on you and yours."[30]

An agnostic could not, I venture, have written about such things with such evident emotion.

ANDREW FISHER (1862-1918)

LABOR: 1908-09, 1910-13, 1914-15

Andrew Fisher was a key figure in Australian history for several reasons. Perhaps most importantly, he brought the Labor Party into the mainstream of our national life. In the words of a biographer, David Day, "with his moderate politics and language, and his upright and handsome demeanour, Fisher made the cause of the workers respectable".[1]

That last word – respectable – is spot-on. Fisher's reputation was as "a man of high principle".[2] But Day's analysis downplayed the most crucial factor of all: Fisher's unimpeachable Protestantism. He represented the strain of "Protestant radicalism which tied the idea of human brotherhood to the moral law and the New Testament".[3] Unlike, say, Joseph Cook, Fisher did not desert the Labor cause in the 1890s over the vexed issue of the Solidarity Pledge (the rule that ALP parliamentarians are bound to vote the party line on pain of expulsion). Tragically, that issue "lessened the links between the [Labor] party and the Churches", because "to Protestantism a rigid discipline of party was a negation of brotherhood and of man's accountability to God".[4] The ALP suffers to this day from this degenerate rule.

As Prime Minister in 1909, Fisher was invited to attend a meeting of the General Assembly of the Presbyterian Church of Australia. For two decades there had been intense internal debate within all the Australian Protestant churches as to the proper attitude to the Labor Party's social justice agenda. The "old" Presbyterian Church clung to 19th-century notions of rugged individualism, and had mostly supported the interests of wealth and privilege during the Depression of the 1890s; the "new" Church was warming to the idea that cold charity was no substitute for justice, and that aspects of Labor's programme deserved support. At the same time, some church leaders were offended by harsh criticism of institutional Christianity levelled by non-believers within Labor ranks.

The Rev. John Ferguson of St Stephen's Presbyterian Church, Macquarie Street (in Sydney), addressed the Prime Minister directly. His words are a testament both to the notoriety of Fisher's personal faith and to the deep schisms at that time within Australian society:

> You and I, Mr Fisher, are brother Scots, and I want you Labour men all in the Church of your fathers and mothers; I want you back to Christ ... Tell us honestly, with straightforward truthfulness from your heart: Seeing as we both believe that Christ is our ideal; seeing we agree to denounce every kind of immorality, and to rescue the poor from their misery, feel with them, pray for them, love them – tell us why so many tens of thousands of your comrades never darken our church doors.[5]

This is a telling early example of the rift that developed in Australia between the churches and the secular Left. But it was never fatal. Despite the Pledge, enough staunch Protestants stayed within the ALP to ensure that it did not expire at birth – as it may well have if people like Fisher and Billy Hughes had left its ranks before Federation. For Fisher, the Labor Party was "an instrument for providing that abundance which Christ had promised to all true believers".[6]

The sincerity of Fisher's Christian faith is beyond doubt. According to his daughter Peggy his everyday speech was peppered with references to the Scriptures.[7] All his life he was a church-goer and a believer in the efficacy of private prayer.[8] He was also a strict teetotaller. He hated bad language and disdained luxury and imperial honours.[9] He could "talk interestingly on metaphysical themes"[10] and once stated explicitly that death ought to hold no fears; indeed, "to the souls of the faithful that would be endless bliss".[11]

Fisher was born in 1862 in Crosshouse, a small town near Kilmaurs in Central Ayrshire. He was the second son of austere working-class parents.

Robert Fisher, his father, was "a sober, temperate Presbyterian".[12] Jane Fisher (née Garven) was a "devoted mother and wife and a devout Christian".[13] Both belonged to the Free Church of Scotland, a hugely influential sect created in 1843 in reaction against the dominance of the wealthy gentry in the affairs of the established church. The "Wee Frees", as its adherents were known, stood for thrift and temperance in private life and encouraged "believing criticism" of the Bible.

These aims were vigorously and rigorously pursued by the Free Church's democratically-elected governors. The Church was an agent of change. It facilitated "the first appearance of the lower classes in Scottish politics, an evidence of the approach of a new age".[14] This severe reformist ethos was at the centre of the Fishers' daily life and stayed with Andrew Fisher for the rest of his days.* Another pervasive influence was the poetry of Robbie Burns (1759-1796), himself an Ayrshireman of renown. In poems such as 'Why should we idly waste our prime', Burns envisioned a sort of Heaven on Earth.[15]

Fisher's childhood was dour but not unhappy. His father was one of ten men who established a co-operative store in Crosshouse in 1863 and young Andrew was an avid user of its library and reading room.[16] His formal education was at the local parish school, but, around the age of 11, his father developed pneumoconiosis and Andrew was forced to commence 13 years of hard toil in the Ayrshire coal pits.

It was a tough life – scarcely imaginable today – but Fisher coped. He grew up into a strapping young man while supplementing his education at night classes in Kilmarnock. Though not possessed of a brilliant intellect, he was capable and confident and determined to succeed.[17] Without fuss he rose steadily in the trade union movement. "He had embarked," in Graham Fricke's words, "on a life of leadership."[18]

---

* In his mid-twenties Fisher – like his contemporaries Alfred Deakin and Chris Watson – briefly became attracted to Unitarianism. This may have come about through his reading of the works of Ralph Waldo Emerson. In any event he seems not to have taken this interest any further in later life. Fisher did not follow the Rev. Charles Strong into the ultra-liberal Australian Church, as Deakin did, but stayed within the Presbyterian Church – albeit its more progressive wing. In Melbourne he found a soulmate in the Rev. Patrick John Murdoch (1850-1940), who became Moderator-General of the Presbyterian Church of Australia in 1905-06. Murdoch taught Fisher to play golf.

In those days, working and living conditions for the workers and their dependants were truly dire. On any fair-minded view, the workers' cause was just. But it still required committed men and women to fight for the cause. According to another of his biographers, Peter Bastian, Fisher's faith was influential in this regard. "He ... found the Calvinist explanation that humans were tempted through their own weakness important in explaining the injustices of the society around them: men were tempted by wealth and privilege to behave badly toward others."[19] In addition Fisher admired the Salvation Army for the practical commitment of its adherents to alleviating injustice.[20]

In August 1881 Fisher became embroiled in a seminal coalminers' strike over wages. He worked closely with Keir Hardie, who later became one of the founders of the British Labour Party and (in 1892) its first member of the House of Commons.[21] Hardie was one of the original "Christian socialists" – the genuine article. He was a member of the Evangelical Union Church, a lay preacher, and a prominent figure in the temperance movement. Famously, he once claimed that "I now understand what Christ suffered in Gethsemane as well as any man living." Yet Hardie expressly rejected the language of class warfare. He admitted that, as a young man, he had been motivated by hatred and envy. But his mindset changed on the day he wrote in his diary: "Today I have given my life to Jesus Christ."[22]

Hardie was a stirring role model for the young Andrew Fisher. They kept in touch. When Hardie arrived in Melbourne in late 1907 during a tour of Australia, it was Fisher who welcomed him. A formal photograph of the two men taken during this visit was used on a postcard sold by Australian labour organisations for fundraising purposes.[23] When Fisher became Prime Minister in the following year, Hardie wrote to congratulate him.[24]

The 1881 strike failed and the Ayrshire Miners' Union disbanded. It re-formed again in 1884 under Fisher's leadership but, at this time in history, a young man's prospects in Crosshouse were grim. Fisher's mother encouraged him to emigrate to Australia and seek a better life. He was torn between a sense of family responsibility and hopeful ambition but, in the end, was persuaded to go.[25]

Fisher and his brother James arrived in Brisbane in August 1885 on the *New Guinea*. In mid-1888, after a few years' on the move, they settled in the gold-mining town of Gympie in Queensland. Andrew Fisher soon became a leading figure in the town. He was a shareholder in the Gympie Industrial Co-operative Society and active in union and church activities. In both capacities he would lament "the commercial spirit of this commercial age".[26]

The centre of his religious life was St Andrew's Presbyterian Church at Red Hill. Fisher was a close confidante of the minister there, Rev. Robert Wallace, who encouraged his protégé to devote his life to Christian evangelism. For a while this seemed a real possibility: in early 1889 Fisher was elected as the superintendent of a large new Sunday school in the Gympie town centre.[27] In that role he served ably and enthusiastically for two years, and at some point Wallace offered to pay for him to study at university in Melbourne. As Peter Bastian has suggested, Wallace presumably had in mind the Presbyterian Theological Hall located within Ormond College at the University of Melbourne.[28]

It was not to be. Fisher was reluctant to leave Queensland. Indeed, by 1890, his Sabbatarian duties had begun to conflict with his expanding duties as a union leader. After rebuke from his church elders, and careful thought, he decided to make his career in the fledgling labour movement. He left Gympie in 1891 but for many years thereafter remained a close friend of Rev. Wallace.[29]

There followed an outstanding political career, beginning in the Queensland parliament in 1893 and including three separate terms as Prime Minister. Fisher led Labor to two thumping election victories, in 1910 and 1914. He stepped down as Prime Minister in October 1915, ostensibly for reasons of ill-health, and was succeeded by Billy Hughes. In between times he sustained an extremely happy marriage and fathered six children. Fisher's wife Elizabeth (née Irvine), whom he married in 1901, had also been a parishioner at the Gympie Presbyterian Church, and, at one time, a Sunday school teacher there.[30])

Kevin Rudd told me:

> The person whose faith I'm always most impressed by is Fisher's. This is a guy who takes the enterprise seriously. And then upon election [in 1914] being confronted with the horrors of the First

World War ... he became very sick; he internalised so much of it. But I think by every reasonable account that I've read he was a very good man, a man who brought himself up by the bootstraps.

The case can be made that Fisher's government of 1910-13 embedded the notion of the "fair go" in our national psyche. Its achievements were formidable: maternity allowances; the liberalisation of invalid and old age pensions; uniform postal charges; a national currency; extensive railway construction; a Workers' Compensation Act; a Land Tax Act; various industrial relations reforms to increase the bargaining power of unions; the creation of the Commonwealth Bank. Fisher even designed the Australian coat of arms.

As D.J. Murphy has pointed out, it is important to recognise that Fisher did these things without becoming a disciple of class warfare: "Fisher's political philosophy contained no [such] concept ... his ideas were based on his background in Ayrshire, his experiences as a miner and his habits of reading and study".[31] And, I would stress, his Christian faith. Like Keir Hardie, Fisher's vision was that of the Wee Frees and of Robbie Burns in 'Why should we idly waste our prime':

> The Golden Age we'll then revive;
> Each man will be a brother;
> In harmony we all shall live,
> And share the earth together
> In virtue train'd, enlighten'd Youth
> Will love each fellow-creature.

It is also worth noting that Fisher had the happy knack of getting along with people from all walks of life. The co-operative ethos of the Presbyterian Church instilled in him "a sense of equality, self-governance and collective decision".[32] He did not have a manic determination to get his own way. His favourite aphorism was modest and non-confrontational: "You do very well ... if you don't do any harm".[33]

Fisher had the dire misfortune of reassuming the Prime Ministerial office at the beginning of World War I. He did not declare war on Australia's behalf – as we shall see, that task fell to Joseph Cook – but he had supported

Cook's decision in sweeping terms. He did so in the context of an election campaign and at the urging of his bellicose and ambitious deputy, Billy Hughes. Fisher himself had little enthusiasm for the cause. In the words of D.J. Murphy, he "saw no advantage in the war to Australia [and] concepts of martial glory were totally absent from his character".[34] One would expect that in a committed Christian man, as Fisher was. On September 23, 1914 he denounced war as "a crime against civilisation and against humanity".[35]

Even so, there was apparently no question in his mind that Australia should fight for the Empire. In an ideal world he might have considered the option of neutrality. But even to voice the suggestion would have been extremely unpopular – politically, in the national mood of naïve and fevered jingoism, it was quite untenable. The only other practical course open to him was resignation as Prime Minister. But he was not *that* principled a Christian.

It would be churlish to judge Fisher too harshly with the benefit of 21st century hindsight. It seems clear that he took no joy in being a wartime leader, and, at least in the early stages of the conflict, honestly believed that the British cause was just – or less unjust than the Germans'. Moreover, and despite his not being kept properly informed by the British High Command (including about the Gallipoli landing in April 1915), Fisher did what he felt he could to support the men at the front.

Overruling British protests, he insisted that the troopships be fully assembled and protected before leaving Australia – there were German cruisers in the Pacific and Indian oceans. He personally put in place arrangements to finance the war effort: Australian soldiers were better paid than their British counterparts (excessively so, thought King George V), and returned soldiers were granted employment and other preferences. When he left for London in late 1915 to take up the post of Australian High Commissioner, he made available his house in St Kilda as a military convalescent home. He visited the troops in France.[36] In November 1920, as High Commissioner, he attended a memorial service at Amiens Cathedral in France for the Australian soldiers who died in defence of that city.[37]

Fisher never supported conscription for overseas service. Indeed he was "irrevocably opposed"[38] and resisted concerted pressure to introduce it while he was Prime Minister. In 1916, as High Commissioner, he refused to sign a public statement of support for the "Yes" case in the first of two conscription plebiscites.[39] He was the only past Prime Minister who so refused: Edmund Barton, Alfred Deakin, Chris Watson, George Reid and Joseph Cook all signed it. No doubt they believed in the cause, but Fisher would not abandon "dearly held principles"[40] despite finding himself in splendid isolation.

Fisher's stance was brave. The howl for conscription came from many influential quarters: the Universal Service League, the conservative side of politics, a vocal faction within the ALP (led by Hughes) and sections of the press. Crucially, too, most of Fisher's co-religionists advocated conscription – at least among the upper levels of clergy.

When the General Assembly of the Presbyterian Church of Australia met in Sydney on September 26, 1916, it voted 92 to 3 for a motion of support. A preamble to the motion listed reasons purporting to show that conscription was just and necessary:

> Since the Empire fought in obedience to Christian principle, it was necessary 'to put forth the full strength of her manhood and resources until her righteous cause triumphs'; the duty of resisting evil and fighting for right was a moral obligation of citizenship; the government could compel people who refused to accept their obligations.[41]

The editor of the *Presbyterian Messenger* also weighed in: "the State is ordained by God to be a lesson to evildoers".

In resisting such blandishments – routinely advanced by all of the mainline Protestant churches in Australia – Fisher was not being "disloyal" to either his church or his country. Rather, he was being true to his own Christian conscience – a more informed and sensitive conscience, I would argue, than that of many ordained ministers. Theirs was an Old Testament view of things, not that of the Prince of Peace. As Michael McKernan has observed, the Protestant leaders concentrated on supposed "moral" duties: of "not deserting the men at the front", of "repaying Australia's debt of gratitude to the Empire": of "acting honourably by fulfilling a pledge". But this was "ordinary civic morality, the morality of boys' magazines, rather than that, specifically, of the Christian religion".[42]

Fisher, I suspect, would have agreed with the tiny minority of Protestant clergyman who spoke out against conscription. Interestingly, among Presbyterians, the most eloquent dissidents were from Fisher's home state of Queensland – men such as the Rev. James Gibson and the Rev. S. Martin. Perceptively, in my view, they feared that the Church was becoming too subservient to the State. They foresaw a future in which "patriotism is the virtue which takes the place of Christian Brotherhood; the State replaces God; and the National flag replaces the Cross. Its supreme law is not the law of God, but the military safety of the country."[43]

In substance, these visionary churchmen foresaw the course of the 20th century. And it here bears mention that, as young men, no fewer than four future Prime Ministers of Australia openly opposed conscription during World War I: James Scullin, Joseph Lyons, John Curtin and Ben Chifley. A fifth, Stanley Melbourne Bruce, was probably against it in his heart. Only Robert Menzies was a supporter.

Fisher lived out his final years in London in South Hill Park. His health declined but his faith never wavered. He regularly attended at the Trinity Presbyterian Church in High Street.[44] A Presbyterian minister attended at his deathbed and recited a prayer which included this Old Testament passage: "The eternal God is thy refuge, and underneath are the everlasting arms" (Deuteronomy 33:27). At Fisher's funeral service at St Columba Presbyterian Church in Knightsbridge, London, the organisers arranged for the singing of two of his favourite hymns: 'Lead Kindly Light' and 'Abide With Me'. There was also a reading from Psalm 46.[45] It was befitting of a man who did so much for social justice that many representatives of the Salvation Army were in attendance.[46]

JOSEPH COOK
(1860-1947)
COMMONWEALTH LIBERAL PARTY: 1913-14

I t has been said of Cook that "his commitment to Methodism was the one continuity in his life".[1] Up to a point, that is true. According to his first biographer, Walter Murdoch, Cook's great pleasures were reading the Bible and singing hymns. He preached on Sundays in a lay capacity and devoured Christian self-help tracts such those of Ralph Waldo Emerson and the Scottish evangelist Henry Drummond. He was an exemplary husband and father to nine children.[2] "All his life, he believed that God and righteousness were on his side."[3]

Like Billy Hughes, his contemporary and sometime colleague, Cook grew up in England and began his career on the Labor side of politics. His origins were extremely humble. Born in Silverdale, Staffordshire in 1860, his father, William Cooke, was a so-called butty miner – one step up from the working class. He leased a coalface from the mine owners and employed his own men to work it.[4] But William Cooke was killed in a coalmining accident in 1873 and this calamity left his bereaved oldest son the main family breadwinner. At the age of 12 Joseph was forced to work in the pits himself, for two shillings and sixpence a day.[5] He soon developed "a high degree of self-confidence and a strong sense of obligation".[6]

He also possessed a brave spirit and an irascible temperament. Outside his family circle he was neither an affectionate nor a trusting man. Hughes once adjudged that his "nature is such that he regards all the world as dishonest, and suspects a trick in everything."[7] (Coming from Hughes, this was rich indeed; but fair comment nonetheless.)

Even so Cook was a tireless worker. In a more generous moment, Hughes extolled him as "the most reliable and helpful of men".[8] Certainly, in the 1880s and 1890s, Cook played an honourable role in the ALP's formation and its early electoral success. But in his middle age, for reasons which seemed compelling to him, he switched his allegiance to the elected representatives of capital and privilege. As he got older, Cook's socio-political views became increasingly reactionary. Indeed, "there is a case for saying that Cook [was] … a founder of the anti-Labor tradition in Australia".[9]

In my opinion there is an even better case for saying that Cook's views became increasingly inconsistent with Methodism – its secondary tenets, at any rate. They were undoubtedly at odds with the views of many leaders of his Church in Australia.

Cook's political metamorphosis must be understood in the light of his religion. In his early teens he was converted to so-called Primitive Methodism[10], a sect formed in the north of England in the early 19th century. It was a response to the well-founded perception that the church of Wesley had become too cautious, money-hungry and status-conscious. As a Primitive Methodist pamphleteer wrote in 1814: "You complain the preachers never call to see you unless you are great folks … Well you may see the reason; you can do nothing for them; money they want and money they must and will have."[11]

The Primitive Methodists (also known as the Ranters or the Clowsites), were drawn disproportionately from the lower echelons of English society. Open-air preaching was encouraged, and a heavy emphasis placed upon education and self-improvement. The teenage Joseph Cooke took these teachings with deadly seriousness. He changed his name to Cook (dropping the "e" in his father's surname, because he thought it pretentious), and knuckled down. By the age of 16 he had joined the Mutual Improvement Society in Silverdale,[12] and was an up-and-comer in the union movement.

It was also at the age of 16 that Cook began preaching. He showed ability and, at 18, to better pursue that calling, joined another breakaway Methodist sect – the "New Connexion" Methodists. There was a New Connexion chapel in Silverdale and it was the minister there, Dr. J. Mellor, who ran the affairs of the Mutual Improvement Society. According to one account Cook "became a popular lay preacher and ... an eloquent speaker showing indications of being a studied and deep thinker".[13] He would have trained full-time for the ministry but for his family commitments.[14]

In 1885 Cook began the next chapter of his life. In August he married a schoolteacher from Chesterton, Mary Turner, at the Primitive Methodist Chapel in London Road.[15] Mary's brother (also a coalminer), had recently emigrated to NSW and settled in Lithgow. The Cooks decided to do the same. Joseph went out first, embarking from England on – appropriately – Christmas Day 1885. Shortly before his departure he had been presented with a gift by his fellow lay preachers, a revised edition of the Bible and a copy of W.J. Conybeare's two-volume classic, *The Life and Epistles of St Paul*. The gift was "expressive of their esteem for him as a Christian".[16]

In Lithgow Cook found work in a clerical/managerial capacity at the nearby Vale of Clwydd colliery. He joined the town's Primitive Methodist congregation, and, in early 1887, Mary arrived in Lithgow with their baby son. For the next eight years Cook devoted his energies to his family and his church. He resumed lay preaching and later became a trustee. He also supported the temperance movement and the cause of organised labour. He was a republican and an early advocate of female suffrage.[17] In June 1891 he was elected to the NSW parliament, and, in October 1893, to the Labor leadership.[18]

It had been an admirable ascension. Yet just a year later Cook left the Labor Party to join "the enemy" – George Reid's pro-business Free Traders. There was, it must be said, a legitimate issue of principle at stake. Cook refused to take the "Solidarity Pledge", insisting that it would "narrow and leg-iron the sphere of any candidate" to an unconscionable degree.[19] More is the pity, his views did not prevail. But to desert his party of origin was an extreme step.

Cook's switch did not immediately put an end to his advocacy for social justice. Reid's pre-Federation government in NSW was reasonably progressive. In the same year as his switch from Labor, Cook expressed himself "pleased that the churches were no longer afraid of socialism".[20] As late as 1896, in his private capacity, he proposed that the Churches carry out sociological studies so as to equip all their members "for works of reform".[21]

The watershed year for Cook was 1901. He followed George Reid to the new federal parliament, where the Free Traders found themselves in Opposition for most of the decade. Cook's style hardened; soon he abandoned any reformist pretensions. In 1908 he succeeded Reid as the leader of the Anti-Socialist Party (as the Free Trade Party was renamed in 1906). Routinely, Cook invoked the verities of moral personal freedom, states' rights and the British Crown in defence of "anything which could help rich men and private enterprise".[22] For example, he opposed direct taxation by the Commonwealth, the only means then available to fund old age pensions on a national basis. The change in him was fundamental, in the manner of another religious conversion.

By the time he became Prime Minister, in May 1913, Cook was a protectionist as well as a conservative and monarchist.[23] His government achieved little of note (it lacked a majority in the Senate), but was still in office in August 1914 when World War I broke out in Europe. It fell to Cook to declare war on Australia's behalf.

Notably, Cook justified the conflict in religious terms, as a defence of Australia against Germany's "putrid morality, an ethic of Hell".[24] No doubt, too, he endorsed the dominant message of the Protestant churches at the opening of hostilities, which was that war would have a "regenerating effect on Australian society" and lead to "spiritual renewal".[25] That was a theme of the sermon delivered on Sunday, August 9, 1914 by Melbourne's Anglican Archbishop, Lowther Clarke, at a special service which Cook attended.[26]

Of course, these were sentiments born in the flush of romantic, patriotic ignorance. Contrary to myth, most of the Catholic churches in Australia also supported the war in August 1914, if not quite so enthusiastically. It was only in mid-1916 – after a plea for peace by Pope Benedict XV, the Easter Rising in Ireland, and two years of horrible slaughter in France – that some Catholic spokesmen changed their stance. Conscription was a discrete though obviously not unrelated issue. Some who believed in the War opposed conscription.

By January 1916 Cook was somewhat more sober. Three of his sons were serving on the Western Front (one was wounded at Gallipoli), and his wife was active in the Red Cross. But Cook suffered no deep *personal* loss and was in no way repentant. He consoled himself as regards the fearful carnage:

"We recognize a Power behind all the strife – a Mind planning the destiny of the world and a Hand shaping it".[27]

Near the War's end, in September 1918, Cook spoke in his native Staffordshire about the purpose of it all:

> This is not a war for arranging and negotiating and fixing up. It is a struggle of two conflicting ideals. You cannot negotiate a thing like that. There is only one thing you can do about it – either the light must drive out the darkness or it must be submerged by the darkness.[28]

By then over 30 million people had perished, including almost 60,000 Australians. Yet Cook was still opposed to negotiation! He wanted a fight to the death. These were profoundly unChrist-like sentiments. They were positively Manichean.

Cook stayed in parliament until late 1921. Following the Labor split of 1916-17, he served in the Nationalist administrations of Billy Hughes as a hamstrung* Minister for the Navy (1917-20) and a tight-fisted Treasurer (1920-21). He accompanied Hughes to the Imperial War Conference of 1918 and the Versailles Peace Conference of 1919. A less convivial pair it would be hard to imagine, though, of the two, Cook was the calmer and more diplomatic.

Some historians attribute Cook's ideological "journey" to sheer opportunism, and no doubt that played a part. As F.K. Crowley once observed, "[a] harsh critic might say that when in office Cook saved the taxpayers' money at the expense of the class from which he had risen".[29] But I would emphasise another factor: Cook's religious allegiance. It also changed – at around the same time as his political allegiance.

In 1902 the Primitive Methodists reunited with the Wesleyans to form the Methodist Conference of NSW.[30] Cook was a strong supporter of union. At a Primitive Methodist gathering in 1895 he had argued:

---

* Typically, Hughes made most of the important decisions himself. Of their time together at Versailles in 1919, Cook made this waspish remark: "I did a lot of the yarding but Hughes did all the barking. That's what little dogs are for." He routinely referred to Hughes as "the little devil". For his part, Hughes derided Cook as a "Bible banging Billy" and "normally the bane of my life".

> The time has arrived when we should join hand in hand for
> the purpose of consolidating the forces of Christianity. I would
> not mind if we could clasp hands with more than our brother
> Wesleyans, if the next day we can clasp with the hand of
> friendship all those who believe in Christianity and hope for its
> advancement.[31]

Those sentiments were admirable, but they were uttered in Cook's left-wing days. By 1902 he was well on the way to becoming a reactionary, and this placed him at odds with his Church. For, to its credit, the new amalgamated body promptly announced its commitment to the "social Gospel":

> The [Methodist] Church should have its eyes wide open to see
> the conditions of things around, its heart should beat strong and
> quick in sympathy for the distressed and suffering.[32]

During the ensuing decade[33] – and beyond – the Methodist Church as a whole supported legislative reform in Australia aimed at ameliorating poverty and injustice. But there remained within its ranks a minority of the "old school", those who held fast to the view that individual salvation and moral probity should be paramount and that attempts by the State to "express the ideal and spirit of Christianity"[34] were counterproductive, if not positively evil. They argued that "no class of society should benefit at the expense of another and that there should be no unnecessary restrictions on personal freedom".[35]

These were Cook's own words and he was a champion of such views. He became, in Graham Fricke's apt phrase, a "puritanical renegade".[36] While he never forgot his Methodist roots, he did seem to forget the plight of the toiling masses – people of the kind with whom, years ago, he had worked in the coal pits, "a nightmare world of darkness and despair and backbreaking labour".[37] And the arguments Cook employed were essentially spurious. A moment's reflection should have told him that the wealthy and privileged classes in society were *already* benefiting at the expense of the working class. What Cook and others like him really objected to, was the prospect that the wealthy and privileged might be required by the State to give up a portion of their existing benefits. That said, the qualifying word "unnecessary" before "restrictions" (in the quotation above) left room for a measure of social reform.

Like too many self-made men, even sincerely Christian self-made men, Cook came to over-value his own achievements. With unseemly relish he accepted appointments as a Privy Councillor (1914), a Knight (1918), and as High Commissioner in London (1921-27). He revelled in the London social round – "the crowning achievement of his life"[38] – before enjoying a restful retirement in a harbourside mansion in Sydney's posh Bellevue Hill. He died a wealthy man in 1947, "satisfied that he had led a worthy and profitable life in the sight of God and man".[39]

One wonders if he ever mulled over chapter 8 of Deuteronomy, especially verses 17 and 18: "You may say to yourself, 'My power and the strength of my hands have produced this wealth for me.' But remember the Lord your God, for it is he who gives you the ability to produce wealth."

Cook was described at his state funeral as a "distinguished Methodist statesman".[40] After his own lights the compliment was merited. But I cannot help thinking that his political career might have taken a very different course had he remained within the Primitive Methodist sect of his youth. The amalgamated Methodist Church gave him respectable cover.

One charming incident late in Cook's life suggests he was not unaware of the ironies of his situation. In late November 1941, at St Andrew's Cathedral in Sydney, Cook attended the state funeral of another Labor defector and former Prime Minister, Chris Watson. The 81 year-old Cook was a pallbearer. Many of his and Watson's old Labor comrades were there, and they came over afterwards to greet him. "It looks," said a sardonic Cook to one of them, "like the day of resurrection."[41]

WILLIAM MORRIS (BILLY) HUGHES (1862-1952)

LABOR: 1915-16
NATIONAL LABOR: 1916-17
NATIONALIST: 1917-23

I t has been remarked with some justice that, as both politician and human being, Hughes "continues to defy definition".[1] The Little Digger, as he became known during World War I, belonged at one time or another to every major political grouping bar the Country Party. In old age, at a function in his honour, this gap in his resume was pointed out: "Good God, brother, you have to draw the line somewhere!" was Hughes' famously blasphemous retort.[2] He had derided the "hayseeds" all his life – at substantial political cost. The Country Party's antipathy towards him was a major reason for his loss of the Prime Ministership in early 1923.

Hughes' life followed roughly the same path as Joseph Cook's, but Hughes was a far more interesting and influential figure. He began his career in the NSW parliament in 1894 as the feisty champion of wharf-labourers and slum-dwellers. He ended it after World War II comfortably ensconced on Sydney's tranquil, blue-blooded north shore. As Prime Minister, his vituperative campaigns for conscription in 1916-17 split the Labor movement and the country at-large. He inflamed sectarianism to a tragic degree, and, ever since, has been pilloried by historians of the left. Donald Horne described him as "a genius in speaking the language of hatred"[3] and "in a sense ... mad, living out his own unrealities".[4] The puritan US President Woodrow Wilson – whom Hughes mocked as the "Heaven-born" – thought him a "pestiferous varmint".[5]

Yet Hughes was a good deal more than the rancorous clown of legend. He served continuously in the House of Representatives for more than 50 years. One of his many private secretaries, Malcolm Booker, judged him a "very complex personality"[6] – and I have come to agree. Hughes was a populist, but an enormously formidable one. He was witty, ruthless, bright, indefatigable and extremely well-read. He had guts, and was a canny distorter of the truth. For good or ill – I would say ill – he argued toe to toe with the Allied leaders at Versailles in 1919 in pressing for punitive vengeance on Germany and spoils for Australia. (We got New Guinea outright and a share of Nauru, but not nearly as much hard cash as Hughes had wanted.)

What of religion? Here, too, the facts are elusive.

Hughes was not a regular churchgoer, except as a youth and an old man. His first marriage was probably never solemnised,[7] and he was notorious for a vile temper and blasphemous language.* What is more, he had a "bleakly Hobbesian view of life".[8] For Hughes, wrote Manning Clark, "life was a savage elemental struggle for survival in which strong men crushed the weak".[9] Certainly Hughes displayed little faith in humanity, individually or collectively. His overriding conviction was that the State was duty-bound to protect its citizens from each other and to defend them from external threat.[10]

Hughes was also a punisher. "Like Jehovah, [he] thirsted for revenge against his enemies."[11] In his advocacy for the pulverisation of Germany in 1918-19 he spoke openly of exacting "an eye for an eye". He called this "the gospel – my gospel".[12] "Let the German people," he said, "work out their salvation by deeds. Let them pay." [13] At Versailles he fought tooth and nail against a proposed Racial Equality Clause in the Covenant of the League of Nations – and prevailed.

---

* Two more examples must give the flavour. When the fresh-faced Malcolm Booker presented himself for a job interview in April 1940, the wizened Hughes grunted: "Jesus, I am getting them straight from school". Another subordinate once copped this serve: "My God, Fry, if I asked you to bring me the Cross of Christ you would bring me a watering can!"

None of this is easily compatible with the New Testament. Nevertheless, I cannot agree with the oft-expressed view that Hughes was either an agnostic or an atheist. For a start, he had a consciousness of his own sin: "It's mercy I want, not justice," he once told a portraitist.[14] Booker attributed to him "a strong religious sense".[15] L.F. Fitzhardinge, his most eminent biographer, went further.

In Fitzhardinge's assessment, Hughes "adhered more or less actively all his life" to the Church of England. Furthermore, he had "a generalised faith in the spiritual values of Christianity" and "a profound belief in the after-life and the all-pervasiveness of God".[16] His infrequent church-going could be put down to "deafness, the hand-to-mouth nature of his early life in Australia and, later, pressure of affairs".[17] The last argument seems inadequate: such hindrances (and worse) have been overcome by countless worshippers down the centuries. I would not go so far as Fitzhardinge, but the evidence establishes that Booker, at least, was close to the mark. Religion was an integral aspect of Hughes' make-up. It is simply not the case, as Manning Clark asserted, that Hughes remained throughout his life "secretive and enigmatic … about metaphysics".[18]

Hughes was born in Pimlico, London, on September 25, 1862, the only son of a respectable couple from the lower-middle class.[19] William Hughes, his father, was a carpenter and joiner, a Tory voter, and a Particular Baptist by religion. He was a deacon at the Welsh Baptist Church at Moorefields in the City of London,[20] and espoused a strict, narrow Calvinism typical of the northern Welsh tradition.*[21] Young Will Hughes endured sermons about "the eternal torments of hell to which sinners were doomed".[22]

His mother, Jane Hughes (née Morris), came from a "mellower religious tradition".[23] She too grew up in Wales, on the land, but her home was only three miles from the English border at Shropshire. Her family worshipped within the Church of England, and Jane's own affiliation must have been strong: she and William Hughes were married according to Anglican rites

---

* So-called Particular Baptism arose in England in the 17th century and spread quickly to northern Wales. Its adherents espoused the doctrine of "particular redemption" – the idea, said to be based on Chapter 10 of John's Gospel, that God's intention is to save only particular ("elected') persons through the Atonement, as opposed to humanity in general.

and ceremonies (at St Peter's in Pimlico), not those of the Welsh Baptists.[24] Indeed, it appears that young Will Hughes' religious sensibilities were shaped more by his mother and her family than by his father. Although she died before he turned seven, Jane Hughes had formed a close bond with her son.[25] She was evidently a much-loved woman – and a devout one. William Hughes Senior arranged for her tombstone to be inscribed with a Biblical text in Welsh, Revelation 14:13: "Gwyn eu byd y meirw y rhai sydd yn/marw yn yr Anglwydd". ("Blessed are the dead which die in the Lord." (KJV))[26]

After his mother's death, Will Hughes was raised for several years by two aunts, one on each side of the family. During school term he lived with his father's sister, Miss Mary Hughes, who operated an apartment house in the town of Llandudno in Wales. In the holidays he visited the Morrises in the border country, where his widowed aunt Margaret and his maternal grandparents had adjoining farms.[27] It seems likely that his identification with the Church of England was fostered by the Morrises.[28] At all events he sang in the choir at the Anglican Holy Trinity Church in Llandudno[29] before, at the age of 11, being enrolled as a pupil at St Stephen's School in Westminster.

St Stephen's was an Anglican institution endowed in 1847 by Baroness Burdett-Coutts, a noted philanthropist.[30] It enjoyed a good reputation and Hughes, after completing his elementary studies at the age of 15, stayed for five more years as a pupil-teacher. These were crucial in his development.

It was at St Stephen's that Hughes came under the tutelage of Matthew Arnold, the great man of letters whose name appears more than once in this book. Hughes admitted in later life to being unaware (then) of Arnold's literary feats – it was as one of Her Majesty's inspectors of schools that the raw pupil-teacher encountered him. Even so, Hughes always claimed that Arnold was a key influence.[31]

In this instance there is no reason to doubt Hughes' word. Arnold was an earnest and effective educationalist. He instilled in his young charge a love of learning for its own sake and – above all – a love of English literature. Paramount were Shakespeare and the King James Bible.[32] Hughes became steeped in both, as well as reading widely in other disciplines. In addition, every Saturday morning, he attended compulsory lectures on church history.[33] Occasionally he rang the church bells – "one of the finest peals in London".[34]

In 1884 Hughes emigrated to Queensland. He spent a couple of rugged years in the outback – his jobs in this period, real or apocryphal, included stone-breaker, grape-picker, tally clerk, boundary-rider, pothole-sinker, seaman, cook, drover and railway navvy. Then, in 1886, he arrived in Sydney. The bare bones of his life over the next 30 years were drolly summarised by Sir Robert Menzies in *Afternoon Light*:

> He followed a variety of occupations, teacher, locksmith,
> umbrella repairer, stage supernumerary, waterside worker, until
> he became founder and leader of the Waterside Workers' Union,
> went into State Parliament and then Commonwealth, and
> became in turn Labour Minister and Labour Prime Minister. ...
> Somewhere along the line he attended [law] lectures and was
> admitted to practice in NSW. But I am bound to say that in my
> later direct experience of him, he struck me as being singularly
> unaffected by any known legal considerations.[35]

Where, during these hectic decades, did Hughes stand religiously? Fitzhardinge would have argued that, whatever outward appearances to the contrary, he was still at heart a Christian. But others have challenged this. Donald Horne intimated that by the time Hughes had spent a few years in Australia, he had lost his Christian faith. "For this dilemma ... he sold answers in his shop [in Balmain], in books about the new secular religions and the heaven on earth they promised".[36]

No doubt Hughes did sell such material in his shop, and read it, but it does not follow that he himself had adopted a secular view of the world. From 1907-11 he wrote a weekly column for the conservative *Daily Telegraph* in Sydney – 'The Case for Labor'. It was highly influential, and for good reason. The pieces were well-researched, sprightly and accessible. Importantly, they were often "religious" in both content and style. As Malcolm Booker remarked, "the Biblical rhythms which [Hughes] had learned in his childhood were much in evidence and must have contributed greatly to dispelling the notion that Labor doctrines were irreligious."[37]

There are parallels with Kevin Rudd's activities from 2005-07. Hughes' pieces were calculated to reassure Christians, especially conservative Catholics and lower-middle class Protestants. He explicitly addressed their fears: socialism, he argued, was "no more atheistical or opposed to religion than is geology or mathematics".[38] Indeed, he went further, maintaining that "socialism itself as a scheme of brotherhood is the outcome of the life and teaching of Jesus Christ".[39]

In 1910, when supporters of the new Fusion Party resorted to a smear campaign against Labor on the grounds of "irreligion" and "disloyalty", Hughes had already blunted their attack. Moreover, he responded on the stump in inimitable style, once quipping (with perfect accuracy) that when he had first joined the NSW Parliament in 1894, "the place was littered with Sunday School teachers and superintendents who were members of the Labour Party".[40]

As an old man, Hughes recalled with evident satisfaction a telegram he received from three Methodist ministers in South Australia, after Labor's big election victory in 1910. "It was couched," he wrote, "in the words of Simeon's prayer: 'Lord, now lettest thou thy servant depart in peace for mine eyes have seen thy salvation'".[41] (Compare Luke 2:29-32.)

Hughes, then, achieved a great deal in his early career for both the underprivileged and for religious tolerance. To say that he undid much of the good work during World War I – and compounded his worst mistakes for another 30 years – is, in part, a political judgment. Many would disagree. Rightly or wrongly Hughes was held in esteem and affection by millions of Australians. He himself was convinced of his own righteousness. "I believe I have a mission and that God gives me strength to do it," he wrote in a letter to journalist Keith Murdoch on November 4, 1916.[42]

There is not room here for a full discussion of the wisdom and morality of World War I – or even of Australian involvement – from a Christian perspective. Michael McKernan's book *Australian Churches at War* (1980) contains a fine survey of the issues. In retrospect, however, Hughes' worst sin seems undeniable: in 1916-17 he sought to exploit, for military and political ends*, a potent strain of anti-Irish and anti-Catholic bigotry in

---

* In the event, Hughes failed to achieve his ends. Both of the conscription plebiscites were narrowly defeated. Even Hughes had no comeback when the ballots were tabulated from the soldiers at the front: the Diggers voted "no" by a 3:1 margin. As the esteemed war historian C.W. Bean explained, a chief reason was that "they would not by their vote force any man into the stream of horrors they had themselves experienced against his will".

the young Australian nation. The cause of conscription obsessed him to the point of hysteria. Hughes always argued that he had tried to get the Catholic churches on side and it is probably true that he harboured no personal bigotry. As Booker explained, "[his] anti-Catholicism was not based essentially on anti-Irish or religious feeling, but upon a quite separate consideration: he strongly resented the intervention of the Catholic hierarchy in Australian politics".[43] This resentment was born in the 1890s when the nascent Labor Party was split between radical socialists on the left and conservative Catholics on the right.

Still the fact remains. By Hughes' conduct during World War I religious sectarianism in Australia was made much, much worse. Hitherto it had been kept in check; thereafter, until the 1970s, it always simmered and occasionally boiled over. James Scullin, a fair and righteous man if ever one lived, believed that Hughes had "very nearly wrecked Australia".[44] Among his most provocative actions were vicious personal attacks on the country's leading Catholic prelate, Melbourne Archbishop Daniel Mannix, and allegations that Catholics were deliberately cooperating with the IWW (Industrial Workers of the World), an organisation dedicated to the abolition of capitalism. Hughes "would have known this to be untrue".[45] He also caused needless turmoil in 1917 by ordering the prosecution of Queensland's Catholic premier, T.J. Ryan, whom he accused of being "Mannix's tool". Hughes formed the Commonwealth (Federal) Police in that year – originally for use only in Queensland – because he "wished to have a group of non-Catholic police under his control". (The Queensland force was dominated by Catholics.)[46]

Hughes died at his home in Lindfield, Sydney on October 28, 1952. His State funeral, at St Andrew's Cathedral in Sydney, was conducted by the Archbishop of Sydney and Primate of Australia, the Most Reverend Dr. Howard Mowll. Dr. Mowll had called on Hughes at his home shortly before he died.

The coffin lay in state for two days, and an estimated 450,000 mourners crammed the city and the route to the Northern Suburbs Cemetery.[47] It was a sultry afternoon, and a crack of thunder rang out as the coffin was being lowered into the grave before a large group of dignitaries. The leader of the Country Party, Arthur Fadden, could not resist a final shot: "He's arrived!"[48]

Arrived where? Where did Hughes stand with God when he died? In his twilight years Hughes wrote two books of memoirs, *Crusts and Crusades* (1948) and *Policies and Potentates* (1950). These were not serious attempts at autobiography and some critics have dismissed them as fable. My own view is that they are two of the most extraordinary books ever written by a politician. Certainly they are among the funniest. Hughes was a master storyteller with a delightful turn of phrase. One thing struck me above all: this man knew his Bible back to front. Both books are laced with Christian phrases.

Two passages bear quoting at some length. They establish to my satisfaction that, by the end of his life, Hughes believed in a Creator God who would dispense divine justice in the afterlife.

In *Crusts and Crusades* Hughes told an anecdote from the 1890s about a speaker he once listened to in the Sydney Domain.[49] It matters not whether the anecdote was true; what matters is that Hughes told it in the way he did. The image he conjured was of a pompous atheist arguing metaphysics with, first, a knowledgeable believer named Jenkins, and, second, a crusty old sea-captain. In Hughes' telling, the notion that Darwinian evolution is a satisfactory explanation of the Universe is exposed as a "pretentious monstrosity". After some bantering Jenkins gets the atheist to concede that, even if life on Earth did emerge from non-life via some process of abiogenesis, "it only pushes the problem one stage further back".

But it is the old sea-captain who steals the show. He quotes Isaiah 49:23 and awes the crowd. "In what did they believe?" he asks the rationalists. "In the protoplasm squirming in the primordial slime, which came they know not whence? Or in an Absolute of which they could not conceive, that must, yet could not be, the First Cause?" Hughes sides with the sea-captain, who believed in "the living God who had inspired Isaiah, who held the destiny of all men in his hands".

Later in *Crusts and Crusades*, Hughes reminisced about his childhood. He recalled his rejection of the "narrow Calvinism" of his father's people, and, in particular, the doctrine of predestination:

> When I was old enough to think for myself I turned away from that terrible creed; I believed that as a man sowed so he should

reap, that the gates of heaven would not be slammed in the face of those who sincerely repented, and that *by faith and works* he might find salvation.[50]

That philosophy is, broadly speaking, one of (high) Anglo-Catholicism.

But what of Jesus Christ? In neither *Crusts and Crusades* nor *Policies and Potentates* did Hughes squarely address the question of Jesus' divinity. It is hard to disagree with Manning Clark's assessment that the mature Hughes appeared "indifferent to the divine example of compassion for the multitude". As Prime Minister, and afterwards, he behaved like an Old Testament tyrant: "to him most of the beatitudes were incomprehensible [and] he saw no reason why the meek should enjoy a state of blessedness – or the peacemakers either."[51] During World War I he even banned the use of the German language in Australian churches.[52] This mostly affected Lutheran and other Protestant congregations, especially in South Australia – on this score at least Hughes could not be accused of anti-Catholicism.

But, yet again, there is another side to the story. Hughes rarely behaved like Jesus, but he professed to believe *in* Jesus as the Son of God. Consider the following passage, from a piece published in the Broken Hill *Barrier Miner* of June 4, 1923. The man who had just recently stood down as Prime Minister of Australia wrote in defence of a popular faith-healer named Hickson:

> He has reminded us all that without faith we perish, and his mission has proved that the people are not only ready but eager to accept Christianity if but those who preach it show by their conduct that they sincerely believe in its great truths. It may be the mark of a credulous and feeble mind to believe in the healing powers of Christ. It may be quite out of tune with the age in which we live to hold that to God all things are possible. But I do not see that any man can be a Christian and not believe these things.[53]

STANLEY MELBOURNE BRUCE (1883-1967)

NATIONALIST: 1923-29

I have puzzled over Bruce. Gerard Henderson once described him as "the embodiment of the Protestant Ascendency in Australia"[1], and arguably he belongs with Reid, Menzies and Fraser – the enigmatic Presbyterians. Bruce's father and mother were both Presbyterians, and initially I assumed that their son must also have been one. However, even as a boy S.M. Bruce seems to have had minimal contact with his parents' church. Most sources specify his religion as Anglican.

Even that is a stretch on the evidence I have seen. Bruce belonged to the Church of England in a formal sense, but that is all that can be said with conviction. Cecil Edwards, in his long and sympathetic biography, made scant mention of *any* religious life. Manning Clark adjudged Bruce "an Australian version of the Renaissance man".[2] Richard Casey, writing in 1973, made this remark: "As for religion, he never seemed to me to be much interested."[3]

Was Bruce, then, just a gentlemanly agnostic, like Barton and Holt? Without doubt he was a gentleman – in the best sense of the word – but I am not convinced he was an agnostic. From time to time he made mention of God, and in later life he espoused a view of the world consistent with the noblest sentiments of the New Testament. He seems best regarded as a fellow-traveller.

As Prime Minister in the 1920s, Bruce led a lacklustre, improvident government. His ascent in politics had been too swift. Preoccupied with cementing a permanent coalition with the Country Party, and with glib notions of law and order, national development and modern business efficiency, Bruce lacked broad life-experience. He was at home among international leaders and had a sweeping vision for Australia, but he "had little understanding of the problems of the common man."[4] His government created the CSIRO, a far-sighted step, but it "stalled on social reform"[5] and saddled Australia with heightened class divisions and substantial foreign debt. In all, Bruce "was fortunate in not having to pick up the burden that he and his government had helped create".[6]

Dame Enid Lyons, who resented Bruce's rather condescending attitude to her husband during the 1930s, summed things up in brisk terms:

What [Bruce] failed to appreciate is that winning elections is not just a gift from God, nor the result of three weeks on the hustings. Some of the qualities of leadership are involved at least, and a presentable record of achievement is not without its value.[7]

Bruce was only 46 when he was pitched from office (and his own seat*) at the October 1929 election. Still a relatively young man, he had ample time to redeem himself – and he did. One of his first acts of atonement was to use his great influence among public servants and bankers in the City of London. Bruce persuaded them to agree to the conversion to lower interest rates of some 400 million pounds' worth of Australian high-interest loans.[8] This saved tens of millions of valuable pounds for Australia at the height of the Depression.

In 1932 Bruce became Australia's representative at the League of Nations and in 1933 he was appointed to a seat on the Council.[9] That same year, 1933, Lyons appointed him as High Commissioner in London. From this base, by dint of hard work and force of personality, he became an eminent world statesman.

Among many achievements was his presidency of the Montreaux Conference in 1936, at which a Turkish border dispute over the Straits of Constantinople was resolved. The Turkish delegation had specifically

---

* Bruce won back his seat of Flinders at the 1931 election standing for the newly-created United Australia Party – he often joked that he had helped his own cause by staying in London throughout the campaign.

asked for Bruce, and the Secretary-General of the Conference, Thanassis Aghnides of Greece, was lavish in his praise:

It is my privilege to bear testimony to the achievement of Lord Bruce. He and the Turks – two ex-enemies – vied with each other in working high-mindedly to buttress a precarious peace … I have rarely seen such a combination of vigour, steadiness [and] fortitude.[10]

In later years Bruce served as the Australian Government's representative in the British War Cabinet and as chairman of the World Food Council. (In the latter capacity, in 1950, he met Pope Pius XII.) He was also appointed a member of the House of Lords and elected to the captaincy of the Royal and Ancient Golf Club at St Andrews – there is a lawn near the first tee named after him.

As he became older Bruce's worldview broadened. Like Malcolm Fraser, he became an "enlightened squire". By 1929 Bruce had accepted privately that governments "must face great expenditure upon social amelioration"[11], and by 1938 it was possible for a close colleague to describe him as "an independent progressive, an individualist with no real political attachment".[12] By 1945, Bruce had become a firm admirer of both Franklin Roosevelt and John Curtin. He felt moved to say that the Liberal Party in Australia was "too reactionary … to swallow".[13]

Stanley Melbourne Bruce was born in St Kilda on April 15, 1883, the youngest of five siblings. Legend has it that his father's side of the family was descended from Robert the Bruce, the medieval King of Scotland.[14] Be that as it may, John Munro Bruce had both Scottish and Ulster roots. Described by Edwards as a "strict Presbyterian" [15], he was a past president of the Young Men's Christian Association[16] and a man of verve and acumen. He was a partner in the Melbourne warehousing company Paterson, Lang and Bruce; a captain in the Prince of Wales Light Horse Regiment; and a leading figure in the establishment of the Royal Melbourne Golf Club. He drew "respect, and almost fear" from his youngest son.[17]

J.M. Bruce may have been a strict Presbyterian, but he sent his boys to Melbourne Grammar (a Church of England school) rather than Scotch College.[18] Whatever the reasons behind it, the choice proved a sound one. Grammar's motto was *Ora et Labora* – pray and work.[19] Students were instilled with a sense of privilege but also of honour and piety and obligation. The school prayer was this:

> May Thy blessing and protection, O Lord, be upon us this day; upon our homes and upon all for whom we are in duty bound to pray ... That those who shall here receive the lessons of piety and knowledge may use the talents committed to their charge to the welfare of their fellow creatures and the honour of Thy great name.[20]

Bruce flourished. He excelled in sport, cadets and debating, and was captain of the school in 1900-01.

During Bruce's final year, his father died suddenly while in Paris on business. In late 1902, accompanied by his mother and sister, he departed Melbourne for England. He studied law at Cambridge and lived at Trinity Hall.[21] This was, and still is, a venerable Church of England college. Another biographer, I.M. Cumpston, has suggested that Bruce's years there "entrenched the social conformity to middle-class respectability and Anglicanism he had learnt at The Grammar School".[22]

It would be nice to relate that Bruce struggled with theology in his university years like a number of our other Prime Ministers. But the record is bare. Bruce's abiding passion at Cambridge was, of all things, rowing. He was a member of the crew that beat Oxford at Henley in 1904 and he came to hero-worship his coach, a charismatic Australian named Steve Fairbairn. Rowing and its collegiate male culture became a kind of substitute religion. After graduation – as a sideline to management of the family firm's affairs and practice at the London Bar – he assumed rowing coaching duties at Cambridge. The Rev. Conrad A. Skinner was the cox of the 1911 crew, and years later he compared Bruce to the author of Mark's Gospel!

Bruce was, wrote Skinner, "the articulate interpreter par excellence (as St Mark was of St Peter in Gospel history) of the coruscating brilliance and genius of Steve Fairbairn. Intuitively and coherently, he expressed, codified and exhibited to the rowing world the revelation and revolution of which Steve was the spearhead."[23]

If Bruce harboured an interest in matters religious as a young man, he kept it well hidden. He was never a wide reader, of theology or much else.[24]

His wedding in July 1913, to Ethel Anderson of Melbourne*, was a quiet affair at a church at Sonning-on-Thames. The site was chosen for its convenience, not because Bruce worshipped there: according to Cecil Edwards, "Bruce had to go over and sleep at Sonning the required number of nights to establish his residence."[25]

World War I was a watershed for the Western world and certainly for Bruce. He served with high distinction in the front lines as an officer in the British Army, winning the Military Cross and the Croix de Guerre avec Palme. But Captain Bruce did not become a Colonel Blimp. Quite the opposite: for the rest of his life he strove mightily to be a peacemaker. It has been suggested that Bruce privately opposed conscription in 1916-17, though he did make recruiting speeches when he returned to Australia.[26]

In September 1921 he was asked at short notice** to be Australia's delegate to a League of Nations Assembly in Geneva. His unscripted remarks on the report of a committee on disarmament made a vivid impression. After bluntly describing the inglorious reality of war ("men mutilated and dying, without the possibility of being helped") he concluded thus:

> I would appeal to those who guide the destinies of the countries
> of the world to try to cast aside their political prudence and their
> diplomatic caution, and think of the matter from the point of
> view of the man who has got to go and endure these things, if
> you will continue to have these ghastly and dreadful wars.[27]

During the 1930s Bruce supported to the hilt all serious efforts to negotiate with Hitler. He championed "long-term economic appeasement ... based in the idea of removing the fundamental causes of war: poverty, ignorance, hunger, poor nutrition, other forms of social and economic deprivation".[28] During World War II itself he tried to mobilise Allied support for "peace aims", beyond "acquisitiveness and vindictiveness".[29]

---

* Ethel was one of seven sisters from a notable Victorian family of Scotch-Irish ancestry – the same as Bruce's own. Also like her husband, Lady Bruce (as she became) had been raised as a Presbyterian. She was an extremely devoted wife but bore no children. Bruce was devastated by her death in early 1967 and outlived her by only a few months.
** At the time Bruce was the only government MP in Europe. He was tracked down on a French golf course.

These were admirably Christian sentiments (cf. Psalm 82; Micah 4:3-4; Matthew 5:9) but other questions arise. Did Bruce truly believe in a (supernatural) God? Did he accept all Jesus' teachings? There are indications both ways.

On the one hand, there is no evidence of regular Sunday churchgoing on his part, let alone of serious metaphysical speculation. As I have said, Cecil Edwards, his first biographer, barely mentioned religion; Edwards concluded that Bruce held an "old-fashioned liberalistic belief in the perfectibility of human nature".[30] Judith Brett has written of his "practical and impersonal rationality … supplemented with a modern faith in experts".[31]

One of Bruce's closest confidantes as Prime Minister – his "evil genius", some thought[32] – was John Greig Latham, the Attorney-General. As we will see in the chapter on John Curtin, Latham was a proselytising atheist "who saw belief in God … [as] evidence of the stupidity of the great mass of human beings".[33] He was also a cold, vain personality. It was he who convinced Bruce in 1929 to try to wash his hands of difficult industrial relations problems, by returning most of the relevant Constitutional powers to the states.

This spineless and ill-conceived move frightened the Australian working class. It was manna from heaven for Billy Hughes, who jumped at the chance to make trouble for the "upstart" who had replaced him as Prime Minister. Hughes precipitated the fall of the Bruce-Page Government by leading a group of dissidents across the floor of the House.[34] Bruce was unrepentant and rashly called an election. It is hard to conceive that a committed, mature Christian would have done so – or have allowed himself to be in thrall to a man of Latham's temperament.

But that was the 1920s, and Bruce mellowed. Moreover there are hints in the record that the older Bruce assumed – or did not reject – the existence of a higher power. Once, in the 1930s, he handwrote a candid 5,000-word letter to Richard (later Lord) Casey. Bruce rued being undecided about his future and living day by day – "not a part I was particularly designed by God to play".[35] In 1965 he told Alfred Stirling, another biographer, that he had referred to God several times in war-time discussions with Winston Churchill – on one occasion Bruce told the Great Man to his face that, "not being God", he should not behave so loftily.[36] Elsewhere Bruce referred to his own even temper as "a gift from God".[37]

The best evidence that Bruce nursed a "religious sense" was presented after his death by Alfred Stirling. In his book *Lord Bruce: The London Years*, published in 1974, Stirling focussed on Bruce's activities in the decade before and during World War II. Stirling's family had been close to the Bruces and Stirling himself worked intimately with Bruce in London from 1936 onwards. The following points are worth noting.

First, Bruce once confided to Stirling that he felt his life had been "saved" during World War I. He suffered bad wounds when many of his comrades were killed outright or survived unscathed – leaving them "ready" for the next futile and often fatal assault. Bruce's wounds took him out of the front lines for extended periods. "This happened twice," he told Stirling. "I began then to think I might be kept for some purpose."[38]

Second, although Bruce was not a regular churchgoer, he was visibly moved and awed on the occasions when he did go. It is true that these occasions were usually to mark secular rather than Christian festivals – Australia Day and Anzac Day, for example. Even so, Bruce treated them with reverent seriousness. He was well-known at St Clement Danes (the "Australia House chapel" before it was bombed in the war) and, later, at St Martin in the Fields in Trafalgar Square.* Bruce always arranged for "the best available preacher" to give the sermon. "He himself read the lessons with clear understanding and deep feeling."[39]

Third, there is the testimony of one of Bruce's closest colleagues, Frank Lidgett McDougall. McDougall worked with Bruce in various capacities after 1923 and once claimed to have been the man who "influenced Bruce to be progressive".[40] Though an agnostic himself, McDougall had been raised in a pious Christian family and was supremely well-versed in the Bible. "The High Commissioner", he once said to Stirling, "is a man who walks humbly with his God."[41] (Compare Micah 6:8.) I. M. Cumpston concurred "very strongly that this was so".[42]

Stirling himself seemed undecided. He proffered the view that "Bruce was not I think a 'religious' man in the outward sense", adding that "I

---

* St Martin in the Fields was the venue for Bruce's memorial service, a month or so after his death. The church was full and members of the Royal Family were represented. The High Commissioner, Sir Alec Downer, read the lesson.

never heard him discuss, or even mention, 'religion', nor did he have clergy among his close friends".[43]

Yet Stirling felt able to adjudge that Bruce held a "reverent attitude to the mystery of the life beyond".[44]

I stand by my evaluation: Bruce is best classed a fellow-traveller. The evidence does not permit a definite verdict of either belief or unbelief, but in a number of respects he thought like a Christian.

Perhaps most tantalising of all is the following passage from *Bruce of Melbourne*. It tantalises on both a religious and a political level. Bruce was asked in 1965 by Cecil Edwards about the British election of July 5, 1945, at which Clement Attlee's Labour Party won an unexpectedly large victory over Churchill's Conservatives, 393 seats to 197 in the House of Commons. Bruce said that "it was providential that it had gone as it had". His reasoning was this:

> If the Conservatives had been returned it would have meant the confirmation of the reactionary element in the party. When Halifax asked about Churchill, I told him that God having intervened in his behalf, Winston was busy trying to upset His handiwork.[45]

In other words, Bruce believed by mid-1945 that it was in Britain's socio-political interests (and Churchill's personal interests) that Labour should form a post-war government. He also believed that God was of a like view – and had, as it were, "approved" the election result.

JAMES HENRY (JIM) SCULLIN (1876-1953)

LABOR: 1929-32

The redoubtable Jim Scullin, who assumed office at the beginning of the Great Depression, was Australia's ninth Prime Minister and the first who was a Catholic. His background was quintessentially Irish and working-class. Both his parents were from County Derry, a place where, in John Molony's words, "the Catholic population kept alive memories of the plantation of Protestant settlers and the ravages of Cromwell".[1] As a little boy Scullin "said his prayers at his mother's knee".[2] There is no reason to doubt Molony's assessment that Scullin "remained committed to his faith and its practice throughout his life".[3]

Scullin's schooling in regional Victoria was rudimentary. As a young man he furthered his education through night classes, voracious reading and – crucially – the activities of the Catholic Young Men's Society. It was at the CYMS, and Ballarat's South Street Society, that he learnt his excellent oratorical and debating skills.[4] His style was both analytical and emotional, and yet "he was very rarely guilty of personal abuse, even in the most trying circumstances".[5] His manners were charming.

It is strongly arguable that Scullin, of all our leaders, was the most conscientious Christian. He "believed in the resurrection of the dead and the life of the world to come".[6] In his personal conduct he came – by fallible human standards – nearer than any of the others to sinlessness. Sir Robert Menzies adjudged that "beyond question, his integrity was absolute".[7] Yet Scullin is generally regarded as a political failure. Does this suggest that the most devout Christians are not cut out for high office?

It is true that Scullin's period as Prime Minister was short. He could not have assumed office at a worse time, just 17 days before the Wall Street crash of 1929. No one blamed Scullin for the Great Depression – indeed, from the mid-1920s onwards, his had been one of the few voices of economic caution and restraint. The people elected him because he was moderate and decent and trustworthy. But, as Molony observed, "in asking a prophet to assume the mantle of leader, they and he were unaware that the times were against them all".[8] For Scullin, his two years in office must have seemed like 20. He aged visibly and came to be dubbed "a prophet destroyed".[9]

By early 1931 he was mournful:

> It has been a bitter disappointment to me that the serious economic crisis prevented the Labor Government upon its assumption of office from putting into effect some of its long-cherished ideals. At the moment all our energies are being devoted to the removal of the acute depression. … This involves patient and unspectacular work.[10]

Scullin did that work. The so-called Premiers' Plan of June 1931 pleased few in the ALP and did little to stifle conservative criticism of the Scullin Government. Even so, it was responsible if unimaginative (deflationary) policy. The great economist John Maynard Keynes, who himself came to prominence during the 1930s, would later say that it "saved the economic structure of Australia".[11]

The problem for Scullin was that his government appeared chaotic. He had to cope with an inexperienced caucus, a hostile Senate, several anti-Labor state governments, a recalcitrant Commonwealth Bank (the Bruce-Page Government had removed it from ministerial oversight[12]), and a suspicious private sector. Worst of all were the sharp ideological divisions within the ALP itself. Scullin declined to fight an early double dissolution election in 1930, at which Labor might have secured a popular mandate to deal with the Depression as it saw fit. Instead he battled to appease the banks and to steer a middle course between the warring factions. But in the end his cautious orthodoxy did him no good. Labor split three ways.

In March 1931 Joseph Lyons defected to the conservatives and in May he became their new leader. In November 1931 several renegades from Labor's far left, led by J.A. (Jack) Beasley, voted with the Opposition to bring the government down.* At the ensuing election Labor was annihilated.

It was a sad end for a capable and diligent man. But it says much for the strength of Scullin's Christian character that even this dreadful experience neither discouraged nor embittered him – at least not for long. He once told fellow Labor politician Fred Daly that, as a Catholic, he was obliged to forgive.[13] Although he was forever ice-cool towards Beasley – and once launched a strong public attack on Beasley's hero, the renegade premier of NSW, J.D. (Jack) Lang – he stayed on as federal Opposition Leader until 1935. Later he became an "elder statesman", a trusted adviser to John Curtin and Ben Chifley. He retired from parliament in 1949.

Again, Menzies' judgment seems astute: though not a political success, Scullin was to be admired for "sensitivity and sensibility of mind, and the high standards by which he guided his own life".[14]

Those standards were high indeed. Scullin and his wife Sarah (née McNamara) were married for nearly 50 years. They had no children – which must have been a source of sadness to them – but were a devoted couple. According to Scullin's most comprehensive biographer, John Robertson, "there is not the slightest suspicion that any irregularity marked [their] married life."[15] Their custom was to attend mass together, usually at St James' Catholic Church in Kent Street, North Richmond (in inner-Melbourne), around the corner from their home.[16] When living in Canberra they worshipped at St Christopher's in Manuka.[17]

In retrospect, Scullin appears something of an ascetic. Manning Clark went so far as to call him "a saint, one of the pure in heart".[18] The only valid criticism ever made of his character was a degree of standoffishness: he "betrayed just a trace, though a forgivable one, of self-satisfaction".[19] He was both a teetaller and a non-smoker in an era when, to say the least, neither was fashionable. His chief recreations were walking, playing

---

* Although Scullin's fellow Catholic Lyons was now the leader of the UAP, sectarianism was still rife among right-wing Protestant voters. In Melbourne, a congregation in the Independent Church in Collins Street burst into sustained applause when told of the division in the House.

the violin (in a duet with Sarah on the piano), and the odd game of bridge or lawn bowls. Another biographer, Warren Denning, recalled "a life … of almost Spartan simplicity".[20] Scullin's work ethic was prodigious, but he had no interest whatever in the accumulation of wealth. Scrupulous and thrifty, he moved out of the Lodge during the Great Depression only to be accused of not being a "gentleman".[21] He died owning little more than his small house in Richmond. Tellingly, his estate included no "watches, trinkets, jewellery".[22]

Scullin, then, set an excellent Christian example by his own conduct. But he was not a noted evangelist. Once, in parliament, after he had lost office, he declared:

> I have only condemnation for those who definitely deny religion, [but] those who do are entitled to their opinions even on that subject.[23]

He made such firm pronouncements only rarely, however. And it will be noted that the declaration I have quoted was against atheists generally: most Christians would have agreed with him, Catholic or Protestant. For decades one of Scullin's most anxious concerns – undoubtedly well-founded – was that encouragements to anti-Catholicism should be minimised. This was necessary, he believed, in order to avert disruption of the Labor movement.[24] Accordingly, "though [Scullin's] parliamentary remarks sometimes revealed that he was a Christian … he did not parade the fact that he was a Catholic."[25] Occasionally as Prime Minister he made a point of stating that his Cabinet adopted a "non-sectarian approach". He even did so while in Rome, in December 1930, during an interview with L'Osservatorre Romano.[26]

It has been asserted by John Molony that "Scullin's knowledge of Catholic social teaching was minimal and had no appreciable effect on his consciousness".[27] This strikes me as an exaggeration; indeed, a far-fetched one. True, Scullin opted for deflationary rather than inflationary policies during the Depression. (Keynesianism was not yet conventional wisdom.) His actions were never guided by any particular member of the Catholic Church, even Melbourne's indomitable Archbishop Mannix. On "day to day political questions", Scullin did not look to a priest to tell him what to do.[28] But his aims and sensibilities were irreducibly Catholic.

Monsignor Arthur Fox (a hard taskmaster) was proud to point this out at Scullin's funeral, a solemn Requiem Mass at St Patrick's Cathedral in Melbourne.[29]

Molony seems to have based his remark on an anecdote from Scullin's early days in Ballarat. Legend has it that he once asked a curate at St Patrick's Cathedral to explain the papal encyclical *Rerum Novarum* (1891) – but neither that august gentleman nor anyone else at the Cathedral could help. Even if some such incident occurred, it beggars belief that so intelligent, well-read and devout a Catholic as Scullin would have remained uninformed about *Rerum Novarum* and other relevant Catholic teachings. Scullin was a personal friend of a prominent Catholic intellectual of the 1930s and 40s, Kevin Kelly, founder of the Catholic Evidence Guild in Melbourne in 1934, and co-founder of the popular newspaper *Catholic Worker* in 1936.[30]

Some of Scullin's opinions clearly *did* reflect Catholic teaching. He strongly supported censorship of "filthy literature" (though not, it should be noted, of political literature).[31] He opposed the death penalty in an era when it was unusual to do so, several times commuting death sentences on natives in New Guinea.[32] His reason was impeccably Christian: "As no man has the power to create a human life, he should not destroy it. The power to create life rests with the Almighty".[33]

Scullin's life-long detestation of war and militarism was another sure sign of the genuineness of his faith. He was not a pacifist: he could countenance the use of force (even conscription) in national self-defence, as in World War II to resist the Japanese.[34] But as regards World War I he was deeply ambivalent from the start. It appalled him that all the great social issues of the day were being "obscured in battlesmoke"[35], and, at war's end, he prophesied correctly that the terms of the Versailles treaty would prove excessively penal – "in them were the seeds of future wars".[36] In 1923 he derided it as "one of the worst huckstering, haggling, sordid pieces of bargaining ever made in the history of the world".[37]

Scullin's Christian instincts were rock-solid. He once said, with exquisite candour: "I do not pretend to be a military expert, and the Lord forbid I ever should be one."[38]

JOSEPH ALOYSIUS (JOE) LYONS (1879-1939)

UNITED AUSTRALIA PARTY: 1932-39

The achievements of this affable yet shrewd Tasmanian are less widely renowned than they ought to be. Yet Lyons' name is venerated among many Australian Christians. In the early 1990s there was a Coalition forum named after him, and it is easy to see why. He and his extraordinary wife Enid* were committed Catholics with 12 children. They were "social conservatives" with a heart.

Lyons' reputation suffered for decades because, at the height of the Great Depression, he defected from Labor to the conservative parties. The then-leader of the Nationalist Party, the dour atheist J.G. Latham, was persuaded to make way for a sure vote-winner – an amiable and respected practising Catholic. Another new anti-Labor party was formed, the United Australia Party (UAP), with Lyons as the standard bearer. Though he was never demonised by Labor to quite the same extent as Joseph Cook or Billy Hughes, he was still regarded ever after as a "rat".

The reasons for Lyons' switch were complicated, but at core there was an issue of fiscal principle.[1] Unlike many of his Labor colleagues – notably the charismatic Treasurer, E.G. ("Red Ted") Theodore** – Lyons thought it

---

* Dame Enid Lyons (1897-1981) went on after her husband's death to be the first female member of the House of Representatives and the first woman in a federal Cabinet. She never remarried.
** Theodore, a practising Catholic like Lyons and Scullin, was the son of a Rumanian immigrant and the grandson of a priest of the Orthodox Church. Like Enid Lyons, his mother had converted from Methodism to Catholicism.

imperative that the government "balance the books" and repay all its debts before embarking on expensive social reform. "Only the Creator," he told Parliament, "could make something out of nothing."[2] As we have seen, Scullin thought so too – but he was a Labor man first and foremost. For Lyons, political loyalties were not paramount. "The promises of Christ and the love of his family always meant more to him than the dreams of the believers in the brotherhood of man".[3]

Lyons' decision to leave the ALP was made neither lightly nor in a mean spirit. He agonised for some months, and consulted his wife regularly. She stiffened his resolve; she saw her husband as an "Aaron holding up the Prophet's hands". (Aaron, of course, was Moses' supportive brother.) Joe and Enid discussed their children's future and eventually Joe decided to take the plunge. "By heaven," he said, "no one is going to spoil this country for them as long as I can lift a finger to stop it."[4]

Of course, we have only Enid Lyons' word for it that these were Joe's overriding motives. But, somehow, the story rings true. Lyons was a unique politician. He was a moral man who prospered in both State and federal politics without ever truly "belonging" on either side of the ideological divide – a very good sign in a Christian, for holistic Christianity is neither "left-wing" nor "right-wing" and the Bible warns against putting one's trust in princes. (See Psalm 146:3-5.)

Even so, the Australian people put their trust in Lyons. He was elected three times by comfortable margins before dying in office, just a few months before the outbreak of World War II.

Just how committed a Christian was he? The evidence suggests that in temperament he was more like Fisher than Scullin: quietly and determinedly devout, but not fiercely so. While not an intellectual lightweight, he was neither as sophisticated nor as anguished a thinker as, say, Alfred Deakin. He was uninvolved – and, it would appear, largely uninterested – in the debates of the 1930s conducted within Australian Catholic-intellectual circles.[5]

For Lyons, Catholicism was a comforting fact of life. He once remarked that "somehow a great peace seems to enter my soul in church".[6] Both his parents had been staunch in their faith. In late 1894, when applying to the Tasmanian Education Department to become a trainee teacher, Lyons included a reference from his local parish priest. Father Cunningham praised him as "a very moral, good young man who will give every satisfaction".[7]

In his mid-twenties Lyons could write – without, it appears, a hint of irony – that his idea of happiness was having "a clear conscience".[8] This was a dependable Catholic lad.

Yet Lyons also once insisted that "I am not extremely religious".[9] The words must be considered in context: when he wrote them in a letter to Enid, on October 13, 1914, she was only 17 and he was trying to reassure her. They had recently declared their mutual love and Enid was, then, a practising Methodist. Nevertheless it was a curious thing to write. Even more curious, given the disparity in their ages and the bitterly sectarian times, is the fact that it was Enid (probably prompted by her mother) who first broached the religious implications of their situation.

Lyons himself "had no quarrel with Methodism".[10] Initially he brushed off the matter: "I am sorry to think that I have been the cause of any unpleasant experience for your mother with the church people, but really if they are so narrow are they worth worrying about?"[11] A month or so later, when Enid complained that some of her Protestant friends were ostracising her, he tried to make a black joke of it: "It seems to me that they would sooner I was a Mohammedan ... personally I would marry you if you were a little heathen."[12]

But Enid persisted, and, not long afterwards, Lyons was forced to reply more thoughtfully. He explained to her why the prospect of a "mixed" marriage was, indeed, terribly fraught: "We recognize the validity of a non-Catholic ceremony for non-Catholics and respect it with the same degree of reverence as our own, but for ourselves, we only recognise our own." (The relevant Papal encyclical was *Ne Temere* (1908) – see further the chapter on Ben Chifley, who disobeyed it.)

The problem thus stated, Lyons continued:

> Therefore you can understand what a position we shall be placed
> in should your convictions be as deep-rooted as mine in regard to
> the matter because no matter how much I care for you I would not
> ask you to do anything that would conflict with your conscience,
> and that is why, though I should like you to be of my religious
> belief so that we might not be separated in any way through life,
> I would sooner lose you altogether than attempt to alter your
> religion in any way.[13]

Enid resolved their dilemma by becoming a Catholic. Encouraged by Joe (who prayed that "the kindly light that led Newman* will lead you too"[14]) she cloistered herself away in a priest's library and stayed there for three days before a breakthrough came. In her words, "the answer was to be found in my Bible, in the parable of the tares and wheat."**[15] Suddenly she was convinced that Jesus had indeed inaugurated "the one true church". Thereby emboldened she overcame other doubts regarding confession, the veneration of Mary, and the sins of the Popes.

I mention this episode because any assessment of Joe Lyons' beliefs must necessarily take account of Enid's. Theirs was a *shared* life-journey. I have dealt with their earnest discussions before Joe's defection from the ALP. Shortly after being sworn in as Prime Minister, in January 1932, he wrote Enid a letter declaring that their "marriage has grown sweeter and more beautiful with the years". He added: "with God's help it will still go on increasing as the years come and go".[16]

According to Anne Henderson, who has written excellent biographies of both of them, "religious faith, a belief that their God would reward their strength of conviction, [took] Joe and Enid through many a sorrow."[17]

Evidence of their shared convictions is plentiful. Enid, in particular, was not shy about sharing them with the public. Campaigning in Tasmania in June 1925, when Joe was the Labor premier of that State, she described Jesus of Nazareth as "the central figure in all history". The fact that He had been a carpenter by trade, she argued, proved "the dignity of labour".[18]

In similar vein, in a speech in Melbourne in November 1932, Enid said:

> I am sure that the greatest philosophy ever propounded to the world was that given two thousand years ago in Palestine. The art of living is not the art of getting but the art of love.[19]

It is to be emphasised that Enid was, at the time, the wife of the incumbent Prime Minister.

---

* John Henry Newman, the Church of England priest who converted to Catholicism in 1845. See the chapter on Alfred Deakin.

** The parable of the tares and wheat is recorded in Matthew 13:24-30 and further elucidated at verses 36-43. It has been interpreted down the centuries in many ways. Sometimes, in my view mistakenly, it is cited in support of the doctrine of apostolic succession. Cf. Matthew 16:18; John 21:17.

For some people, Enid went too far. Several rich and hard-headed powerbrokers within the United Australia Party grew increasingly dissatisfied with both her and her husband – especially those who were beating the drums of war. Throughout the 1930s Lyons supported every attempt by the British government to negotiate peace with Nazi Germany. Lyons' most recent biographer, David Bird, has described him as "a peacemaker let loose in the lion's den of his time".[20]

The Biblical allusion is apt. In 1935, and again in 1937, Lyons utilised his ties with the Vatican to obtain audiences with Italian dictator Benito Mussolini. In September 1938, during the crisis over Germany's re-occupation of the Sudetenland, Lyons drew upon his close friendship with the British Prime Minister, Neville Chamberlain. He urged Chamberlain to use Mussolini as a go-between with Hitler – and Chamberlain did.

At the time, the last-gasp preservation of peace at the Munich Conference was greeted almost everywhere with joy. But, as I have said, Lyons was gathering enemies. In January 1939 Keith Murdoch wrote in exasperation to a like-minded friend:

> I don't know what we can get out of Lyons, but his wife is an ardent pacifist, even a belligerent pacifist; when he speaks she speaks; when he gives a Christian message she gives one. … Her message always, if we love our neighbours enough there will be no war. It is very pitiful.[21]

The wisdom in retrospect of appeasement – and Britain's sudden abandonment of appeasement in September 1939 – is a massive and controversial subject.* But in my opinion the "message" of Joe and Enid Lyons, far from being pitiful, was sensible and judicious.

Joe Lyons has been accused of naivety on this score even by his admirers, but it seems to me that at all times he behaved *as a Christian*.

---

* Apart from David Bird's study, there is a dispassionate overview of the arguments in Christopher Waters' valuable book, *Australia and Appeasement: Imperial Foreign Policy and the Origins of World War Two* (I.B. Tauris, 2012). For two rather different American perspectives, both supportive of appeasement but for very different reasons, see Nicolson Baker's *Human Smoke: The Beginnings of World War II, the End of Civilisation* (Simon and Schuster, 2008), and Patrick J. Buchanan's *Churchill, Hitler, and the Unnecessary War: How Britain Lost Its Empire and the West Lost the World* (Crown Publishers, 2008). Baker is a left-wing pacifist; Buchanan a right-wing isolationist.

He vetoed conscription for overseas military service because "he had such a strong belief in the sanctity of human life and the sanctity of individual conscience".[22] At every turn he urged consultation, concessions and compromise, rather than the "brave" path of war.

The prospect of a repeat of World War I literally sickened him. After a visit with Enid in 1935 to the war graves of France and Belgium, which left Enid in tears, he pronounced at a press conference:

> I think that the statesmen of the world should be brought here regularly to ensure that this great tragedy is never repeated.[23]

Lyons was not blind to the Nazi menace. He was acutely aware of the persecution of German Catholics, condemned by Pope Pius XI in his March 1937 encyclical *Mit brenneder Sorge* ("With burning concern"), and also of German Jews.[24] Lyons instigated modest Australian rearmament during the 1930s as a precautionary measure. But he accepted, like his predecessors James Scullin and S.M. Bruce, and most Western statesmen of the day, that Germany bore genuine grievances. These dated back to the punitive Versailles treaty of 1919.

Hitler's evident paranoia was all the more reason to tread carefully. "In these times," Lyons said in February 1939, "we must keep cool heads and not be swayed by passion and prejudice."[25] History, I would argue, proved him right. Passion and prejudice held sway later in 1939 when most it was needed. I will return to this subject in the chapter on Menzies.

As Prime Minister, Lyons was less forthcoming than Enid with public protestations of faith. Like Scullin, he was ever-fearful of inflaming sectarianism. But his many letters to Enid were full of references to God, and every Sunday when he was in Canberra he worshipped at St Christopher's Catholic Church in Manuka.[26] In Melbourne he often visited St Francis' Church in Lonsdale Street or Pellegrini's Catholic bookshop. He took Communion when and where he could.[27] He was an honorary member of the St Vincent de Paul Society in Launceston from its inception[28], and, in his private capacity, gave countless gifts to charities.[29] At his house at Home Hill in Devonport there was a reproduction of Fra Angelico's *Mother and Child*.[30]

The one time that Lyons went fully public with his faith was September/ October 1938 – during and immediately after the crisis over the Sudetenland.

On September 3, 1938 he called for a "Day of Prayer for Divine Intervention and Guidance":

> At times national viewpoints become so irreconcilable that it would seem that no human agency could devise a solution and our hope of achieving a lasting peace must emanate from the intervention of a Higher Power.[31]

Shortly after the Munich Conference, Lyons nominated Sunday October 9, 1938 as a "National Day of Thanksgiving".[32]

Despite all this, David Bird has contended that Lyons was a "liberal Catholic who considered himself alienated from the Church hierarchy by 1939".[33] Possibly, although Bird does not make this clear, Lyons' sense of alienation stemmed from differing attitudes towards appeasement. His calls in 1938 for national days of prayer went largely unheeded in Catholic and Protestant churches alike.

A final question: appeasement aside, how did the Lyons' religious beliefs impact on Australia? There is much to be said. In the limited space available I will proffer a few brief thoughts.

Anne Henderson has opined that Lyons "never allowed his private religious beliefs to dictate his political directions".[34] If that were so, it would seriously undermine his claims to be being considered a deeply religious man. But it was not so. As Enid wrote in her memoir, *So We Take Comfort*, she and Joe took the view that "if religion mattered at all, it mattered in every department of life".[35] True, Lyons skirted the State aid debate. But everything he did in politics – especially his commitment to appeasement – was driven by his conscience. In my opinion Henderson came closer to the mark later in her biography. Lyons, she there wrote, was a man "whose religion … dominated his sense of charity and generosity of spirit, but … never played an *institutional* role in his politics".[36]

It could never have played an institutional role and Lyons surely knew it. When he was still in the ALP his priority had been to avert or defuse sectarian ructions. (Tasmania, by the way, was the least Catholic of all the states.) Once he was ensconced in the Protestant-dominated United Australia Party he could not possibly have championed State aid even if he had wished to.

Perhaps Lyons' greatest achievement was to *begin* the slow and painful resolution of sectarian discord. Prejudice continued to run deep throughout the British Empire. Once at a banquet Lyons was seated with the Prime Minister of Northern Ireland, Lord Craigavon – a fierce anti-Catholic who knew nothing about Lyons' personal background. "Have you got many Catholics in Australia?" his Lordship asked. "Oh, about one in five," Lyons replied. "Well watch 'em! They breed like bloody rabbits!"[37] After Lyons' death, Richard Casey made an offer to Enid to pay for the education of one of the Lyons boys at Xavier College in Melbourne. In doing so Casey admitted that he had needed to overcome "residual anti-Papist scruples".[38]

At the federal election of December 1931 the central issue was the dire state of the economy. Lyons had no obvious credentials as an economist – other than a belief in thrift – but people sensed that his heart was in the right place. As Menzies observed in his memoirs: "The instinctive feeling he evoked from the public was that he could be trusted to do his best for the unfortunate, and for households grievously afflicted".[39]

Lyons drew hundreds of thousands of Catholic voters to the UAP, mainly but not exclusively from the middle class.[40] After his death, it took the Coalition parties another 35 years to lure these voters back in substantial numbers. Of course, in the 1950s and 60s, many of them came "halfway" back via the DLP. But Lyons had won their *primary* votes, despite never pitching for them on religious grounds. He did not need to, and it would have been counterproductive to try. Sectarianism was still boiling. When he took his first Prime Ministerial oath on January 6, 1932 he held, in a gesture of unity, a Protestant Bible.[41]

It is beautifully apt that Lyons died on Good Friday. His obsequies were fitting. On Easter Monday 1939, from 10am to 10pm, his body lay in state at Sydney's St Mary's Cathedral. A wisp of Enid's hair was placed in his right hand, a set of rosary beads blessed by the Pope in his left. On Easter Tuesday, Archbishop Michael Kelly presided at a full requiem mass. The next day, in Melbourne, Archbishop Daniel Mannix conducted a memorial mass at St Patrick's Cathedral. The coffin was then flown to Devonport and met by Archbishop Justin Simonds. Lyons was buried from Our Lady of Lourdes, the Catholic church in Devonport.[42]

JOHN JOSEPH AMBROSE (JACK) CURTIN (1885-1945)

LABOR: 1941-45

Australia's leader during most of World War II is rated highly by almost all historians. Some – including political opponents[1] – consider him our greatest-ever Prime Minister. Curtin's story is remarkable on many levels, not least because he was dogged by insomnia, heart disease and (undiagnosed) bipolar depression. He was also a reformed alcoholic who displayed, among men, "a bullock driver's command of banned adjectives".[2] He died in office on July 5, 1945, just six weeks before the end of the war in the Pacific.

As his biographer John Edwards has observed, Curtin was "a complicated man … not as he seemed and not as we remember him".[3] In appraising his religious life it is especially important to avoid a rush to judgment. The standard view is that Curtin renounced his childhood faith as a teenager and never regained it – indeed, that he became an atheist or something close. In Manning Clark's words, "he abandoned his Catholic hopes in the resurrection of the dead and substituted instead the utopian socialist dream of the perfection of man on earth".[4]

My own view is that the truth is less clear-cut and more interesting. Curtin certainly fell out with the Catholic Church. But as another of his biographers, David Day, has pointed out, it does not follow that Curtin "rejected the notion of a Supreme Being".[5] He was searching for meta-physical truth in his final years and may well have made a late conversion.

In any event, he was far from an irreligious man. One admirer suggested in 1969 that Curtin "never repudiated the Christian philosophy. Indeed, it influenced his everyday life more deeply than it did the lives of many churchmen of his era."[6]

Apart from anything else, Curtin was a life-long social conservative as regards such matters as sex and family.[7] At home in Perth with his wife Elsie and two children, away from the dreadful responsibilities of politics and war, he "did not tell *risqué* stories and 'bloody' was almost his only swearword". According to historian Geoffrey Serle, Curtin's marriage was "happy and stable" and he "enjoyed bringing up the children, surfed with them, often walked on the beach, cheerfully did household chores, pottered in the garden and kept a dog".[8] In 1944 he compared family life to "the earthly locale of what we mean by heaven".[9]

Curtin was born in Creswick, Victoria on January 8, 1885, the eldest son of Irish-Catholic immigrants.[10] John Curtin Senior was a policeman, but ill-health forced him to take early retirement from the force. He took a gratuity in 1890 and started a second career as a publican. For almost a decade he tried his luck managing various hotels across Victoria, but none of these ventures succeeded. It was a peripatetic and precarious existence for him, his wife Kate (née Bourke) and their four children.

Catholicism played a big part in the Curtin family's life. John Curtin Senior was "a good Irish Catholic"[11] and Kate was "devout".[12] At her insistence all of the children went to mass each Sunday. Jack (as the future Prime Minister was known), was baptised at St Augustine's at Creswick[13], and was an altar boy at the Catholic Church in Charlton[14], one of the Victorian towns in which his father later ran a pub. The priest at Charlton, Father Michael Costello, was "a commanding presence and strong personality".[15]

According to his daughter Elsie, it was around this time that Curtin nursed a plan to become a priest himself.[16] In that era, given his family's circumstances, such an ambition would have been commonplace – "priest, publican or policeman" were three of the main options for young Catholic men with no money behind them.[17] If Jack had entered the priesthood the Curtins would have covered all three bases.

It was not to be. By 1898 John Curtin Senior was completely incapacitated by ill-health. The family returned to Melbourne and settled in the working-class suburb of Brunswick – an enclave known derisively as "Paddy town". (B.A. Santamaria also grew up in Brunswick.) The Curtins now lived "in poverty".[18] It was a cruel setback for proud people who had struggled to remain in the middle class, and it was during the next few years that young Jack became deeply disillusioned with his Church.

For a time he still attended mass on Sundays, at St Ambrose's on Sydney Road, Brunswick. He also went to its parish school in 1899.[19] But his faith waned. Why? An early biographer, Lloyd Ross, asserted that "there seems to be no evidence of his reasons".[20] Ross, however, cannot have delved hard enough. The record establishes that there was an instructive combination of reasons.

First, Curtin's education. He attended seven schools, and he enjoyed the four state schools much more than the three* run by the church. Curtin's favourite school was the one at Charlton, which he attended for three years. The District Inspector at the time, Frank Tate, was an enlightened and diligent man. Later he became the Head of the Victorian Education Department. Though a committed Anglican, Tate ensured that students imbibed "the religion of rationalism, of science, and of empire".[21] The school at Charlton was of above-average quality and the headmaster, Charles Phillips, was a disciple of Tate. He encouraged independent, enquiring minds. Curtin emerged "distrustful of dogma".[22]

Second, and not coincidentally, Curtin became a voracious reader. He remained one his whole life: it complemented "the restless quality of his intellect".[23] Of course, reading is not necessarily antithetical to faith. But especially when you are young and impressionable, it can lead you down many a tangential path. Curtin began reading some radical political tracts.

Third, it appears likely that the teenage Curtin began to harbour resentment towards his parents. As a result of his father's incapacity, Curtin was compelled to become the main family breadwinner**, and the loss of

---

* Curtin went to the parish schools attached to St Francis' in Lonsdale Street, Melbourne; St Bridget's at North Fitzroy; and St Ambrose's at Brunswick. St Francis' was the first Christian Brothers school in Australia. In Curtin's time it was run by a Father Tracey, according to a "strict religious creed and rigid discipline". Work ceased on the hour when students stood to say the "Hail Mary".
** After a succession of odd jobs Curtin found secure employment in 1903 at the Titan Manufacturing Company in South Melbourne, as an estimates clerk. He stayed there until early 1911.

independence was severe. For some years his mother effectively garnisheed his wages.[24] Kate Curtin was by most accounts a hard taskmaster and suggestions have been made that, from infancy, her eldest son felt ambivalent towards her.[25] It is possible that – consciously or otherwise – he was rebelling against her or his father, or both.

Fourth, Curtin began to bristle at sectarianism. Small towns like Charlton were riven by it[26], and, once he was in the workforce in Melbourne, he may well have experienced its effects more directly.[27] This was another reason to distance himself from Irish-Catholicism. (In due course, it may here be noted, Curtin developed sectarian feelings of his own. In the words of David Day, as an adult Curtin "had such an aversion to the church of his birth that he rarely entered a Catholic church".[28] After his marriage in 1917, another factor in the mix was the anti-Catholicism of his wife Elsie.[29] And as federal Labor leader in the late 1930s he had to grapple with the emerging schism between conservative Catholics and left-wing secularists, a problem brought to a head in 1937 by the Spanish Civil War and exacerbated further by the Nazi-Soviet Pact of 1939. In this period, Curtin himself was an isolationist.)

Fifth, there were the insidious effects of poverty. As a boy Curtin endured it himself in no small measure; as he grew older he noticed suffering and deprivation almost everywhere he looked. It was "sorrowful and maddening".[30] Curtin came to regard the major churches as "unseemly supporters of capitalism"[31] – a commonplace reaction, then and now, among young idealists of left-wing bent.

Curtin's initial response to these influences was logical enough. In or about 1899 he joined the Salvation Army. The Nathanielites, as they were known, had a prominent presence in Brunswick. They preached abstinence and self-discipline – and sported a spectacular marching band. Curtin carried a torch in it and later played a cornet.[32] But in the event, for whatever reason, his spiritual needs were not satisfied. He stayed in the band for two or three years before moving on, dabbling briefly with the Free Religious Fellowship of an ex-Unitarian pastor in Melbourne, the Rev Fredericke Sinclaire. But that too was a passing phase.[33]

At some point in the early to mid-1900s Curtin began attending meetings of the Melbourne Rationalist Society. Prominent members included Bernard O'Dowd, the socialist poet, for whose work Curtin had developed an admiration. But perhaps the key figure was an up-and-coming conservative lawyer named John Grieg Latham, a lecturer at the Society. (I have already discussed Latham's role as Attorney-General in the Bruce-Page Government; subsequently he served as the leader of the United Australia Party and as Chief Justice of the High Court.) According to Curtin's Prime Ministerial secretary, Don Rodgers, "it was Latham who Curtin would later claim to be responsible for leading him away from religion, something for which Curtin never forgave Latham".[34] Jack Hunter, an old friend of Curtin's from Sydney, told a similar story.[35]

To my mind the charge seems unjust. Curtin had already begun moving away from religion, though Latham's lectures may well have accelerated the process. The most interesting thing about this anecdote is that Curtin *regretted* his loss of faith: "Although abandoning Catholicism, [he] keenly felt the void that it left."[36] This feeling of emptiness was exacerbated in 1906 by the death at 16, from pneumonia, of his sweetheart Nancy Gunn.[37]

It appears that Curtin was sufficiently self-aware to realise his predicament. Some years later he confessed to admiration for "men and women that 'are born again'".[38] On October 3, 1941, shortly after learning that he would soon become Prime Minister, Curtin said to his secretary: "I will need all your prayers, Gladys, taking this job."[39]

John Curtin found his calling – or thought he had – in the Labor movement. He started out in the Victorian Socialist Party, where characters such as Frank Anstey and Tom Mann inspired their followers with flowery and fiery rhetoric. From 1911-15 Curtin was the Secretary of the Victorian Timber Workers Union; he spent much of 1916 campaigning against conscription, and actually spent three days in gaol for failure to enlist. (Billy Hughes had introduced a requirement that single men go to camp. Curtin was convicted in his absence to three months' imprisonment but was released after three days when all such prosecutions were withdrawn.[40]) In early 1917 he accepted an offer to become editor of the *Westralian Worker* and stayed in the post for 12 years.[41] He was first elected to federal parliament in 1928 as the member for Fremantle.

Until the mid-1920s there was a fundamentalist fervour to Curtin's language and behaviour. As David Day has observed, part of the attraction of socialism was the "religiosity of its discourse and the churchlike manner of some of its organisations".[42] The VSP had a Sunday school, baptisms and funerals; its members sang hymns.[43] Curtin became a sort of secular evangelist.

In this regard he found a kindred spirit in his father-in-law, Abraham Needham, a former Methodist preacher. Though his faith had withered by the time he met Curtin (in 1912, in Hobart), Needham had once likened the role of socialist reformers to that of the early Christians. Both were "the prophets, priests and kings of hope and liberty for men ... who fought a fight for Truth and Right." On other occasions Needham had proclaimed that "Christ of Nazareth is my standard" and that Christ was a symbol of "the vast toiling masses".[44]

These were sentiments to which Curtin related. But he twisted them around. In the middle of his life, it appears to me, Curtin was trying to convince himself that political activism was a proper substitute for faith. "If you love justice and honour, [and] work," he once insisted, "you need not bother about God."[45]

But he protested too much. Curtin never stopped bothering about God. His library included well-thumbed copies of John Ruskin's *King of the Golden River* and *Foxe's Book of Martyrs*.[46] His career in federal politics, while momentous, did not slake his thirst for spiritual nourishment. That thirst gradually increased as he descended into a "loneliness of mind and spirit".[47]

Some might question this thesis, and it is true that outward appearances were a long time to the contrary. When Curtin married Elsie Needham in 1917 it was not in a church – Catholic or Methodist – but in the dining room of a house in West Leederville (in Perth), owned by a Justice of the Peace. (Curtin had made an arrangement with the Registrar-General of Western Australia – evidently he did not wish to offend his Catholic family by marrying in a Methodist church.[48]) Neither of the Curtin children was christened and, at least until the war years, neither Curtin nor Elsie was a churchgoer of any frequency.[49] Near the end of Curtin's life, old Jim Scullin is supposed to have made an attempt to draw him back to the Catholic fold: "I know you don't believe much in God, Jack, but don't you think it's time you made your peace with your maker?" Curtin responded: "I've seen it through like this so far, and I'm not going to change now."[50]

And yet, there is another side to the story. Curtin's state funeral service in Canberra was conducted at Parliament House by the Rev Hector Harrison*, a local Presbyterian minister.[51] His body was then flown to Perth and buried in the Presbyterian plot at Karrakatta cemetery.[52]

Some tricky questions arise here. Why Harrison? Why the *Presbyterian* plot? There is tantalising evidence that Curtin had been trying for several years to regain his Christian faith. In Geoffrey Serle's expression, he was "groping towards religious consolation".[53]

Towards the end of his life Curtin began adding the words "God Bless You" at the end of his speeches.[54] In his 1943 New Year's message he explicitly invoked Christianity:

> We must be bigger Australians in every way in the year ahead. We must fix our minds on the tasks at our hands to the exclusion of everything that is paltry and miserable and self-seeking. If we fail we fail not only ourselves and our children, but we fail in the face of an enemy who has no regard for the Christian way of life and all that 1942 years of Christianity have stood for. That will be swept away and our memorial tablet will be written in slavery.

Curtin concluded:

> Resoluteness must be the keynote of the Australian character. I am confident that that will be manifested throughout the land, and that with God's blessing 1943 will be a better, a more victorious, year than was 1942.[55]

This, of course, was for public consumption. But there is other, better, evidence that Curtin regained a form of Christian faith. Without doubt, various people were pushing him in that direction.

For a start, there was his wife. As a girl and a young woman Elsie had been an active Methodist[56] – she played the organ at the Needham family's

---

* Hector Harrison (1902-78), relatively young when he knew Curtin, went on to become a prelate of considerable eminence. He was the Moderator of the Presbyterian Church of NSW in 1950-51 and Moderator-General of the Presbyterian Church of Australia in 1962-64. In 1964 he was appointed a vice-president of the World Presbyterian Alliance.

churches in Cape Town and Hobart.[57] Although she and Curtin were very infrequent churchgoers during most of their marriage, it appears that in private they still shared certain religious assumptions. At Christmas in 1941, Curtin sent Elsie a telegram lamenting the fact it was the first Christmas they had not spent together since their wedding. It ended: "I pray you a good Christmas Heaven guarding you always".[58]

David Day has suggested that Elsie, by 1945, was worshipping within the Presbyterian Church. She was certainly involved with the Subiaco Choral Society and was a sometime member of the Women's Christian Temperance Union. On December 9, 1944, the Curtins' son John was married by Presbyterian rites – to Catherine Neill at the Ross Memorial Presbyterian Church in West Perth. The Prime Minister was there.[59]

Aside from Curtin's nuclear family, there were other influences working upon him.

His closest mate during the war years was a man named Fred Southwell – the brother of Belle Southwell, manageress of the legendary Hotel Kurrajong.[60] The Southwells worshipped at St Andrew's Presbyterian Church in Canberra[61], where Hector Harrison was the minister from May 1940. Curtin was never a member of Harrison's congregation, but he did know him as a near-neighbour in Canberra and they were on amicable terms. In early 1942, Harrison invited Curtin to attend a re-dedication ceremony at Canberra's original ("pioneer") Presbyterian church. Afterwards, Curtin was prevailed upon to give an impromptu speech – during which he observed that "the fatherhood of God [is] closely related to the brotherhood of man".[62]

Another religious influence on Curtin in the war years was F.A. (Fred) McLaughlin, his private secretary. A deeply pious Protestant involved in the Moral Rearmament Movement, McLaughlin made active attempts to bring Curtin back to Christianity.[63] The conventional wisdom is that he failed, yet, according to McLaughlin's daughter, the Prime Minister would frequently ask for her father's company when he was feeling very low – "Fred, come and see what you can do." The two men would sit and pray together.[64] It was McLaughlin who arranged for Hector Harrison to conduct Curtin's funeral service. He did so at Curtin's request.[65]

Some historians have belittled the influence of Fred McLaughlin. Curtin, they say, may have been "humouring" him. But Kim Beazley Senior – who knew McLaughlin well and succeeded Curtin as the member of Fremantle in 1945 – doubted this hypothesis. In his view, "though Curtin never lost his distrust of religious institutions, faith grew within him."[66]

There was also an old friend of Curtin's named Jim Hunter, a former Country Party MHR from NSW, whose brothers were Presbyterian ministers. When Curtin visited Sydney, he liked to meet up with Hunter and take a walk with him; often the subject turned to religion. In a letter written to Lloyd Ross in 1958, Hunter claimed that Curtin had once confided to him that he was looking for "Truth". The Prime Minister complained that his life was "worse than any religious hell" after having "lost the faith that he once had" and being left with "an aching void".[67]

The Catholics around Curtin did not give up. I have mentioned Scullin. Curtin's brothers and sisters also urged him several times to return to the church of his youth. But Curtin refused to see a priest. One who came to the Lodge in his final days was turned away. It seems incontestable, then, that Curtin had renounced Catholicism forever. But what of a Protestant form of faith?

At Curtin's last meeting with Jim Hunter, in March 1945, the two men parted company at Sydney's Circular Quay. Curtin said: "You are right, Jim. It doesn't matter what Church a man belongs to. The main thing is for him to live a decent straight keen life as near to Christ's as humanly possible."[68]

At least for orthodox Protestants, that is *not* the main thing. One's conduct is relevant, certainly, but "it is by grace you have been saved, through faith – and this not from yourselves, it is the gift of God – not by works, so that no-one can boast" (Ephesians 2:8-9). It is doubtful that the Rev. Hector Harrison would have agreed to conduct Curtin's funeral service on the basis of his statement to Hunter. Why, then, did Harrison agree?

It seems that Harrison and Curtin had never discussed religion in any detail.[69] The subject was not broached by Harrison during his visit to Curtin's sickbed in early May 1945.[70] Two months later, at Curtin's deathbed, Harrison merely held Curtin's hand and told him that "a lot of people are praying for you".[71]

But a week or two earlier, as a precondition to conducting the funeral service, Harrison had asked Fred McLaughlin to provide some evidence of Curtin's religious beliefs. McLaughlin decided against asking Curtin directly – probably he was doubtful what answer he might receive. Instead, he gathered second-hand evidence sufficient to satisfy Harrison. There was an anecdote about Curtin's sanguine conduct on an aeroplane. More persuasive was the testimony of Norman Makin, a senior minister in Curtin's government. Makin (a Methodist) swore that Curtin had once said to him during a chat: "I am aware that there is a hereafter and that men are required to account for their misdeeds in this life."[72]

Had he known of it, McLaughlin might have added Curtin's rejoinder to his siblings when they urged his return to Catholicism: "I think I've led a good life and I believe that Almighty God will find a place for me."[73]

JOSEPH BENEDICT (BEN) CHIFLEY (1885-1951)

LABOR: 1945-49

F ew leaders of any era have been as fondly regarded as Chifley. Many disagreed with his policies, notoriously his ill-fated attempt in 1947-48 to nationalise the private banks. But almost nobody – among colleagues or opponents, journalists or voters – seems to have disliked him as a man. He was that rarest of rare birds, a humble soul who reached the top in politics despite having no desire to lead. Robert Menzies, who sobbed on the night of his death, thought Chifley "the most authentic Labour leader in Australian political history".[1]

Chifley had no false pride. He always paid his own fare on trams and trains, though he could have brandished his politician's Gold Pass.[2] He rarely submitted claims for ministerial expenses.[3] For many years he served on both the Abercrombie Shire Council and the board of the Bathurst Hospital. He continued to serve in both capacities throughout World War II – in between discharging his duties as Treasurer and Minister for Post-war Reconstruction.[4] He became Prime Minister reluctantly, after John Curtin's death in July 1945.

There is an old story that Chifley's telephone number in Canberra was one digit removed from that of the local butcher. When a customer rang him by accident the Prime Minister did not stand on ceremony; he just wrote the order down (mincemeat, lamb chops, etc.) and rang it through to the shop.[5]

Chifley was neither a deep thinker nor a saint, but he was a hard worker, a peacemaker* and a quietly inspiring leader. He was also – so I shall contend – a good Christian. To be sure, he had a strained relationship with the Catholic Church. He defied its edicts to marry a Protestant and then was unfaithful to her. But he believed in the key tenets of Christianity and, all things considered, adhered to them better than most men. It was Chifley who coined the phrase which is still the ALP's catchcry: "the light on the hill". He drew it, of course, from the Sermon on the Mount: "Ye are the light of the world. A city that is set on a hill cannot be hid" (Matthew 5:14 (KJV)).

For Chifley, Christianity was not wholly or even mainly a private matter. He once explained to a friend that he wanted as many people as possible to "have a little of Heaven on earth".[6] As treasurer under Curtin, and then as Prime Minister, he converted that noble ideal into practical reality. A Labor colleague, Norman Makin, once compared him to Joseph of the Old Testament, for his combination of wisdom, generosity and compassion.[7]

His government provided generously for returned servicemen (in the form of housing, retraining, employment, etc.), and expanded the social safety net. It legislated for free medical treatment in public wards. It raised old age pensions and child endowment payments. It introduced sickness and unemployment benefits (filling a gap in the social safety net that had caused untold misery during the Depression). Unemployment was kept at or around 1 per cent.[8]

Chifley's government also presided over key "nation-building" projects. Two – the Snowy Mountains Scheme and the launch of the Australian car industry (the Holden) – are now iconic. But most significant of all was the post-war immigration programme, which he began. About a third of the new arrivals were British; most of the rest were from Southern, Eastern and Northern Europe.[9] The long-term effects on Australia were utterly profound, but, for present purposes, I would emphasise two things. First, many of those who came in the 1940s and 1950s were "displaced persons", refugees brought to Australia under the auspices of the International Refugee Organisation.

---

* The Bathurst Hospital board was a disparate group of Protestants and Catholics who regularly bickered amongst themselves. Only Chifley – diplomatic and respected by all – could get things done. In the words of David Day, "with a Presbyterian wife, a Masonic father-in-law, and a problematic relationship with the Catholic church, Chifley was well-placed to bridge the religious divide".

Second, a sizeable proportion of these people were practising Christians – and stridently anti-Communist. Chifley extended charity to people who would not, in the longer term, prove to be natural allies of his party.

That – very briefly – is the political side of Ben Chifley's Christian story. What of the personal side?

He was born in Bathurst, NSW on September 22, 1885, the oldest of three boys in a solidly Catholic family.[10] Mary Chifley (née Corrigan), the matriarch, was raised in Ireland before her family emigrated. As a young woman she had lived and worked at the Convent of St Benedict in Queanbeyan. Established in 1879 by nuns from the Sisters of the Good Samaritan, its declared purposes were to "teach in the schools, to visit and assist the sick in their own houses and in hospitals, to instruct penitent women and to apply themselves to every charitable work".[11]

This was the ethos that Mary Chifley helped to instil in her oldest son. Indeed, Joseph Benedict Chifley took his middle name – the one he used all his life – from the Convent.[12] He was baptised in christening robes which had been lovingly embroidered there.[13]

Patrick Chifley, Ben's father, was a blacksmith. Seven years younger than Mary, he married her in May 1884 in Bathurst's Cathedral of St Michael and St John. The ceremony was conducted by Father Joseph Byrne, a stern enforcer of the Vatican's teachings. According to David Day, Chifley's most recent biographer, it is likely that Father Byrne counselled the newly-weds as to the evils of birth control and the dangers of educating their children anywhere other than in Catholic schools.[14]

The evidence shows that neither piece of advice was followed to the letter. Although Patrick Chifley was a regular at mass and a prominent member of the local branch of the Australian Holy Catholic Guild [15], he was neither a zealot nor a sectarian. In this respect his famous son would take after him.

Ben's early education was mostly secular. Between the ages of five and 13 he lived with his grandfather on a property at Linekilns, 40 kilometres from Bathurst. The local State school at which he was enrolled proved to be rustic[16], yet Ben was not switched to the nearby Catholic school at Wattle Flat run by Mary MacKillop's Sisters of St Joseph. It is likely, however, that he travelled to see the Sisters periodically – to receive instruction before his Confirmation and his First Communion and Confession[17] – and, once back in Bathurst in 1899, he attended St Patrick's Boys' School. Run by the Patrician Brothers, it also was scholastically sub-standard, but the Brothers did take pains to instil Catholic doctrine and Ben was an apt pupil. He won the prize for Bible study.[18]

Chifley was radicalised as a teenager. He joined the NSW railways in September 1903 and worked his way up from shop-boy to cleaner to fireman to engine-driver.[19] Simultaneously he educated himself through wide reading and advanced in the union movement. But before that, his first paid job was as a cashier's assistant at a Bathurst department store. The proprietor, one John Meagher, was a wealthy Irish-Catholic businessman and a pillar of the local church. But he mistreated his workers shamelessly. Chifley was rebuffed when he tried to improve conditions for himself and his mates.[20]

This was a formative experience – politically and spiritually. Chifley was appalled by the hypocrisy of Meagher and two other rich local scions. According to another biographer, L.F. Crisp, Chifley disdained them as "three of the greatest exploiters of labour he had ever known".[21] He regarded "[the] reality behind their Sunday facades [as] one of the most damaging influences he had known to the link between organised religion and the people of Bathurst".[22] I believe Chifley had imbibed one of the most important messages in the Gospels: the gulf between sanctimonious Pharisaic "religion" and genuine Christian piety.

In early 1914 Chifley faced a serious dilemma. He wished to marry a woman named Elizabeth (Lizzie) McKenzie, the daughter of a fellow train-driver in Bathurst. There was one huge barrier: she was a Protestant.[23] Her father was a seat-holder and elder at St Stephen's Presbyterian Church in Bathurst, and, according to the church history, led "a consistent Christian life".[24] He was also an active member of the local Masonic Lodge.[25] There was no prospect whatever of Lizzie converting to Catholicism.

What was Chifley to do? He loved Lizzie, but so-called "mixed marriages" were frowned upon, even castigated, in those sectarian days. By a papal decree of 1908, Ne Temere ("Not Rashly"), Catholics were forbidden to be married in a Protestant church or by a Protestant minister. If they did, they would be denied the sacraments.[26]

There were two questions: whether he and Lizzie should marry at all, and where to conduct the ceremony if they did. Chifley agonised for several months before deciding. The wedding took place on June 6, 1914, at a Presbyterian church in Glebe, Sydney. It was a small and discreet affair: neither of the families attended, though they adjusted to the marriage in due course.[27] Years later Chifley gave his reasons, which were chivalrous and stoic: "One of us has to take the knock. It'd better be me."[28]

Not a few commentators over the years have questioned the sincerity of Chifley's faith in the light of this decision. He should have walked away, they say, or somehow prevailed upon Lizzie to convert to Catholicism. He risked damnation of his soul.

This strikes me as too severe. In any event, as David Day has pointed out, "even though Chifley had agreed to be married in a Presbyterian church, he had not agreed to become a Presbyterian. He had defied his church but had not deserted it."[29] He remained, for 25 years, a member of the Australian Holy Catholic Guild[30] and continued until his death to worship at Catholic churches.

When he was in his hometown he went to St Philomena's in South Bathurst. According to a former altar boy there, Chifley's custom was to stand at the back with his hat in hand. His church-going was anything but casual and irregular down the years. He went *every* weekend when he was home in Bathurst, and also took the trouble to drive Lizzie to and from St Stephen's Presbyterian.[31]

In later years, whenever he was in Canberra on a Sunday, Chifley attended early-morning mass at St Christopher's Church in Manuka. A chair was kept for him at the back, which became known as "Chif's chair." This is not legend but historical fact, attested to by a number of witnesses.[32] Archie Cameron, leader of the Country Party for a short while during World War II, and later a Speaker of the House, was in the habit of observing Chifley at mass. He once reported to a Coalition colleague that Chifley "did not take part in the service." During prayers he closed his eyes rather than kneeling and "always slipped away to avoid the priest's greeting."[33]

Beyond attendance at mass, what other evidence is there of Chifley's faith?

I would highlight a number of private and public statements, starting with three from the war years. When the Japanese bombed Darwin in February 1942, Chifley told his sister-in-law to "keep up the prayers and the Rosary, Molly, and we will do the best we can – with a bit of luck we will win.

Keep up the prayers."[34] In September 1942, presenting the federal budget, he congratulated the Australian people for their improved "spiritual zeal ... the readiness to sacrifice money, goods, labour and even life itself ... to uphold the faith that is in us."[35] And on August 15, 1945, announcing the end of the war, he called on everybody to "give thanks to God."[36]

There are two more examples from 1949. At an ALP Women's rally in Perth, Chifley said that "the endeavour to make a little happiness in the world is the very spirit of Christianity."[37] And at an ALP caucus dinner in Canberra he alluded to Jesus' explanation at the Last Supper of how divine justice will be dispensed in the afterlife (cf. Matthew 25:31-46):

> When one reaches the end of one's life one should be able to say that the world is a little better because one has lived. Bringing a ray of happiness to some mother in a back street, who has a family to rear and has to cope with sickness, may tip the scales in our favour.[38]

In a letter in 1950 he was still more explicit:

> All those who seek to spread the Gospel of Christ are, I feel, dutybound to follow his own rule of life to help the lowly to better things, which was shown I think in the New Testament.[39]

It is also to be emphasised that Chifley's concern for "the lowly" extended beyond Australia's borders. Once, when he lamented the extent of poverty in Asia, someone in his presence remarked that "they have never known anything better." Chifley replied: "These people are God's people."[40]

Chifley was also a Bible-reader. He poured over Scripture in a thoroughly Calvinist way. According to L. F. Crisp, who knew him well, this may have been a reason for his less than reverential attitude to the Vatican: "he read [himself] out of the church's discipline". Chifley studied the Bible often and systematically, "in later years traversing it from cover to cover some 11 times". And he was interested in the various translations. Near the end of his life a parish priest at Kandos lent him a copy of Ronald A. Knox's book, *On Englishing the Bible*. When returning it to the priest, Chifley remarked that he "found [it] very interesting and, for a work on the subject of the Bible, containing much humour".[41]

Why, then, is there any doubt at all about Chifley's faith? There are three main reasons.

First, the weight of evidence suggests that – during the last 20 or so years of his life – he had two mistresses. They were sisters: Nell and Phyllis Donnelly, whom Chifley had known since his childhood in Bathurst. Phyllis, the younger of the two by 15 years, was also his secretary. Although Chifley's surviving relatives would mostly deny any sexual relationship, the Donnelly family did not.[42]

It seems likely that either woman would have made a more suitable wife than Lizzie. For a start, they were Catholics. They were also committed to the Labor movement and everything Chifley stood for. Sometime in the late 1920s, in Canberra, his friendship with Phyllis developed into something more. His relationship with Nell, maintained mostly in Bathurst, was of even longer standing.

It is easy to be censorious about such things, but if ever a man might be forgiven for adultery, it was Ben Chifley. Lizzie was unable to give him children. Much more than that, it appears that, not long into the marriage, she became unable or unwilling to engage in sexual relations. She was, in effect, a semi-invalid. She rarely left Bathurst and was disengaged from Chifley's political activities. She did not share his steely commitment to social justice. And, of course, she remained a Presbyterian.[43]

This is not to say that the marriage was miserable. When Chifley was in Bathurst, their home life was serene. Lizzie was not a shrew. Indeed, Chifley was devoted to her and on amicable terms with her family (from 1932, upon the death of George McKenzie, Lizzie's mother lived with Ben and Lizzie at their house in Bathurst). Lizzie appears to have been a kind-hearted if limited person, content in her cosy life. Divorce would have had dire social and religious consequences for both of them. Chifley's hopes of a political career could well have suffered too, but there is no good evidence to suggest this was his overriding motive.

What was Chifley to do? Resigning himself to lifelong abstinence was the Christian ideal. But it seems he could not. Sometime in the 1920s he faced the fact he did not possess the willpower to live like a monk. To do so would have gradually warped his personality and sapped his physical and mental strength. It must be doubtful he could have remained on such sweet terms with Lizzie, who probably understood his predicament and turned an understanding blind eye. A Labor colleague of Chifley's in Bathurst, Frank Slavin, would later claim that Lizzie knew the score: "Just because he doesn't love me," she is supposed to have said to Slavin, "doesn't mean that he can't love other people."[44]

During Chifley's life these facts were not in the public domain. But they were probably known to a good many people in Bathurst. David Day has speculated that Chifley's defeat in his seat of Macquarie at the 1931 and 1934 federal elections may have been attributable in part to gossip about the Donnelly sisters. A local priest, Father Frank King, wrote after Chifley's death that he (Chifley) had adopted "a way of social life at variance with what his high position would seem to require".[45] Possibly Chifley received some such admonition during his lifetime.

Paul Hasluck wrote in his private diary that the mature Chifley "still loved God (or was still interested in God) but hated the priests".[46] "Hate" was too strong a word, and the generalisation too sweeping. Indeed, Chifley himself once claimed that he had "been unable to hate anybody ... the only things I hate are the want, misery and insecurity of any people in any country".[47] It is nevertheless true that he frequently felt uncomfortable in the presence of some men in the Catholic hierarchy. He was certainly sceptical of Pope Pius XII, whom he regarded as "extraordinarily conservative in his outlook on world affairs".[48]

The last comment is revealing. It highlights the second major reason why doubts were cast upon Chifley's Catholicism. He distrusted B.A. Santamaria and other right-wing "Groupers" who had begun to infiltrate the ALP. In the words of a modern-day Labor historian, Jenny Hocking, these men were "unashamedly sectarian"[49] – not so much anti-Protestant (though that strain existed), as stridently Catholic and fanatically anti-Communist. As Archbishop Daniel Mannix wrote in a supportive letter to Menzies and his Cabinet in January 1950: "With me the Communist menace is no mere political matter: it threatens the Christian way of life."[50]

At the beginning of the Cold War – in certain influential quarters – Labor was painted as "soft on Communism". In Chifley's case the charge was demonstrably unfair. As early as 1931 he had publicly denounced communism as "one of the most evil forces that has ever crept into the life of

Australia". What is more, he did so on *religious* grounds: "it preaches nothing but materialism and completely neglects the spiritual side of the nation's existence".[51] By 1948 he disdained communists in the West as "fools and traitors to democracy".[52] Even so, in 1950-51, Chifley was privately opposed to the Menzies Government's attempt to ban the Communist Party. On that score he was overruled by the ALP federal executive but ultimately proved right: the High Court declared the Act unconstitutional, and a subsequent referendum (held a few months after Chifley's death in 1951) was narrowly defeated. The concept of making a person's *beliefs* subject to criminal sanction was plainly illiberal. It flew in the face of basic notions of freedom of conscience. B.A. Santamaria himself had initially opposed the idea.[53]

The worst that can be said of Chifley is that he was given to overstatement about the deficiencies of the churches. On March 3, 1950, in Parliament, he sought to draw a link with the rise of communism:

> With great regret I point out that that the Christian churches,
> which had the greatest influence in Europe in the past, did little
> if anything to ensure that justice was done to landless farmers
> and the poor sections of the community. They never gave
> assistance towards righting the wrongs that should have been
> righted long ago. As a result of that inactivity, or failure to exert
> the influence they could have exerted, communism has crept
> into Italy, France and all the countries of Central Europe.[54]

This was careless hyperbole. Chifley's words were attacked publicly by Catholic spokesmen and, in Parliament, by one of his own backbenchers – a Santamaria acolyte named S.M. Keon. In a private letter, Chifley responded:

> Of course I am not any way unmindful of what has been done by
> the various Christian Churches in charitable works amongst the
> poor, but I hold the view that charity is not enough and that some
> measure of security must be given to the great mass of the ordinary
> people if the causes which enable Communists to create discontent
> are to be removed.[55]

The third reason for Chifley's chequered reputation within the Catholic Church was his approach to State aid. He never ventured into the debate.

Rightly or wrongly, like Scullin and Lyons, he was afraid of fanning the flames of sectarianism. He took the position that church schools were better off remaining unindebted to the State, however under-resourced they might be.*[56] It was pointed out to him that the Commonwealth was already involved in pre-school and tertiary education: why not, then, primary and secondary education? Chifley's droll reply – "that's different – they're for kids before they've got souls and after they've lost them"[57] – was not apt to amuse people like B.A. Santamaria.

The Catholic Church did not desert Chifley at the end. When he suffered a heart attack in his room at Canberra's Kurrajong Hotel, on the evening of June 13, 1951, a priest was called. Fred Daly, a fellow Catholic who adored Chifley, asked later whether he had "got there in time" to give extreme unction. The priest hoped so: "I might have been," he said to Daly, "because, under certain circumstances, it's difficult to assess when life actually leaves the body".[58]

Likewise, the church's representatives back in Bathurst behaved well. Father Dunne was at the town's main Catholic Cathedral when told the news by telephone. "God rest his soul," he pronounced, before declaring stoutly that Chifley was "not going to be buried by the Presbyterians!" He wanted "the biggest funeral Bathurst has ever seen"[59] – and it was.

---

* Andrew Fisher and James Scullin, Protestant and Catholic respectively, were also of this view.

ROBERT GORDON (BOB) MENZIES (1894-1978)

UNITED AUSTRALIA PARTY: 1939-41
LIBERAL: 1949-66

Australia's longest-serving Prime Minister – and beyond argument one of the most distinguished – was fond of calling himself a "simple Presbyterian". Yet doubts have been expressed about his faith. He has often been described as a "nominal" or "formal" Christian, and before doing research for this book I held that assumption myself. The image I had of Menzies was as a gifted but self-centred man, prone to haughtiness and condescension. Admittedly my thoughts had been coloured by a disturbing book about the Vietnam War*, to which I may have overreacted. But there were also his dire-sounding compliments to Hitler and the Nazis, paid on several occasions until the late 1930s, and his life-long support for

---

* The book I had read was Michael Sexton's *War for the Asking: How Australia Invited Itself to Vietnam* (New Holland, 2002). Sexton's discomforting thesis, including his account of Menzies' role in the relevant events, still strikes me as persuasive. It is indisputable that Menzies was responsible for the notorious "birthday ballot" – selective conscription among men turning 20, announced in November 1964. However, I am now convinced that he believed in good faith – albeit, with the benefit of hindsight, mistakenly – that the larger cause was just. He placed reliance on a system of so-called "forward defence" (fighting communist insurgency wherever it happened in the region) and took the view that if Australia expected American help in the future it was obliged to "do its bit" in the present. The same attitude undergirded his approval of British nuclear testing in outback South Australia between 1955 and 1963, which left the area dangerously contaminated and had dire long-term consequences for the local Indigenous population. In some respects Menzies was naïve. He failed sufficiently to take heed of two of the plainest lessons of World Wars I and II (and, as it happened, of Vietnam and Iraq). The Great Powers are capable of brazen deceit and massive blunders, and always look out for themselves.

the "autonomy" of white South Africa. He campaigned loquaciously for conscription in World War I, yet declined to enlist himself.

In temperament, Menzies was a strange mixture. At times he was unscrupulous; at other times honourable. He enjoyed the comforts of life but was a true puritan in his distaste for profanity, obscenity and ostentatious money-grubbing. He was capable of both tender kindnesses and cold-hearted wit. I agree with the assessment of his fair and sympathetic biographer, A.W. Martin, that there was a diffident side to him: a "private nervousness, and ... glimpses of a thirst for approbation by others, almost needed to integrate and confirm his picture of self".[1]

At the core of this dichotomy was a simple fact. Menzies was streets ahead of most of his colleagues in intellect, learning and sensibility. In the words of a veteran Canberra journalist, Wallace Brown, he was "a whale among minnows".[2] Menzies knew it and – at least as a young man – did not bother to hide the fact that he knew it. He once said bluntly to the Country Party's Archie Cameron: "I do not suffer fools gladly."* Cameron shot back: "It might be news to you to know that bloody fools have a lot of trouble putting up with you too!"[3] Such barbs wounded Menzies.

The same sentiments were echoed by many on the Labor side. John Curtin admired and liked Menzies, but he too commented once that "if Bob has a fault it is that he does not suffer fools". Curtin (who was Prime Minister at the time) added sagely: "I am afraid that you have to learn to do that in this job."[4] In due course, to his great credit, Menzies did learn.

Overall, the mature Menzies was cultivated and astute and basically fair-minded. But was he a Christian? My own conclusion is that his faith was very real. Having examined the record and talked with his daughter, it seems plain that Christianity was an integral aspect of his life – especially in his early and late years. As an adult his church-going was sporadic, but he knew his Bible, believed in the Gospel and cherished the Scots Presbyterian tradition. Given Menzies' stature and importance, it is appropriate to make this case in a little detail.

---

* The expression "suffer fools gladly" is Biblical. It was first used by St. Paul in his second letter to the Corinthians: "Ye suffer fools gladly, seeing ye yourselves are wise." (2 Corinthians 11:19, KJV) Of course, Paul was being sarcastic. Like Menzies he was a giant among many Lilliputians.

His father, James Menzies, was a Presbyterian by birth and upbringing. According to his famous son, he was possessed of "a deep-seated faith and belief".[5] As a young man in Ballarat in the 1870s and 1880s, James Menzies had been a prominent elder at Scots Church, Soldier's Hill.[6] His sister, Belle Menzies (Bob's aunt), was a Presbyterian missionary in Korea.[7]

Presbyterianism was, then, in Menzies' blood. But there was no Presbyterian Church in the small Victorian town of Jeparit in which he grew up.[8] On arriving there in late 1893 James Menzies had "[thrown] in his lot with the Methodists, who were the strongest non-Catholic group, with their own church building, which had been erected in 1891".[9] James, indeed, was one of the first trustees of the Jeparit Methodist Church[10] and a lay preacher given to "highly emotional" sermons of a stern, Old Testament flavour. His was a "narrow Calvinism".[11]

Menzies recalled his father's ethos less than fondly ("whom the Lord loveth, he chasteneth"[12] – cf. Hebrews 12:6), but his mother's was very different. A miner's daughter of Cornish descent, Kate Menzies (née Sampson) had a whimsical sense of humour and a kind heart. Menzies extolled her as "calm, human and understanding" – a paragon of "sweet reasonableness". She doted on her youngest son and he routinely sought comfort from her.[13] It is sobering to imagine what might have become of Menzies had he not experienced another, gentler side of Christianity in his mother.

Church-going was a part of family life. As an old man, Menzies retained a vivid childhood recollection of the little Jeparit church: "The pews … were of varnished pine, and, as money was scarce, the varnish was cheap and sticky. I can remember sitting forward after the sermon and disentangling my hair from the varnish with considerable difficulty!"[14]

Another key influence upon the boy Menzies was his paternal grand-mother, with whom he lived for some years in Ballarat while attending school*

---

* In Ballarat Menzies attended a privately-owned secondary school called Grenville College. He was best known at Grenville not for his grades – which by his lofty standards were disappointing – but his superb mimicry of a prominent Methodist reformer of the day, the Rev. William Henry Judkins. Judkins was once described as "an aggressive Protestant, a crusading prohibitionist, [a] symbol of … political complacency and puritanical arrogance". It says a lot for the importance attached in those days to Christianity that Bob Menzies was repeatedly asked *by teenage schoolboys* to imitate a prominent religious figure.

in the town. She was a frugal old lady, somewhat narrow-minded and lacking in humour. But she was also devoted and devout. According to A.W. Martin, "the only books permanently permissible in [her] house were the Bible, the Presbyterian Hymn book, *The Ingoldsby Legends* and *Pilgrim's Progress*".[15]

Books, indeed, were crucial to Menzies' development – intellectually and vocationally, as well as spiritually. As a child he grew up immersed in the written word, and the Bible was central. So too was the evangelistic theology of the Scottish writer Henry Drummond.[16] Menzies was a voracious childhood reader and – not coincidentally – a phenomenal student. He won several scholarships, which were immeasurably precious in those days. In Menzies' case they were a passport to two elite institutions: Wesley College in Melbourne, where he was exposed to three more years of Methodism; and the University of Melbourne, where he studied arts and law as a non-resident at the Presbyterian college, Ormond.

Many people down the centuries have lost their childhood faith at university, but Menzies was not among them. If anything his faith became more intense – though not more mature. He attended a Bible class at North Carlton while maintaining a close involvement with his family's local churches. On one occasion at Kew Presbyterian Church he delivered a lay sermon on 'The Sacredness of the Secular'.[17] On campus he was President of the Students' Christian Union[18] and wrote spiritual articles for *The University of Melbourne Magazine*. His support for conscription in 1916-17 was couched in explicitly Christian terms: Britain stood "for the world's best civilisation and the spread of the world's purest religion".[19] All those who volunteered to fight could, he believed, "go with God's glory on [their] face".[20]

He also wrote a series of pieces about the wonders of Nature, each focusing upon a mystical, epiphanous moment when "My spirit bows down and worships in silence and alone". A.W. Martin sensed in these pieces "some strain, as if in the experiences [Menzies] talks about he is almost pathetically grateful for the imagined 'signs' of faith confirmed".[21] I get no such impression: so-called natural theology, while unfashionable today, can have a very powerful effect upon those who experience it. The heavens declare the glories of God, says Psalm 19.

The influence of the Presbyterian Church upon Menzies' life continued after graduation – and in a vital way. He met and married Pattie Maie Leckie, the daughter of a Deakinite Liberal MLA. As teenagers they had periodically attended the same churches, but they did not meet properly until 1919, at a party at Camberwell. Pattie later insisted that Menzies strode over to her and declared: "You're Pattie Leckie; you used to make eyes at me at church!"[22] The impish opening gambit succeeded: he and Pattie were married the following year, on September 27, 1920, at Kew Presbyterian Church in Melbourne. With remarkable prescience, the Rev. J. Ringland Anderson predicted that "the bridegroom of today will one day be Prime Minister of Australia".[23]

It was at this stage of Menzies' life that his commitment to Christianity may have waned somewhat. Certainly he became less outwardly observant. His daughter, Heather Henderson, suggested to me that her father may have been "over-burdened with religion" in his early life – "churched out". During the 1920s he was concentrating six days a week on his flourishing career at the Bar; the rest of his time was largely devoted to his young and growing family. Then, in 1928, he entered the Victorian Parliament and became immersed in political affairs. In this period he and Pattie worshipped occasionally at Kew Presbyterian Church, but they did not take part in wider church activities.[24] However, during 1929 he became a regular – and popular – speaker at the Methodist Central Mission's Pleasant Sunday Afternoons. He continued this activity well into the 1930s.[25]

One of his speeches bears mention. Delivered on May 3, 1931, at the height of the Great Depression, it was entitled "Politics and the Church" and contained this sentence:

> If Australia was to surmount her troubles only by abandonment of British standards of honesty, justice, fair play and honest endeavour, it would be better for Australia that every citizen within her borders should die of starvation within the next six months.[26]

One hopes that Menzies did not mean this literally. His argument – on that occasion and others – was that "no good turn can be done to the underdog in a community which is insolvent".[27] Menzies did not lack a sense of private charity: at the Bar he took on *pro bono* cases including a big one for the Melbourne City Mission's maternity home.[28] Even so, his priorities during this period seem to have been rather skewed. He deprecated the importance of public works as a partial solution for unemployment. Once, bizarrely, he denied that the Depression was due to "monetary factors".[29] He often denounced strikes and opposed most proposals by Labor or the unions to ameliorate working conditions.[30]

It was a case of the company he was keeping. Menzies had become close to key figures in the Melbourne business and financial establishment, and his faith and his humanity had not yet fully flowered.

In 1934 he moved to the federal Parliament and became Attorney-General and Minister for Industry in the Lyons Government. His family still lived in Melbourne, and at some stage in the 1930s they began going to the West Hawthorn Presbyterian Church rather than the one in their own suburb of Kew. Menzies went more often than Pattie: he was often accompanied by Heather, who attended Sunday school there. Heather recalls bringing along her French Bible to services, at her father's suggestion, so that she could follow the readings in that language and improve her command of it!

In 1935, having just turned 40, Menzies made his first trip overseas – to Britain, for trade talks and King George V's silver jubilee. Menzies was in Heaven. He kept a diary and it is fascinating on many levels. But two entries are especially illuminating for what they say about his engagement at that time with matters religious.

In one he mocked the dry, affected Christianity of certain English country squires, those who believed that one "must attend to the rites of the church but leave the public discussion of religion to the non-conformists".[31] Menzies much preferred the huge football crowd at Wembley which spontaneously sang 'Abide With Me', Henry Francis Lyte's beautiful Christian hymn. "An irreligious communism", wrote Menzies approvingly, "has no chance with these people".[32]

What of irreligious *fascism*? Menzies' conduct during the 1930s as regards Nazi Germany has often been remarked upon. He has been denounced over the years by historians from the right (for appeasement) and the left (for supposed Nazi-sympathising). What is almost always lacking in such analysis is the Christian angle.

The key issue with which Menzies had to grapple could not have been more momentous. The deteriorating situation in Europe terrified almost everybody. Memories of 1914-18 were still horribly fresh, and the prospect of another war, fought with modern weapons, was close to unthinkable. As we have seen, Joe Lyons supported to the hilt the official British policy of appeasement – as did S. M. Bruce, by then High Commissioner in London, and the ALP. Their stance had Menzies' public and private backing. He made long trips to Britain in 1935, 1936 and 1938 – on the last occasion he also visited Germany – and in May 1939 he succeeded Lyons as Prime Minister.* His thoughts and actions during this period have been thoroughly documented by Christopher Waters in *Australia and Appeasement*.[33]

In retrospect, Menzies paid some sinister-sounding compliments to the Nazi regime.

It is true that, from time to time, he also expressed serious reservations about it. But the record, in parts, makes embarrassing reading. For example, in mid-1938 – not, let be noted, 1933 or '34 – Menzies wrote to his sister and appeared to make light of Hitler's brutal suppression of dissident Christian voices:

> The Germans may be pulling down the Churches, but they have
> erected the State, with Hitler as its head, into a sort of religion
> which produces a spiritual exaltation that one cannot but admire.[34]

---

* There was a brutal fight within the Coalition before Menzies got the job. One of his most venomous critics was the leader of the Country Party, Sir Earle Page. Following Joseph Lyons' death, which affected him deeply, Page was commissioned as a stop-gap Prime Minister pending the UAP caucus electing a new leader. Page promptly announced that he would bring the Coalition to an end if the UAP chose Menzies. Menzies was elected anyway, but on the third ballot, and by a bare four votes over the 78 year-old warhorse Billy Hughes. Unrest continued. Senior Coalition figures including Page, Richard Casey and Hughes sought to persuade S.M. Bruce to return to Australia and lead his country again. In Parliament, Page as *Acting Prime Minister* kept up the pressure on Menzies by questioning his "courage, loyalty and judgement". Menzies' failure to enlist in World War I was used against him: Page implied that he could not hope to be a respected war-time leader. But the charge was below the belt: Menzies responded with measured dignity, and his aged mother backed him up in a rare public statement: "We told him again and again that two sons from a family was as much and more than a country expected ... We needed someone at home to look after us ... and I think that is why he was perhaps the bravest of all my boys." This testimony – and generous support from some notable ex-servicemen – elicited sympathy for Menzies and shored up his position. When, in the end, Bruce declined to return to Australia, the die was cast. On April 26, 1939, Menzies was sworn in as Prime Minister, together with an all-UAP cabinet.

On August 8, 1938 he said:

> I do hope that we British people will not too easily accept the
> idea that because personal liberties have been curtailed in
> Germany the result is necessarily a base materialism. There is a
> good deal of really spiritual quality in the willingness of young
> Germans to devote themselves to the service and well-being of
> the State.[35]

On October 15, 1938, back in Australia, he praised the fascist governments
of Germany and Italy for having fostered "enthusiasm for service to the
State". Although "it perhaps went too far," he admitted, such patriotism
"could well be emulated in Australia".[36]

Of course, it is vital not to take such snippets out of context. Heather
Henderson insisted to me that her father was "not in the least racist or anti-
Semitic", and, even making allowance for her natural loyalties, the sincerity
of her testimony was impressive. It must be stressed that views of the kind
which Menzies expressed about Nazi Germany were not uncommon in the
1930s throughout the British Empire. Hitler was tolerated or indulged by
many well-meaning people because of his trenchant anti-Communism.
For the same reason, Mussolini – and General Franco in Spain – had
support from many conservative Catholics. All democrats of that era were
faced with an unpalatable choice between totalitarian evils.

Even so, the conclusion seems inescapable that Menzies' anti-war
stance was the product of mixed motives. He was not, like Lyons or
Scullin, and probably the latter-day Bruce, "honestly pacifist at heart".[37]
He believed that, provided the cause was just, war might be converted
"from a brutal deflowering of humanity into a good *and holy* thing".[38]
But unless and until Britain declared war on Germany, Menzies could not
discern any sufficiently just cause.

Up until September 3, 1939 he followed the Christian precept that – at
a minimum – war should be treated as the absolute last resort. "To talk at
any stage except at the last moment of a preventative war is the very ecstasy
of despair."[39] Menzies uttered those wise words on October 3, 1938, and
he behaved accordingly for another 11 months. "No nation," he wrote to
Chamberlain in August 1939, "should ignore real efforts at settlement because

of false notions of prestige".[40] He deplored war as "the greatest possible calamity"[41], and defended Britain's "magnificent efforts to avoid the insanity and injustice" that, inevitably, war would bring.[42] Indeed, on the weekend of September 2-3, 1939, Menzies kept urging negotiations with Hitler even after Chamberlain himself had abandoned the idea. (So did S. M. Bruce.)

As soon as Britain declared war, however, Menzies did too for Australia. On Sunday evening, September 3, 1939, he began his famous radio address to the nation as follows: "It is my melancholy duty to inform you officially that in consequence of a persistence by Germany in her invasion of Poland, Great Britain has declared war upon her and that, *as a result*, Australia is also at war." (My emphasis.) For Menzies and the UAP, there had never been any question of Australia breaking with Britain. Menzies saw no need to recall Parliament, and he defended this stance in his memoirs on three grounds: public opinion in Australia as he assessed it, the need to "encourage" the British people, and the indissoluble bond of the Crown.[43]

Views can reasonably differ as to the wisdom and morality of Menzies' declaration of war – and, for that matter, Chamberlain's. For present purposes, the point I would stress is that Menzies hated doing it. This was to his credit: it bolsters his credentials as a serious Christian. Unlike, say, Winston Churchill*, Menzies utterly dreaded the prospect of war. The conclusion of

---

* Churchill died an atheist. That he relished war seems to me incontestable, since examples of his blood-lust abound. In September 1914, a month into World War I, the British Prime Minister H.H. Asquith wrote: "I am almost inclined to shiver, when I hear Winston say that the last thing he would pray for is peace". After the first Battle of Ypres, with tens of thousands dead, Churchill confessed: "I am so happy. I cannot help it – I enjoy every second." Churchill's adulators argue that, during the 1930s, he was one of the few voices of courage and good judgment. This is nonsense. His tactical acumen was poor and, on several occasions, he expressed fulsome admiration for Mussolini and Hitler. He gave every appearance of wanting war for the sake of war. By early 1938 he was agitating for it, notwithstanding Britain's military unpreparedness, and he was elated when it came ("the glory of Old England thrilled my being"). After succeeding Chamberlain as Prime Minister in May 1940 he vetoed any idea of peace negotiations with Germany, interned all "enemy aliens and suspect persons" in England (mostly Jewish refugees), and ordered a starvation blockade of the continent (including occupied France). Worst of all, he ordered the bombing of German cities, not in accordance with old rules of siege bombardment (that is, to assist troops fighting their way into an urban area), but as a deliberate, cold-blooded strategy – to kill civilians on a mass scale. This was a tragic first in the history of warfare. In the words of the English Catholic-conservative historian Paul Johnson, Churchill's decision "marked the point at which the moral relativism of the totalitarian societies invaded the decision-making process of a major legitimate power."

Menzies' September 3 announcement is much less well-remembered than the beginning: "May God in His Mercy and compassion grant that the world may soon be delivered from this agony."

At a very early stage Menzies was urging consideration of "peace aims". This was an unpopular view at the time in Australia and Britain, but Menzies was prescient. In effect, he anticipated the spirit of charity inherent in the Marshall Plan and the formation of the United Nations. Also sound were his first instincts about Churchill. In February 1940 he wrote to the former British Prime Minister Stanley Baldwin:

> I cannot tell you adequately how much I am convinced that Winston is a menace. He is a publicity seeker; he stirs up hatreds in a world already seething with them and he is lacking in judgment ... We have tried [in World War I] to alter the German spirit by force. Is it not possible that it might be more effectively altered by conspicuous generosity following on conspicuous defeat?[44]

These were Christian sentiments. And Menzies concluded his letter to Baldwin in overtly Christian terms: "If only a kindly Providence would remove from the active political scene a few minds which are heavily indoctrinated by the 'old soldiers' and by the 'Versailles' point of view, my task here would be easier."[45] Clearly enough he had in mind the likes of Billy Hughes.

Menzies' war leadership is generally regarded as a failure. Paul Hasluck's broadly sympathetic thesis was that Menzies tried his best and did some sensible things but was engulfed by the torrent of events. What was lacking was something intangible: the Australian public's enthusiasm for the war effort remained low.[46] Menzies admitted in *Afternoon Light* that he lost their confidence – "if I ever had it".[47]

It seems tolerably clear to me that throughout 1939-41 Menzies' heart was never fully in the job. He was like Andrew Fisher in 1914-15: miserable and conflicted. As the media proprietor Warwick Fairfax observed, Menzies' state of mind at the outbreak of World War II was like Hamlet's after the appearance of his father's ghost: "The world is out of joint/O cursed spite that ever I was born to set it right."[48] This seems a just assessment and it weighs *in favour* of Menzies as a conscientious Christian man. He wrote in his diary shortly after the war commenced:

> I know that there is probably no answer to it all – except just to go on fighting until the other country goes down into a state of starvation and riot in which the seeds of another war, in which my grandchildren will fight, are sown. But at the same time I see no sanity in it.[49]

The prophet Micah could not have put it better. But Micah, one suspects, would not have prospered as a wartime leader.

The result of the Federal Election of September 1940 was a hung Parliament. There were shades of 2010: the Menzies Government was reliant thereafter on the support of two Independents, Arthur Coles and Alex Wilson.

Unwisely, perhaps, Menzies left Australia in late January 1941 on another extended visit overseas, this time to confer in person with Churchill and the War Cabinet. Questions loomed about the threat to Australia posed by Japan.[50] Menzies was away until May. The Allies' prospects in Europe were then at their lowest and the months during and immediately after this trip were filled with anguish for him. Ultimately he lost the confidence of his colleagues, and, on August 29, 1941, resigned as Prime Minister. The government fell soon afterwards when the two Independents withdrew their support.

Three incidents from this period are worth noting for the light they cast upon Menzies' faith.

First, the circumstances of his arrival in the Middle East on February 2, 1941. He landed in a flying boat on the Sea of Galilee! "I had never been there before," Menzies noted in his memoirs, "but I had been well-schooled in the Bible, and was excited at all I saw." Two days later he visited the old City of Jerusalem. He was fascinated by the "complicated rules" of conduct expected of visitors there, but accepted them, "since Jerusalem is not only the Holy City for both Christian and Jew, but is also one of the three holy cities of the Mohammedans". Of the experience in general, he wrote simply: "I will never forget it."[51] Fleetingly, he had been able to put the War from his mind.

A second incident of note is Menzies' meeting in Ottawa in May 1941 with the Canadian Prime Minister, W.L. Mackenzie King. A shrewd and eloquent man, Mackenzie King noted afterwards in his diary that the Australian leader had "reveal[ed] his Scotch Presbyterian origin in his thoughts and views generally".[52]

Third, and most tellingly, Menzies' mother wrote to him on July 11, 1941 to convey "how much we sympathise with you in your very difficult position" and to remind him that "the Lord God omnipotent reigneth". She acknowledged that this could be hard to accept "at times when one is passing through the valley" (an echo, of course, of Psalm 23).[53]

It is now a matter of legend that Menzies revived his career in mid-1942 with a celebrated series of radio talks. There were 37 in all, and Christianity was often mentioned directly or in passing.

In 'The Forgotten People', his first and most famous talk on May 22, 1942, Menzies outlined a vision for post-war Australia. He argued powerfully that society had to be constructed around the middle class ("the backbone of the nation"). He emphasised the virtues of "thrift" and "independence" and "free enterprise" – and the concomitant dangers of excessive government intervention. God helps those who help themselves.

But also central to Menzies' analysis was a Biblical proposition: "we are all, as human souls, of like value". This required a temperate, *moral* liberalism – not dog-eat-dog. Menzies spoke movingly of the less fortunate in society and of the critical importance of education. He laid heavy emphasis on family and the arts. He lauded "homes material, homes human and homes spiritual". As to the last:

> This is a notion which finds its simplest and most moving
> expression in 'The Cotter's Saturday Night' of Burns. Human
> nature is at its greatest when it combines dependence upon God
> with independence of man.

('The Cotter's Saturday Night' is a poem by the Scottish poet and lyricist, Robert Burns. Written in 1785-86, it celebrates a humble hard-working family's reading of the Bible. It was one of the favourite poems of Menzies' father.)

On July 3, 1942 Menzies's address was entitled "Freedom of Worship".

It contained a beautiful passage going directly to his belief in the numinous:

> With all our modern cleverness ... we are still only on the fringes
> of the universe of thought. We grope out towards the light,
> seeing the occasional flash of beauty or understanding, hearing
> occasionally the penetrating voices of reason. ... [In] the heart of
> every man, whatever he may call himself, is that instinct to touch
> the unknown, to know what comes after, to see the invisible.

In the same speech, Menzies ventured the view that "there is a consciousness in most of us that someday all will come to light and he shall be judged". He quoted Christ's words in John 14: "In my father's house there are many mansions."

These speeches were the turning point of Menzies' career. He had struck a nerve. His arguments gained force when the moribund UAP was thrashed at the 1943* election under Billy Hughes' quixotic leadership. In late 1944 Menzies launched the Liberal Party of Australia, pronouncing that "there is no room in Australia for a party of reaction".[54]

The full story of the Liberal Party's genesis is told in Gerard Henderson's book *Menzies' Child*. As Henderson explains, the links between the new party and the Protestant churches were vital from the start. There was a key conference in Canberra over three days in late 1944: Friday October 13, Saturday October 14, and Monday October 16. A religious flavour was lent to the proceedings by the venue – Canberra's Masonic hall, a nondescript building near Old Parliament House. In Henderson's sardonic yet perceptive words, "It was a reflection of the Protestant allegiance of many of those attending the Canberra conference that it was decided to keep preference to keeping holy the Sabbath over the immediate need to establish a nationwide non-Labor organisation in Caesar's realm."[55]

---

* Menzies identified 1943 as the year in which he "turned the corner". Many years later, scoffing at rumours that he was about to stand down as Prime Minister, he invoked a Biblical metaphor. "'He that setteth his hand to the plough and looketh back is not fit for the Kingdom of Heaven,'" he told a Liberal Party meeting. "And I haven't set my hand to the plough, as I did in 1943, to take it away again because there are a few ruts and stones and obstacles in the furrows". The allusion was to Luke 9:62, though in most translations (including the KJV) Jesus refers to "putting" rather than "setting" one's hand to the plough.

There was a follow-up conference in Albury from Thursday December 14 to Saturday December 16, 1944. "Once again," noted Henderson, "the Sabbath was not violated."[56]

The new party endured a disappointing loss to Labor at the 1946 federal election. (Menzies' friend Lionel Lindsay complained that the people had chosen Barabbas rather than a Saviour.[57]) But then a kindly Providence set in. In August 1947, Prime Minister Ben Chifley decided to try to nationalise the banks: although the legislation was struck down in the courts it remained a political albatross for Labor. So too was petrol rationing. Menzies won office in December 1949 on an "anti-socialist" tide and thereafter bestrode Australian politics like a colossus.

In its domestic policies the Menzies Government was sound rather than spectacular. Nevertheless it could boast several lasting achievements. For present purposes, one stands out.

In 1963-64 Menzies finally began the process of defusing the State aid debate. In the lead-up to the November 1963 election he promised to give £5 million to both government and independent schools for the building of science blocks.[58] He was accused of cunning and expediency, and no doubt there were political considerations in the timing of his action. (The Coalition had been clinging since 1961 to a one-seat majority, and Labor was hopelessly split over State aid.) Even so, the time had come to heal wounds. And I venture to say that in 1963 *only* Menzies could have done so. He had immense authority within the Coalition and the country at large and was unimpeachably Protestant. He also had a most respectable record as regards sectarianism.

Growing up, Menzies had witnessed a good deal of religious intolerance – some within his own family. In *The Measure of the Years* he recalled that "from my earliest days it nauseated me".[59] As late as 1928, he had been rebuked by older relatives for having attended the opening of a Catholic school in his electorate of East Yarra.[60] As the Victorian Attorney-General in the early 1930s, he attracted criticism in some quarters for opposing Protestant efforts to ban a large Catholic Eucharistic procession through the streets of central Melbourne.[61] In May 1939, as Prime Minister, he spoke at a bi-partisan peace rally at Melbourne's Exhibition Hall organised by the Australian National Secretariat for Catholic Action. He emphasised the shared faith of all present: "That is why I, a Presbyterian, can stand here, a non-Catholic on a Catholic platform."[62] On June 4, 1939 he gave an address at the opening of the newly-built St Christopher's Catholic Church in Canberra, and in his "Freedom of Worship" radio address in 1942 he denounced sectarianism in plain terms as "the denial of Christianity, not its proof".

All this was admirable. Yet it must be said that, during his 16-year reign as Prime Minister after December 1949, Menzies' tolerant personal views were not reflected in the make-up of the Liberal and Country Party caucuses. Perhaps Menzies was not sufficiently proactive. At one stage there was just a single Catholic MHR from the Liberal Party: J. O. (later Sir John) Cramer.

In his memoirs, Cramer made some revealing remarks about sectarianism within the Coalition. He "noticed that if a discussion was going on in the ministers' private rooms that touched on religion, discussion immediately ceased when I entered the room although no doubt what was being said was in good humour".[63] (I interpolate here that Cramer was almost certainly being charitable; he must have overheard some objectionable comments.)

As for Menzies himself, Cramer acknowledged that he was "never openly hostile to adherents of the Catholic Church". However, Cramer added this observation:

> I was sensitive about and rather hurt by the quite frequent
> remark of [Menzies], 'Be careful boys, here comes the Papist'. For
> some reason I cannot understand, it always seemed uppermost
> in his mind that I was a Catholic and therefore in some way
> different from the others.[64]

No doubt Cramer heard what he heard. But the clear weight of evidence suggests he was mistaken as to the true state of Menzies' mind. Menzies may have cracked some distasteful jokes but he was *not* a sectarian. Certainly he was not by 1960. In that year he wrote a letter to his daughter Heather concerning the presidential election campaign in the United States. Menzies doubted John F. Kennedy's prospects of victory because of his Catholicism. But Menzies addressed the "sectarian issue" in terms which indicated that he *disapproved* of religious prejudice (and understood how it worked in practice). "[It is] the kind of issue which lends itself to a whispering campaign," he wrote. "By the time a lot of folk over their teacups or otherwise have been able to say, 'But of course, my dear, he is a Roman Catholic and would have to take orders from the Pope,' it may very well turn out that a considerable number of Democrats won't vote at all".[65]

There is other evidence. As I have said, in 1963-64 Menzies intervened decisively in the State aid debate. Later in the decade he became a friend of B.A. Santamaria, and at the 1969 and 1972 federal elections he voted for the DLP.[66] There was also this passage in *Afternoon Light*: "Protestant and Presbyterian as I am, I long since learned that there are some Protestants whose Protestantism is an expression of hostility rather than of faith."[67]

That disposes of sectarianism. But where, it might be asked, is the proof that Menzies remained a serious Christian? When I broached the matter directly with Heather Henderson, she was careful not to gild the lily. Although Presbyterianism was "an important part of his whole make-up", and his "moral and ethical standards of behaviour went back to Christianity", she could not recall discussions about theology. She would be "guessing", she said, as to his positions on particular matters. Her father was a "private and reserved" man in some respects, at least in the company of his children, though he may well have had such discussions with his sister Belle.

I would draw attention to Menzies' public and private professions, written and oral – some of which are little-known. Considered collectively (and examples could be multiplied) these seem inconsistent with anything other than a living faith. Mrs Henderson confirmed my instinctive impression that Menzies was not the sort of man to have mouthed confected views about things so sacred. His sinful tendency was toward excessive bluntness, not insincerity. (That is my judgment, not hers.)

In 1940, during his first term as Prime Minister, Menzies spoke on the occasion of the Centenary Thanksgiving of the British and Foreign Bible Society of Victoria. He lauded the King James Bible not only for its immense literary and cultural influence but as "the greatest storehouse of enthusiasm one can discover".[68]

On Sunday, March 14, 1954, during his second term, Menzies spoke at the opening of St Edmund's Christian Brothers Memorial College in Canberra:

> I do not believe that education can be pagan without being
> destructive. The 20th century has proved that to the last limits of

disaster. I think that the great thing in the world today is that we have our children grow up, not only learning of their relationship to their fellow men, *but even more of their relationship to God.*[69]

Later in 1954, in June, Menzies was present in Alice Springs for a ceremony to mark the laying of the Foundation Stone of the John Flynn Memorial Church. He praised Dr Flynn – the founder of the Royal Flying Doctor Service – as a "modern Apostle Paul". Like St Paul, Menzies said, Dr Flynn not only had vision but "the executive ability to get things done". Two years later, in May 1956, Menzies returned to Alice Springs to attend the first service conducted at the Church, at which he read the lessons.[70]

Also noteworthy is his Sir Henry Simpson Newland Oration of March 5, 1958, on "Modern Science and Civilisation".[71] In the course of an argument about the ethical responsibilities of scientists in the nuclear age, he quoted St Paul: "Hath not the potter power over the clay?" (Romans 9:21. See also Isaiah 29:16, 45:9, 64:8.) For Menzies, the achievements of science were to be marvelled at, but "a moral and mental philosophy" was needed to "give … balance". His overarching point was that technological advancement is only ever a means to an end, and he quoted from Browning's poem 'Bishop Blougram's Apology' (1855). "And body gets its sop and holds its noise/And leaves soul free a little."

In retirement, on August 11, 1974, Menzies gave a speech at the conferring upon him of the Freedom of the City of Kew. He was moved, and paid tribute at one stage to the essential decency of the Australian people. He continued:

> You know, I think it was the Apostle Paul who said that 'we are all members one of another'. It is a lovely phrase, you know. It is a lovely expression. It means that no man can live to himself, that every man who lives in that community is a member of that community. He shares his membership with other people.[72]

Of course, these were all public occasions. But similar sentiments and preoccupations are discernible in Menzies' private correspondence.

In 2011 his daughter Heather Henderson published a book containing a selection of her father's private letters between 1955 and 1975. They are remarkable for their emotional candour and – because Menzies was not aware he was writing for posterity – excellent evidence of his true beliefs. It emerges clearly that Christianity was a subject with which he was extremely familiar and assumed Heather was familiar. (The same is true of his wartime letters to his son Ken.[73]) A few snippets from his letters to Heather must suffice to give the flavour.

In September 1961 he wrote about one of his grandchildren*:

Edwina's question "Was God born?" has filled me with delight. This, in my opinion, is the most profound theological question ever put. It suggests to me that this girl should end up either as the first female president of the Rationalists' Association or as the first female Primate of Australia.[74]

On July 11, 1967, *apropos* the modest monetary inheritance that he would one day leave his family, he quoted from Proverbs 15:17: "Better a dinner of herbs where love is, than a stalled ox and hatred therewith."[75] And on November 8, 1967, writing from England, he described a dinner with his son Ken, his niece Margaret, their spouses, and a special guest:

We dined ... with the new Presbyterian Minister at Brighton, an Irishman called McRae and his wife, and sister Belle. The dinner was quite hilarious.

McRae is a youngish man with a light Irish brogue and a keen sense of fun. He is a good storyteller and accepted with relish a martini before dinner and some wine with it. There is hope for the Presbyterian Church yet![76]

Mention must also be made of Menzies' close and trusting friendship with the Rev Dr J. Fred McKay (1907-2000), an eminent figure in the history of the Presbyterian Church of Australia. They first got acquainted in 1954 during Menzies' visit to Alice Springs, and their respective families became close. Menzies told Heather during that visit that McKay had impressed him greatly as a "good, practical Christian". When Menzies suffered a stroke in November 1971 he was paralysed down one side for many months afterwards.

---

* Menzies doted on his grandchildren and sang them hymns on request. He once boasted publicly of a bedtime rendition of 'Shall We Gather at the River?'

Rev. McKay frequently visited the Rehabilitation Centre at Parkville in Melbourne and was with Menzies when he showed the first sign of regaining movement. The two men said a prayer of thanksgiving together.[77]

McKay's testimony about the aged Menzies is invaluable, and, in my judgment, decisive. McKay knew him intimately for 24 years. He officiated at the services for Heather Menzies' wedding in 1955 and Ian Menzies' funeral in 1974. He also led the service at Menzies' own state funeral in 1978 at Scots Church in Melbourne.

In the last few years of Menzies' life, McKay often came to dinner at Menzies' home.[78] There was a ritual: those at the table joined in prayer while Menzies recited Robbie Burns' Selkirk Grace:

> Some hae meat, and canna eat,
> And some wad eat that want it,
> But we hae meat and we can eat,
> And say the Lord be thankit.

Shortly before Menzies' death, McKay gave him a copy of William Barclay's recent book *Testament of Faith*. They then "shared an interesting theological discussion".[79] Possibly it was about the afterlife, for Barclay (a prolific Christian author who also died in 1978) had come to believe in universalism, the idea that all souls will eventually be re-united with God. In any event, by this time, it seems overwhelmingly probable that Menzies trusted in an afterlife. In 1970, he had concluded the chapter about his parents in *Afternoon Light* with this sentence: "I owe an immense debt to both of them, and, now that they are long since dead, I send my love to them in heaven."[80]

Menzies and McKay parted in touching circumstances. McKay clasped Menzies' hand and said, "God be with you, Bob." According to McKay's biographer[81], this is what came next:

> Robert Menzies replied: "And with you, and may He make His face to shine upon you, and be gracious unto you." Fred continued the blessing: "The Lord lift up the light of his countenance upon you." Then both friends said together, "And give you peace."*

---

* See Numbers 6:22-27.

HAROLD EDWARD HOLT (1908-67)

LIBERAL: 1966-67

Holt was Minister for Labour and National Service in the first Menzies Government. In that capacity, during 1940-41, he oversaw the introduction of universal child endowment. It was a hugely popular reform and Holt was dubbed affectionately "the godfather of a million Australian children".[1]

That label was the closest Holt ever came to public association with religion. Theologically, he had more in common with the "average" Australian than any Prime Minister in our history. Like most of his fellow citizens – then and now – he was an apathetic agnostic. His biographer, the Anglican academic and author Tom Frame, adjudged that Holt's abiding belief was "in the individual's right to live his own life in his own way."[2] He also had "a simple buoyant faith in progress".[3] One of his closest friends, the Melbourne businessman Simon Warrender*, believed that Holt's *raison d'etre* was "dedication to his career".[4]

Warrander also revealed that his friend's primary guide to life was Rudyard Kipling's ubiquitous secular poem, 'If'. This is an overrated text if ever there was one. Yet, according to Warrender, for Holt it was a creed: "In

---

* Simon Warrender (1922-2011) was a notable character in his own right. According to his obituary in the *Sydney Morning Herald*, he was the great-great grandson of the Seventh Earl of Shaftesbury, the 19th-century English aristocrat and Christian social reformer who fought for (among other causes) the abolition of slavery in England and the restoration of the Jews to the Holy Land. Warrender himself was the first member of the Melbourne Club to resign in 132 years – he did so in 1971 "when the Club refused the nomination of his wife's relative, Baillieu Myer, seemingly on the grounds of his Jewish heritage".

his soul-searching moments he always returned to its four short stanzas and used their sentiments as a guiding light in his political and private life."[5]

By worldly standards, Holt's life was a great success. He did well at school, in the law, and in business. He served in the Federal Parliament for 33 years, many of them as a minister. He was abstemious, disciplined and hard-working; and ambitious without being ruthless. Among colleagues and opponents alike he earned a reputation as a decent and tolerant man. Gough Whitlam considered him "a truly civilised human being who was in a very real sense a gentleman".[6] Kipling would have approved.

But Holt's life-story is also a cautionary tale. From a Christian perspective it illustrates the precept that a wise man builds his house upon the rock. For all his fine qualities and impressive achievements, Holt built his house upon sand.

In Manning Clark's opinion, Holt nursed "a desperate drive to … be loved".[7] It is an opinion borne out by the ethical contradictions evident in Holt's character. Although he was a loyal friend and a kind stepfather, he was also an inveterate womaniser – discreet, up to a point, but often unfaithful to his wife Zara. She remained stoic and silent while Holt was alive, but confessed some of her feelings in her 1968 memoir, *My Life and Harry*, and in subsequent public statements.

The key to Holt was his chaotic upbringing – in which religion played a negligible role. He was baptised an Anglican but seems never to have attended Sunday school or to have received Christian instruction at home. As a teenager he boarded at Wesley College in Melbourne (Methodist); he also lived for several years at the University of Melbourne's Queen's College (also Methodist). But at no stage was God on his radar. In Tom Frame's assessment, he was "never troubled by … religious doubt".[8]

Holt's parents set a dissolute example. T.J. (Tom) Holt was variously a school sportsmaster, publican, theatrical manager and film producer. He and Holt's mother, a widow named Olive Mary Pearce, were married when Olive was already pregnant. As young boys Harold and his brother Cliff were palmed off to relatives; Tom and Olive moved interstate and later divorced.[9] When his mother died in 1920, Holt did not attend her funeral.

For a long time his own personal life was problematic. In the early 1930s, pleading poverty, he had declined to marry Zara. She promptly married someone else (a British army officer named James Fell) and for well over a decade Holt stayed single. Though outwardly suave and handsome, "the most eligible bachelor in Parliament", inwardly he grieved. He confided to one of his wealthy patrons, the influential Melbourne socialite Dame Mabel Brookes, that politics was "all he had".[10]

Things changed on October 8, 1946, when, aged 38, he finally married Zara. She had divorced James Fell a couple of years earlier.[11] The ceremony was held at the home of Zara's mother in Toorak, "with Congregational forms"[12], but these were a formality. Zara's father had been a very religious man – she recalled in her memoirs that as a girl she and her siblings "all had to read one chapter of the Bible every night"[13] – but Zara herself was as spiritually apathetic as Holt.* Certainly theirs was not a "white wedding". Holt had probably fathered Zara's twin boys, Sam and Andrew, while she was still married to Fell.[14]

There was a hedonistic side to Harold Holt. He cared little for wealth *per se*, but he liked parties, dancing, restaurants, travel, spear fishing and gambling at cards.[15] And the company of attractive women. In 1962, he made this revealing diary entry about a female dinner companion: "[She] is still a lovely woman, but like a very ripe peach which should be eaten without delay".[16]

None of this was known to the Australian public in January 1966 when, unopposed, Holt succeeded Menzies as Prime Minister. He was a popular choice. In his own accurate boast he "had won the job without stepping over a single dead body"[17] and his reputation was as a "with it" modern man.[18] His lack of religious faith (or even religiosity) was not much remarked upon: indeed, as Tom Frame has observed, it was emblematic of the changing times. Australia was entering an era when the "unifying symbols of Crown, religion and race were becoming less relevant to an

---

* In *My Life and Harry*, Zara devoted several florid pages to an account of the Queen's coronation in 1953, which she and Holt attended. The setting – Westminster Abbey – did not inspire her to any ruminations of a Christian nature. The closest she came were some remarks about protocol and spectacle. For Zara, a boutique operator, there was nothing "more beautiful or more impressive" than "ecclesiastical clothing". Perhaps Zara's religious temperament was more Eastern. In the 1960s she reacted emotionally during a visit to Angkor Wat (Hindu) temple in Cambodia.

increasingly multi-cultural society".[19] John Warhurst has identified 1966 as the first year of a new period in Australian history – one of "ecumenicism and secular humanism" as opposed to sectarianism.[20] Holt's accession was the turning point.

Holt, however, did not have an overarching secular vision. He was energetic and well-meaning and took the first significant steps to dismantle the White Australia Policy (a move, incidentally, that was first advocated by the DLP). But he was also an unquestioning supporter of the Vietnam War ("All the way with LBJ!") and conscription. Nor was the economy his strength: Ian Hancock has maintained that he had "little interest … and no conceptual grasp".[21]

In truth, Holt had a limited imagination. Apart from newspapers and political briefs he did very little reading. On the day after his accession to the Prime Ministership the *Australian Financial Review* called him "a plasticine man – imprinted with the philosophy, beliefs, arguments of the last person with whom he came in contact".[22]

During 1967 Holt was ill-equipped to deal with a series of personal and political setbacks. He had always been sustained by cheerful optimism, which Paul Hasluck compared to a sort of secular "fundamentalism".[23] But then the rain came down, the streams rose, and the winds blew and beat against Holt's house. He began to brood. Kipling's 'If' seems to have become a slender reed, of limited utility and comfort. Holt staggered, then fell with a great crash. (Cf. Matthew 7:26-27.)

In March 1967 his brother Cliff died. Hard upon that blow came several others. The Vietnam War began to go wrong – terribly wrong – sparking bitter public protests and dissent within Cabinet about the commitment of further Australian troops.[24] There were recriminations over the tragic HMAS *Voyager* incident of 1964, culminating in the public embarrassment of Holt by a Liberal backbencher, E. H. (Ted) St John.* The so-called VIP

---

* Infamously, Holt interrupted St. John during his maiden speech. St John's dead-pan remark – "I did not expect to be interrupted by the Prime Minister" – was an enormous embarrassment for Holt. He was restrained by a squeeze on the arm from his Attorney-General, Nigel Bowen, before slumping back "red-faced" into his chair. As regards St John, see further the chapter on John Gorton.

aircraft affair led to accusations that Holt had misled Parliament, a charge then regarded much more seriously than it is today.[25]

Colouring everything was the emergence of Gough Whitlam as a formidable Opposition Leader. In mid-1967 Labor secured two important by-election victories and in November there was a big swing its way at a half-Senate election.[26]

Holt's prestige had been battered. As the year drew to a close there were Liberal leadership rumblings.[27] On Friday December 15, 1967, Holt said goodbye to Zara in Melbourne – "Before God, you're a rose of a woman" were his last words to her[28] – and drove to his Portsea beach house on Victoria's Mornington Peninsula. Within 48 hours he was dead. Late on Sunday morning, December 17, 1967, he went to Cheviot Beach with Marjorie Gillespie (his then-mistress) and several other friends. Soon after midday he strode alone into rough and unpatrolled surf and was never seen again.

Did Holt commit suicide? There is a school of opinion that such speculation is cruel.[29] Tom Frame considers the idea ill-founded, as does Ian Hancock. But the evidence is not clear-cut.

Zara's third husband, the Liberal MHR Jefferson (Jeff) Bate, insisted it was suicide. Marjorie Gillespie said in 1985 that Holt had "put himself in a situation where he was almost certain to die".[30] A shoulder complaint had caused him bad physical pain throughout November.[31] Gough Whitlam has always taken the suicide theory seriously; indeed, there is evidence that Whitlam feared for Holt's state of mind in the weeks preceding his disappearance. According to Wallace Brown, one day in November 1967 Whitlam answered a private phone call from Holt in Brown's presence. Whitlam asked Brown to leave the room while he took the call. When Brown returned 15 minutes later, Whitlam remarked: "I am a bit worried about him".[32]

At the least, there was a fey recklessness about Holt's conduct. Although his mind was weighed down with problems it would not have occurred to him to pray to God for strength and wisdom, when most he needed it. Holt's refuge was not God but escapist fun. He was a fatalist and often quoted a verse of Marvell's: "But at my back I always hear/Time's winged chariot hurrying near."[33]

The case for suicide, whether by negligence or design, is strengthened somewhat by Holt's unbelief. Modern knowledge of mental illness makes it dangerous to moralise, but for Christians suicide is a grave sin. It amounts to self-slaughter and flouts the Sixth Commandment. This would not have been a consideration for Holt, whose thoughts "lay in this world not the next".*[34] He had no fear of Divine judgment.

Holt's state funeral took place on December 22, 1967 at St Paul's Anglican Cathedral in Flinders Street, Melbourne.[35] It was attended by numerous world leaders including US President Lyndon Johnson, with whom Holt had formed a genuine friendship. Archbishop (Sir) Philip Strong spoke of "fidelity" as the mark of Holt's life.[36]

In the days and weeks that followed the tributes were warm and generous. Senator Vince Gair, the leader of the DLP, expressed the opinion that "Holt's main aim in life … was to serve God and his country".[37] No doubt Gair was sincere, and correct as to Holt's patriotism. But he attributed to the man a faith which there is no evidence he had.

---

* Holt's Cabinet colleague Sir Alec Downer (father of Alexander) made this observation. Curiously, Sir Alec regarded it as a factor pointing *away* from suicide. Even more curiously, for an Anglican bishop, so did Tom Frame.

JOHN GREY GORTON
(1911-2002)

LIBERAL: 1968-71

J ohn Gorton was not, in any conventional sense, a "religious man". Like Harold Holt, he endured a fractured upbringing. He was a womaniser, and rather less discreet about it than Holt. He could be stubborn and intemperate. Even today, the suggestion that Gorton was at heart a Christian would be laughed at in some quarters. But the possibility is more than tenable.

Gorton had compassion, vigour and a bold imagination. He also had great respect for Christianity and "a little-known spiritual side of his character".[1] Some of his most fervent beliefs were moulded during his youth by men of the Church of England.

He was an Oxford graduate and a brave fighter pilot during World War II. Before entering federal politics he had been an orchardist by occupation, and an extremely popular figure in the Victorian rural district in which he lived, near Kangaroo Lake. Though he cultivated a low-brow larrikin image* and could be erratic in his work habits, he read widely and had "a first rate intellect".[2]

He was also his own man. During the 1950s and early 1960s he was a Cold War "hawk". He went as far as arguing that Australia should develop its own nuclear weapons[3] and rejected the view that "survival is all". A man

---

* At the 1970 World Expo in Japan, Gorton declared that "Australia has more to it than bloody boongs and pop singers!" On another occasion he said: "I like my TV ... with redskins biting the dust, some violence mixed in, and a certain amount of sex. I am not a boor but I am not a culture-vulture either."

who thought that, "and not that survival in free conditions is all", was, in Gorton's view, "morally dead".[4] Yet by the mid-1960s he was equivocal about the Vietnam War. This was at a time when many in the Coalition (and, even more so, the DLP), were fervent champions of both the conflict itself and Australian involvement. Gorton expressly refused to give the United States "a blank cheque", but he was constrained from going much further by practical politics. (The DLP's right-wing Catholic leadership threatened not to direct preferences to the Coalition at the next general election – preferences which had been decisive in 1961 and which would again be decisive in 1969.[5])

Gorton also openly disagreed with church strictures on what were and are, for some Christians, critical issues. On abortion, for example, Gorton often said he was against "compulsory pregnancy". He believed that "when it was not against a woman's conscience to have an abortion, she should be allowed to have one, provided an abortion was not against the conscience of the medical staff in attendance".[6]

Likewise, in October 1973, as an Opposition backbencher, Gorton moved a motion that: "In the opinion of this House homosexual acts between consenting adults in private should not be subject to the criminal law." Gorton drew a distinction between conduct "which may be held by some to be sinful and conduct which ought to be held by the state to be criminal".[7] (Many agreed with him: the motion was passed 64-44, with support from over 20 Coalition members.)

Within Coalition circles, a good number of the objections to Gorton were not on public policy grounds. They were personal. Malcolm Fraser deprecated his dictatorial style and famously pronounced in Parliament in 1971 that he was "not fit to hold the great office of Prime Minister". Others felt the same way. It is notorious that Gorton "liked the company of women and liked talking to them, [and] was sufficiently uninhibited to parade this liking".[8] During his Prime Ministership there were various "scandalous" incidents.[9] Most (not all) of these were trivial, but, collectively, they took their toll on Gorton's reputation. By early 1969 opinions within his Cabinet ranged from "near hero worship, through hopelessness to every degree of doubt to downright despair".[10]

One of Gorton's sternest critics was a backbencher in his own government – E. H. (Ted) St John. In his book *A Time to Speak*, published in late 1969, St John alleged that "we are now under the Prime Ministership of … a man quite inadequate in character, training and temperament to meet the demands and challenges [of his office]".[11] The overused term "Puritan" was not, in St John's case, inapt. He employed the righteous language of an Old Testament prophet. St John saw Gorton less as the cause of Australia's problems and deficiencies than as a reflection of them. His conduct was emblematic of Australia's "spiritual unhealth".[12] Within the Coalition St John had few friends, and those he had were fellow members of a tiny parliamentary Christian group. Eventually, early in the election year of 1969, the Liberal Party closed ranks around Gorton. St John was blackballed.

The whole saga was tragic in its way, because Gorton and St John were both decent men who emphasised quite different features of a broadly Christian vision. St John placed high, possibly excessive, importance upon "proper" personal conduct: temperance, discretion, modesty and so forth. His critique was one-dimensional. It was also, to an extent, uncharitable, considered in the light of Gorton's fraught and disrupted childhood. The full story is convoluted and sad, but for present purposes there are two points of relevance.

First, in the blunt phrase of biographer Alan Reid, Gorton was "a bastard by birth"[13] – conceived and raised out of wedlock. In the early 20th century, illegitimacy carried a very real stigma, societal and religious. Gorton's parents, John Rose Gorton and Alice Sinn, were "anxious to hide it".[14] With some ingenuity they succeeded in doing so, but no doubt the strain told on everyone. Gorton did not mention the matter publicly until he was 58, almost two years after becoming Prime Minister.

It is also important to understand why Gorton's parents were not married when they conceived him – and why they could never marry. Simply, John Rose was already married when they met, and his estranged wife – an "imperious" Irishwoman named Kathleen O'Brien[15] – would not agree to grant him a divorce. She was a strict Catholic. The trauma was compounded by the fact that Alice, the mother whom Gorton adored, died young. Gorton was only seven and he had to go and live with Kathleen.

These and associated experiences coloured Gorton's views about marriage and the churches. This was evidenced in 1959, when he was given the task of securing passage through the Senate of the Government's Matrimonial Causes Bill. This was an important piece of legislation – a unification of divorce laws throughout Australia – and its terms were not especially liberal. Nevertheless there were strenuous objections made to it by the Catholic Church, some Anglican clergy, and not a few parliamentarians.

Speaking in the Senate, Gorton was forthright. While respecting the views of those who opposed the Bill on religious grounds, his respect did "not extend to a belief that a party to a marriage who does not hold those convictions ought to be in any way bound by another party to the marriage who does hold them".[16] He pointed out that dysfunctional marriages caused misery not only for the parties to them but for any children of the marriage. The task of senators was "to decide where the greatest injustice really lies".[17]

There is another point to be made in Gorton's defence, as regards his sexual infidelities and his attitude to marriage generally. For a start, as C.S. Lewis once wrote, "the sins of the flesh are bad, but they are the least bad of all sins".[18] Gorton believed that his affairs were inconsequential because, in his mind, they never threatened his marriage. Bettina (Betty) Gorton was a sophisticated woman. A Quaker by upbringing, she tolerated her husband's dalliances.[19] The marriage* lasted for almost fifty years, ending on October 2, 1983, when Betty died of cancer.

For the next decade Gorton lived alone in Canberra. His health declined and he became something of a recluse.[20] Then, out of the blue, at the age of 82, he announced his decision to re-marry.** His bride, Nancy Home, had been a friendly acquaintance for many years. They lived together contentedly until Gorton's death in 2002.

Gorton's sins, then, should be seen in perspective. And there is another side to his story which is not well-known.

---

* The wedding took place on February 16, 1935, at St Giles (Anglican) church in Oxford. To avoid the need for parental consent, Gorton had lied to the Rector, telling him that Betty was 21! He and Betty had tried to get married first at the local registry office, but were rebuffed on account of Betty's age.

** The wedding took place on July 24, 1993, in Sydney, at St Michael's Anglican Church in Vaucluse. At least on the surface, it was a thoroughly religious occasion. There were readings from Scripture (including Psalm 121), and several hymns were sung ('Jerusalem', 'The King of Love My Shepherd Is', 'Praise My Soul the King of Heaven').

As a boy he imbibed Christian teaching. After his mother's death he attended three elite Anglican schools. The first two were in Sydney: Headford Preparatory School in Killara ("a quiet and genteel Anglican establishment"[21]) and Sydney Church of England Grammar School (Shore). But it was during his four years at Geelong Grammar (as a boarder from 1927-30) that Gorton's religious consciousness was shaped.

The headmaster during Gorton's first three years was the Rev. Dr. Francis Brown (1869-1939), who, like Billy Hughes, was an admirer of Matthew Arnold. Brown was "a painstaking and God-fearing man" with "a mission to implant a Christian education among the boys".[22] Though generally regarded with affection, Brown ran a tight ship and his Sunday sermons were "interminable".[23] One can imagine young Gorton squirming in his seat. Even so, the message seeped through.

In Gorton's final year, 1930, a new headmaster arrived – and he made a huge impression. James Ralph Darling (1899-1995), an Englishman, was young and idealistic. He had been strongly influenced in his theology by two headmasters of Repton, the venerable Church of England grammar school in Derbyshire (est. 1557) that Darling attended as a boy.[24] Both of these headmasters, William Temple and Geoffrey Fisher, were future Archbishops of Canterbury. It was Temple who once said: "It is a mistake to suppose that God is only, or even chiefly, concerned with religion."

This might have been Gorton's credo; it was certainly Darling's. He had a decided social justice streak, tempered by belief in self-help, and he displayed it during the Depression year of 1930. Every Friday, Darling arranged for boys from Geelong Grammar to distribute food hampers to local families where the breadwinner was unemployed. According to Gorton's most comprehensive biographer, Ian Hancock, "years later, and on numerous occasions, Gorton would refer to this experience as shaping his political outlook".[25]

Darling remained headmaster at Geelong Grammar until 1961 and Gorton kept in touch with him for decades. They exchanged friendly letters shortly after Gorton's election to the Senate in December 1949. Darling congratulated his former pupil, but urged him to become "more liberal" (that is, left-wing). Gorton replied that he would do so "at drop of a hat", subject to one crucial proviso: "you cannot help men *permanently* by doing things for them which they should, or could, do for themselves".[26]

This was Gorton's worldview. He was true to it all his life, and, in my judgement, it was a view shaped by his understanding of the Gospels.

On two separate occasions in the 1940s, before he entered politics, Gorton delivered speeches at the Mystic Park Hall near his home in northern Victoria. These were functions held in his honour – the first when he was leaving for war, the second after he returned. They are revelatory of the man. Remember, these were not calculated political speeches; they were spoken from the heart.

The first was in June 1941, at Gorton's "farewell" send-off. Gorton declared that if the war was won, "there must be a new order, one that will take the place of the old order permanently".[27] He expanded on this theme on April 3, 1946, at the "welcome home" function. It was a longer and more considered talk, indeed a superb piece of heart-felt oratory, well worth reading in full.[28]

Gorton began by observing that "there has been a good deal of confusion as to why we went to war, and as to what we can reasonably expect as the result of our military victory". Gorton's view was that the war had been fought – rightly – to preserve a democratic system of government and "a conception of justice in which the humblest one amongst us has equal rights before the law". But these were but "the foundation" of a just society, not its actualisation. Material living standards needed to be raised *for all*.

Importantly, he referred to the "spiritual" aspect of the challenge:

> We must raise the spiritual standard of living so that we may get a spirit of service to the community and so that we may live together without hate, even though we differ on the best road to reach our objectives.

In conclusion, in a general "call to arms", he made specific mention of the duty of Christians:

> We must do this. For no person of susceptibility, no soldier who has seen his comrades killed, *no Christian*, above all no mother with growing children can stand idly by and see the chance which we have once more won, once more wasted.

Fifteen years later, after the Coalition's election victory in December 1963, Gorton was appointed by Menzies as Minister-in-charge of Commonwealth

Activities in Education and Research under the Prime Minister. In this capacity Gorton had responsibility for implementing the Coalition's promises on State aid. In the first instance it was Catholic schools that stood to gain the most. Gorton was an excellent choice, for he was "clearly devoid of any religious prejudice himself".[29] Appropriately, on November 30, 1970, it would fall to him (as Prime Minister) officially to welcome Pope Paul VI to Australia. It was the first-ever Papal visit to this country.

Gorton had done an able job for Menzies as regards State aid, and after the December 1966 election he was rewarded with a promotion. Harold Holt made him Minister for Education and Science. The subject of education was dear to Gorton. It was in the context of education policy that he made the most explicitly "religious" pronouncements of his career.

On August 19, 1948, shortly before entering Federal politics, he gave a long speech at the Regent Theatre in Kerang. It contained a passage on religious instruction which, if nothing else, gives the lie to any suggestion that Gorton was uninterested in matters metaphysical. In it he doubted the value of exposing young children to religious instruction – not because the subject-matter was frivolous but because it was so profoundly important:

> The story of Christianity is the most tremendous in the history of the world. To appreciate it properly a fully developed mind is absolutely essential. Its teachings run counter to natural instincts and to what a child can see of the world. It is probably the ultimate in philosophy, and no child can understand it. I do not mean that it is bad to tell a child that there is such a thing as Christianity, that it is good, and that it will be a wonderful experience for it when it grows up. I do not mean that simple stories and such comments as "God is love" should not be taught. What I do mean is that to drag a child step by step through the gospels when it doesn't understand, to make it learn extracts by heart instead of in the heart; to introduce a sanctimonious and false aura of "good" and "bad" and wickedness; and to insist that everything that appears in the Bible is literally true and can't even be questioned. To do these things is apt to make the child lose interest in the subject for ever, though he may pay it lip service.

That is quite possibly the reason why we have today so many professing and so few practising Christians.[30]

These were thoughtful musings. By the 1960s Gorton had decided that there was certainly a place for religious instruction when children were older – though precisely where he placed the cut-off point is not clear.

Ian Hancock, after reviewing all of Gorton's speeches and memoranda in the National Library pertaining to education, summarised his views thus:

> He argued that 'the primary function of education' was to translate into reality Christ's words from the Sermon on the Mount: 'Be ye therefore perfect as your Father in Heaven is perfect' (Matthew 5:48). It was 'better to fail in the attempt to make a perfect human being than to succeed in making a fully competent technician'.[31]

For Gorton, the most crucial subjects at school were history, literature and religion. The technical subjects – science, mathematics, economics and so on – had their place. But they "were not the factors which made the difference". Religion, Gorton thought, "imposes a discipline and reveals a philosophy that breaks the shackles of the present". Via these influences, society could nourish a child's "soul".[32]

In what state, when he died, was Gorton's own soul? It would be unwise to rush to judgment.

WILLIAM (BILLY) MCMAHON (1908-88)

LIBERAL 1971-72

H istory has not been kind to Sir William McMahon. Known by most Australians as "Billy" (though he preferred "Bill"), his failings and foibles are the stuff of legend. Yet he was, in several respects, a substantial and important man. For present purposes, one little-known achievement stands out. McMahon took the trouble coherently to explain the connection between his religious and political beliefs – in writing, in public, and at some length.

In September 1953, as a relatively junior MHR in the Menzies Government, McMahon presented a paper at the First Winter Forum of the Victorian Group of the Australian Institute of Political Science. It was subsequently published in book form, along with other papers presented on that occasion.[1]

McMahon insisted that his paper was not about the relationship of ethics or theology to politics.[2] He did, however, spell out four "basic assumptions" about human nature, which, he said, influenced his views concerning political action.[3]

First: "The Christian World in which we live has as its sustaining principle the idea of the individual as the central feature of society. We therefore reject the proposition that the "State" has some inherent value and can be of greater consequence than the individuals who compose it. We reject the view of Plato in his "Republic" and consequently abandoned in his later works, notably the "Laws". We reject the philosophical basis of Marx and Hegel."

Second: "Man alone possesses the capacity to think and act purposefully. Although the implication is over-simplified because the causes of change are highly complex, this implies that the primary driving force throughout history has been the individual man and woman. I accept the idea that the individual determines change in society. Consequently I reject the materialistic thesis of Socialism and Communism that the forms or conditions of production are the fundamental determinants of social structure and change. As the individual is the driving force in society and undoubtedly responds to external stimuli – of rewards of one kind or another – he must have satisfactory incentives for effort and achievement."

Third: "The Doctrine of Original Sin. Following St. Paul that Man is born with the tendency to sin, of hereditary weakness, which, if not disciplined, will lead to excess or sin of one kind or another. This implies, of course, that too great power must not be placed in the hands of the exceptional individual. If this principle is accepted, it demands distribution of power and deterrents to the arbitrary abuse of authority. By the tests of fact alone and logic a more persuasive case can be made out for this Doctrine than for Rousseau's fantasy of the Noble Savage or Marx' version of the classless society."

Fourth: "The Doctrine of Free Will, a will that belongs to man alone; the ability to choose; to express within limits a free choice, and therefore to be able to choose between right and wrong, good and evil. Without free will there can of course be no evil."

McMahon concluded: "Thus, in the widest sense, freedom of choice implies the Parliamentary Democracy and a market economy."[4]

Of course, views may reasonably differ as to the strength of McMahon's thesis. Some might argue that he was trying a bit too valiantly to reconcile his religious beliefs with his political beliefs – when, for any Christian, it should always be the other way around. But it was a thoughtful contribution.

How did McMahon get to that stage? It is a story full of interest.

The marriage of his parents was "mixed". His mother was an Anglican, but she died when he was four.[5] His father, W.D. McMahon, was a Sydney solicitor of Irish-Catholic heritage and considerable inherited wealth. There were, as a result, "religious differences between some members of the family".[6] It seems, however, that W.D. McMahon's faith – such as it was – at some stage lapsed. By the end of his life he was a "rationalist".[7] He was not close to his children and they were raised by a disparate collection of relatives and guardians.

Young Bill McMahon was a lonely, solitary boy – in effect an orphan.[8] The dominant figure during his childhood and adolescence was his maternal uncle, Samuel Walder, his mother's older brother. Sir Samuel, as he later became, served in conservative interests as Lord Mayor of Sydney, as a member of the NSW Legislative Council, and as a vice-president of the United Australia Party. His influence upon his nephew was considerable. Bill adopted both his entrepreneurial, free-trade philosophy and his Church of England affiliation. Reflecting back on his early life, McMahon once described Sir Samuel as both a mentor and a good Christian – "a very tolerant Anglican".[9] "That must," McMahon said on another occasion, "have had a good effect on me."[10]

In his late teens McMahon became keenly interested in dogmatic theology – the result, perhaps, of his father's premature death. Until then his religious practice had been formal only: "there had been a vacuum there before," he conceded in 1972, "a pretty big vacuum".[11] He did not go to Sunday school as a child[12] and once recollected that it was doubtful whether he had ever seen a Bible until he was 17[13] – though given the schools he attended this sounds unlikely.

At all events, at 16 or 17, he began investigating God. He read extensively and, in the end, was converted. "I sort of proved to myself that there was a God," he once explained, "and that I was ... able to make up my mind about it".[14] In short, he now believed. Looking back in 1963, McMahon described his teenage experience as of being "twice born".[15]

McMahon's was not a static faith. For the rest of his life he continued to read widely, and his evolving views were shaped by an eclectic mix of English Protestant theologians: C.S. Lewis, J.B. Phillips, Cyril Garbett (*Church and State*), John A. T. Robinson (*Honest to God*) and Claude Beaufort Moss (*The Christian Faith*).[16]

The Christian whom McMahon held in the highest esteem was William Temple (1881-1944), the great English bishop and philosopher/theologian who became Archbishop of Canterbury in 1942, as mentioned previously. Speaking in 1965, McMahon nominated Temple's *Christus Veritas* (1924) as a key influence in his journey to faith. He also admired

Christ's Revelation of God (1934). These texts could, he said, "be read and re-read".[17] It was a just observation: these are classic theological works.

The basics of McMahon's career can be shortly outlined. He studied law at the University of Sydney from 1924-27 while boarding at St Paul's, the most prestigious Anglican college on campus. Somewhat surprisingly, in view of McMahon's later persona, he acquired a reputation at Paul's as a "wild man". He was described in the college magazine *Pauline* as a "cheerful rowdy extrovert" with "a fondness for night-life". According to this source, young Bill McMahon "would talk volubly and hyperbolically on most subjects, with or without any knowledge of them".[18]

After graduation he worked solidly for 12 years as a city solicitor. He became a partner at the eminent Sydney firm of Allen, Allen and Hemsley*, and came under the influence of some cultivated, intelligent – and decidedly Protestant – men. Sir Norman Cowper and Arthur Hemsley were two who exhibited, in McMahon's words, a "generous liberalism". They were not obsessed, like so many leading corporate lawyers today, with the narrow business of money-making. Cowper especially, McMahon once recalled, "tried to give you every opportunity to study and understand" in a broader sense.[19]

During World War II McMahon enlisted in the Army, but, due to deafness, was confined to staff jobs. At war's end he did not return to the law. He travelled widely in Europe and North America before re-enrolling at the University of Sydney to take a degree in economics.

During these studies he came under the influence of Francis Armand Bland (1882-1967), a noted lawyer and academic who later served (from 1951-61) as the Liberal MHR for Warringah. Bland was also prominent in Sydney Anglican circles. For many years he was a lay reader and a member of the Synod, and he served on the council of The King's School at Parramatta and of Moore Theological College.

---

* In case it seems to the knowledgeable reader that I have an unusually soft spot for McMahon, I should here make a disclosure. I too worked at Allens as a young man, from 1987-2006, the last ten years as a partner. I was always fascinated by the presence of McMahon's name on the roll of partners in the entrance foyer. Norman Cowper, incidentally, was the great grandson of William Cowper (1778-1858), a noted Evangelical who arrived in Sydney in 1809 as an assistant chaplain to Rev. Samuel Marsden. Cowper served as the minister at St. Philip's (Anglican) Church in the city and later as an Archdeacon. His son, Charles Cowper, was an early Premier of NSW.

McMahon was particularly impressed, he would later recall, by Bland's views on "free men and free institutions".[20]

In December 1949 McMahon entered federal politics. He won the seat of Lowe, in Sydney's inner-western suburbs, and held it for 33 years until his retirement in 1982. In a long career he served in various senior portfolios in the Menzies, Holt and Gorton governments. He succeeded Gorton in March 1971 after ugly machinations within the Liberal party-room long since dissected by political experts.[21] For me, the most intriguing thing about McMahon's accession is a comment he made during his first press conference as Prime Minister: "I believe in the Liberal Party and I believe it is the organ by which the national will *and conscience* can be put into effect."[22] Deliberately or not, he used the language of faith.

In the event, his record in office was undistinguished. As is well-known, he led the Coalition to defeat at the "It's Time" election of December 1972. But he had started behind the eight-ball. Alan Reid, a hardy veteran of the Canberra Press Gallery, once drew upon an Old Testament metaphor: McMahon "would have needed the wisdom of a Solomon … to re-establish the Coalition as a united, coherent fighting force."[23] McMahon could take solace from the fact that the election result was closer than expected. Thereafter, for ten years, he sat on the backbench. He became increasingly disenchanted with the Liberal Party and with the spitefulness of political discourse.

In any hard-headed assessment of McMahon's Christianity, three further matters should briefly be mentioned. Interested readers can investigate for themselves and decide whether they cast reasonable doubt on the genuineness of his faith.

First, it cannot be denied that McMahon was disliked and distrusted – even reviled – by many of his Coalition colleagues. These feelings were harboured at the very top. Famously, after the death of Harold Holt, the Country Party leader John McEwen blackballed McMahon for the Liberal leadership. Menzies, too, was not a fan. In a letter to his daughter on October 24, 1969, he dismissed McMahon as an "untrustworthy little scamp".[24] Paul Hasluck's comments about McMahon in his private diaries were positively scathing.

It is still not entirely clear to me why McMahon was so unpopular with his peers, but it seems that he acquired a "reputation for being a stranger to the truth".[25] He had "an inclination to show off and exaggerate, and [to make] weak attempts at humour".[26] He was a frequent "leaker" to the press and a reluctant delegator. On the other hand, he was known by his personal staff and by acquaintances around Parliament House as "a friendly, approachable man".[27]

Second, McMahon had an unfortunate tendency to exploit religion for political advantage. Certainly he could be gauche. One example among many: during an interview in 1971 with David Frost, he said he was "a religious man" and that he would pray for a Liberal election victory.[28] Worse, in the closing stages of the 1972 campaign, he did not intervene to prevent or disown a great deal of anti-Labor invective on ostensibly "religious" themes – homosexuality, abortion, pornography, Asian immigration and such wise. Much of this was instigated by a junior member of McMahon's cabinet, the Rev. Dr. Malcolm Mackay*, and/or the Liberal Party premier of NSW, Sir Robert Askin. The DLP, as might have been expected, was also in the thick of it. Some of these arguments were fair comment but others were downright scurrilous.[29]

A third issue pertaining to McMahon is his sexuality. He married late, at the age of 57, and there is circumstantial evidence he was gay – or bisexual. To be sure, a good many people down the years have asserted or insinuated the fact.[30] Once, when McMahon belatedly announced that he would set up a Royal Commission on the Status of Women, Gough Whitlam quipped cruelly: "It takes some political leaders some time to show an interest in women."[31] In 1972, a Gay Liberation candidate ran against McMahon in his seat of Lowe under the slogan "Vote for the poofter who lives in the electorate".[32]

Such rumours are still current today, despite an indignant public rebuttal in 2007 by McMahon's widow, Lady Sonia McMahon (née Hopkins), with whom he had three children, and of whom he always seemed very fond.[33]

---

* Malcolm George Mackay AM (1919-99) was McMahon's Minister for the Navy from 1971-72 and an ordained Presbyterian minister. Before entering federal politics in 1963 he had served as the Australian General-Secretary for the World Council of Churches (1954-56) and as the first Australian-born minister at Scots Church in Sydney. He was defeated in his seat of Evans at the December 1972 election. Subsequently he served as the assistant minister at Scots Church in Melbourne (1975-76 and 1982-84). He was made an officer of the Order of Australia in 1986 for "services to the community particularly in the fields of religion, education and politics."

To me the allegation is a long way from proved, and I hesitate even to raise it. But in the context of this book it seemed unavoidable, given the trenchant views about homosexuality held by a good percentage of practising Christians. For many it is a litmus test issue. Put to one side more nuanced contemporary questions concerning gay marriage and gay ordination. Even in Australia, the majority Christian view (which personally I do not share), is that all homosexual acts are sinful *in and of themselves*. Reliance is placed upon Leviticus 18:22 and 20:13 and Romans 1:26-27, among other passages.

As far as I have been able to ascertain, McMahon never discussed homosexuality from a Christian perspective. In 1973 he abstained from a conscience vote in the House of Representatives on the question of decriminalisation. But the year before, in answer to a direct question from a journalist, he said this:

> Homosexuality I haven't expressed an opinion about. What little reading I've done about it has given me the impression that it's more due to physiological causes than anything else. Consequently you must look at it from a medical point of view rather than a political one.[34]

My own guess is that McMahon was not gay. Far too much seems to have been made of his smart clothes and querulous voice. It seems most unlikely that a conservative Christian such as Dr Malcolm Mackay would have supported McMahon so avidly had he believed or even suspected that he was homosexual – let alone put his name (unless he was a total hypocrite) to full-page advertisements during the 1972 election campaign denouncing the ALP and Gough Whitlam for "moral permissiveness". On November 28, 1972, the *Sydney Morning Herald* reported on its front page that Dr Mackay had issued a statement signed by ten leading Protestant churchmen declaring that "Australia's future depends on national leaders who respect traditional Christian values".

Of course, even if McMahon had been gay, and pretended for political reasons to be something he was not, it does not follow that he was not a good Christian. At the very least he was a seeker. The only thing that gives me pause (about McMahon's faith, not his sexuality), is the fact that his widow did not mention Christianity when she defended him. Then again, she herself was not "religious" [35] – the point simply may not have occurred to her.

It would be uncharitable to speculate any further. "For all have sinned and fall short of the glory of God" (Romans 3:23). While he was no Alfred Deakin, the evidence suggests that Billy McMahon searched hard for the Divine.

EDWARD GOUGH WHITLAM (B. 1916)

LABOR: 1972-75

T o some he was a "political Messiah".[1] To others he was the Devil Incarnate. Opinions about Whitlam have always diverged sharply, and probably always will.

Today, I venture to guess, a dim view would be held of him by a majority of practising Christians – certainly by those of conservative Protestant bent. Whitlam has referred to "the Jensenite heresy" in Sydney[2] and "the climate of wretched religiosity prevalent in the United States".[3] He is not a humble man, and his frequent self-comparisons with Jesus, though tongue-in-cheek, could verge on the blasphemous.

But Whitlam's irreverent humour masked sober thinking and seriousness of purpose. As Opposition Leader in the late 1960s, he resolved, by sheer force of will, the decades-long rift within the ALP over State aid to religious schools. In government, on any fair-minded view, he achieved a great deal for social justice – one-vote-one-value, Medicare*, the Trade Practices Act, needs-based education funding, and better sewerage for Australian cities, to name but five of his legacies. The Family Law Act of 1975 is often invoked

---

* The universal health insurance scheme that Whitlam instigated in 1974 was called Medibank. After being gutted by the Fraser Government it was resurrected as Medicare during the Hawke/Keating years. John Howard pledged to dismantle it during the 1987 election campaign and John Hewson made similar noises in 1993. Labor won both times. Medicare is now an untouchable component of Australia's social fabric.

against him, and with some justification; so too his permissive views on abortion. On balance, however, his achievements hold up well to Christian analysis.

In any case, it cannot be disputed that Whitlam was a titanic figure in the history of modern Australia. And – a little-known fact – his knowledge of Christianity exceeded by some margin that of any other Prime Minister since Alfred Deakin.

Whitlam was an expert in both history and doctrine. In his book *Abiding Interests,* he treated readers to the observation that, in the Balkans, "Orthodox Christians believe that the Holy Spirit proceeds from the Father, and Catholic Christians believe that the Holy Spirit proceeds from the Father and the Son (*filioque*)".[4] That is one example among hundreds.

I can also speak from personal knowledge. One morning in June 2008, when my book *God, Actually* was published, Whitlam rang me out of the blue to offer congratulations. For 20 minutes, in a kindly and respectful tone, he proceeded to dissect the passages about extra-Biblical sources for the life of Jesus. He knew his stuff.

Of course, knowledge is not the same thing as faith: there is no clearer message in the Gospels (see John 20:29). Whitlam was raised in a devout Baptist household, but he ceased to believe in Jesus' divinity at the age of 11 or 12. He admitted in 1973 that this happened "probably for spurious reasons"[5], but, even so, his faith has never returned. Yet he has remained fascinated by all things Christian, and, over the course of a long life, some of his closest relatives and friends were believers.[6] Margaret, his beloved wife for almost 60 years, was one of them.[7]

According to his most recent biographer, Jenny Hocking, Whitlam's Christian upbringing is crucial to a full understanding of his character. The "two great constants" of his childhood were politics and religion.[8]

The religious aspect can be traced to his grandfather, Henry Hugh Gough (Harry) Whitlam. A market gardener by trade, from 1877-81 Harry served a prison term at Pentridge Gaol for the forgery of cheques. Then came redemption. Shortly after his release, he married into one of Melbourne's most prominent Baptist families, the Steeles, and turned his life around. His religious conversion, wrote Jenny Hocking, "brought him a measure of salvation [and] ... would be felt through ensuing generations."[9]

Both of Harry Whitlam's sons – Fred (Gough's father) and George (Gough's uncle) – were raised as Baptists. Fred Whitlam was "deeply religious, diligent and dutiful".[10] Highly respected on both sides of politics, he served for 12 years as Commonwealth Crown Solicitor and was a legal adviser to the Australian Council of Churches.[11]

Fred's wife, Martha, was also devout. She met Fred when she was 16 at the Murrumbeena Baptist church in Melbourne. They were married seven years later, in 1914, at a ceremony conducted by Fred's maternal uncle, the Baptist minister Alexander Steele.[12] Their first child and only son, Edward Gough Whitlam, was born on July 11, 1916 at their home in Kew.[13] Gough's sister Freda followed in 1920.

Fred and Martha Whitlam were pious church-goers[14], and raised their two children in a God-fearing, disciplined home. There was a focus on reading and conversation rather than frivolous games. One of Gough's favourite childhood books was an annotated French translation of the New Testament![15] Tellingly, one of the first movies to which he and Freda were taken was the silent epic *Ben Hur: Tale of the Christ* (1925). Freda recalled many years later that her brother, 12 at the time, "was really quite affected by the cruelty, the treatment of the Christians".[16]

According to Whitlam, his father Fred was a "philosopher" who almost certainly believed in the Resurrection (that is, as an actual, historical, miraculous event). Fred also believed that "religious faith underpinned social morality as well, naturally, as personal morality".[17] He regarded "spiritual virtues [as] marks of a society that is great"[18], and had "a deep, abiding abhorrence of war".[19] In his personal life Fred was a modest gentleman who had "little interest in material things", though he was neither a wowser nor sanctimonious.[20]

Jenny Hocking points out that Fred Whitlam was "an unusual believer". Although raised a Baptist, he did not confine himself to Baptist churches. In Sydney in the 1920s, he attended both Anglican and Presbyterian services: "he went primarily to the nearest church and then if it was full of rubbish he would go to one where he found the services more interesting".[21] In Canberra, Fred preferred the Presbyterian church at Ainsley.[22] Clearly enough he was a discerning seeker of spiritual nourishment and inspiration, not a habitual attendee of "church" for the sake of appearances or the rigid re-enforcement of doctrine.

Freda Whitlam was also a Christian. Unlike her older brother, she never lost her childhood faith. In later life she was a missionary in France. She also served as the Moderator of the NSW Synod of the Uniting Church in Australia, and as a lay preacher. From 1958-76 she was the headmistress of Presbyterian Ladies College in Sydney (PLC Croydon).[23]

George Whitlam, Gough's uncle, was another staunch believer. His was a sterner form of Baptism, and it was he who took young Gough to Sunday school each week, and first noticed his emerging scepticism. After a time George reported to Gough's parents that their impudent son was making waves: "[Gough] could not see how the whole world could have been created in seven days".[24] Worse, he had the temerity to question his teacher, a Dr Waldock, on the point. Dr Waldock's reply – "But you'll notice the sequence is correct" – was unavailing.[25]

At this time Fred Whitlam's overarching decency may have been an evangelical drawback. He continued to ensure that Gough attended church on Sundays (even though Gough objected to the "windbag Presbyterian sermons"), and he consented to Gough's request to be confirmed as an Anglican.[26] But one gets the sense that Fred was a somewhat passive man. "He did not try to force his beliefs or way of life on others, *even his children*".[27]

For some Christian tastes, Fred Whitlam may have been too tolerant:

> Fred would have been horrified if either of his children had shown any sign of racial or religious prejudice. On one occasion when [a Parsee] was dining with the Whitlams, young Gough asked his father, 'Is Mr Lalkaka's god the same as our god?' Without hesitation his father replied, 'Of course'.[28]

As a boy Gough attended an unusual variety of schools, including Knox Grammar preparatory school in Sydney. His favourite by far was Telopea Park High School in Canberra. He excelled there but acquired a reputation for insolence[29], and, at the beginning of 1932, his concerned father moved him to Canberra Grammar. This imposing institution was "private, selective, elitist, boys only … and conservative". It was, moreover, proudly Anglican. This may have been an attempt on Fred Whitlam's part to revive his son's faith.

If so, it did not work. In 1934 Whitlam attained the top mark in the Divinity exam (92 per cent), only to miss out on the Divinity prize. The headmaster, Canon William John Edwards, was an ordained priest of the Church of England. While conceding that Whitlam's paper was "a magnificent forensic effort, splendidly written"[30], he decided that there was a more deserving recipient – the second place-getter in the exam, a boy named Francis James. "James actually believes it," the Canon ruled.[31] Asked in 1987 by Barry Cohen to verify the story, Whitlam replied with mock indignation: "Yes, the old bastard!"[32]

As it happened, Francis James was later expelled from Canberra Grammar.[33] But he went on to an eminent, if eccentric, career. Among myriad pursuits and adventures he was a publisher of *The Anglican*. He also spent three years in a Chinese gaol for alleged espionage. In November 1973, in his capacity as a journalist, he attended a Whitlam press conference and the following remarkable exchange ensued:

> **JAMES:** It's not generally known, but I hope you don't mind it being known that you are a fairly learned bloke in matters of theology, with as much knowledge of doctrine and history as any man I know who is in holy orders.

> **WHITLAM:** Bless you.

> **JAMES:** In this sub-Christian country in which we now live, but above all in this period when people have arrived at the idea of God which you arrived at many years ago – where we're getting to the essence of what Christian belief is, would you agree that in China there is in fact a spirit of applied Christianity? Quite obvious throughout all Chinese life – economic, social and political – of the kind that we in this decadent, bourgeois Western democratic state…

> **WHITLAM:** You can call me bourgeois, but not decadent…

> **JAMES:** The point I would like to make is whether you would agree that there is an extraordinary parallel between Chairman Mao's dictum: "We must be modest, prudent, avoid arrogance and serve the people".

> **WHITLAM:** I follow it myself constantly.[34]

In his final year at Canberra Grammar, Whitlam won a tertiary scholarship. In 1935 he commenced an arts degree at the University of Sydney, living on campus at St Paul's College. According to Jenny Hocking, Whitlam's attendance there "was due to the still guiding hand of Fred Whitlam and his determination to provide for the spiritual welfare of his brilliant but ecumenically unbiddable son".[35]

The warden of St Paul's was Arthur Henry Garnsey, canon of Sydney's St Andrew's Cathedral (and, in April 1942, the presiding prelate at Whitlam's marriage to Margaret Dovey). Whitlam admired Garnsey enormously – "he was a fine man … a Christian socialist in the Kingsley* tradition".[36] But not even Garnsey could re-spark Whitlam's faith. He was another tolerant soul who preferred that "students would go to chapel because they chose to, not because they had to".[37]

Whitlam attended the minimum number of services allowed. He volunteered as a chapel warden, but not for selfless motives: at choir services he got to choose the texts and the hymns.[38] Nevertheless the experience stood him in good stead. During World War II Whitlam served in the RAAF as a navigator and occasionally presided at funeral services at Gove airbase in the Northern Territory as a sort of lay minister.[39]

After the war Whitlam studied and practised law until 1952. Then he entered Federal politics, winning the south-western Sydney seat of Werriwa for the ALP. It was a diverse electorate and Whitlam decided early in his tenure that he "could not be uninformed or insensitive about the ethnic or religious backgrounds of my constituents". He and Margaret accepted numerous invitations to churches. As Whitlam recalled in 1997:

> There were always Anglican, Catholic and Protestant churches in the electorate. By 1952 the Catholics were already attracting large numbers of parishioners from all parts of Europe and from European colonies in Asia.

---

* Charles Kingsley (1819-1875) was an English priest of the Church of England, notable for being one the first churchmen to praise Darwin's *On the Origin of Species*. He was also a university professor, historian and novelist.

There was a synagogue on the boundaries of the electorate. Orthodox churches, one Russian and two Serbian, were soon built within the boundaries. Just before I retired, a Macedonian Orthodox Church was built. Since then many mosques have been built, Hindu and Buddhist temples, a Zoroastrian shrine and Antiochian and Greek Orthodox churches.

(He added – a respectful if pedantic qualification typical of the man: "Although I am aware of the historic differences between the respective Orthodox communities I have used the titles which they themselves use."[40])

As a politician, most of Whitlam's public forays into religion were inconsequential. The huge exception – State aid – was a triumph of courage, patience and skill.[41] During years of internal debate within the ALP, he battled against bigoted Protestants and irreligious secularists alike. He secured party support for his policies at the 1969 Federal conference, and then appointed as his Shadow Minister for Education a genuinely serious Protestant Christian, a man steeped in the Moral Re-Armament Movement* – Kim Beazley Senior. Over the next six years, in opposition and later in government, Whitlam and Beazley managed to convince a sufficient number of Church leaders that Labor could be trusted on State aid.

A pivotal figure on the Catholic side, especially in NSW, was Archbishop James Patrick Carroll (1908-95). On the eve of the December 1972 election, Carroll paid public tribute to Whitlam, and to "our men of state" in all parties, for having made such progress in resolving this hitherto diabolical issue.[42] Once Labor was in office, it still needed to secure the support of the Country Party (which broke ranks with the Liberals) in order to pass the Schools

---

* Moral Re-Armament (or MRA) was an international spiritual movement launched in 1938 in response to the looming threat of another world war. Its leader was the Rev. Frank Buchman, an American Protestant (Lutheran) evangelist whose so-called "Oxford Group" had been active since the 1920s in Europe and the United States. In launching MRA in 1938, Buchman declared: "We need a power strong enough to change human nature and build bridges between man and man, faction and faction. This starts when everyone admits his own faults instead of spot-lighting the other fellow's. God alone can change human nature. The secret lies in that great forgotten truth, that when man listens, God speaks; when man obeys, God acts; when men change, nations change." Followers of MRA, such as Kim Beazley Senior, committed themselves to "the Four Absolutes": absolute honesty, absolute purity, absolute unselfishness and absolute love.

Commission Act of 1973. Beazley regarded his role in ending sectarianism in education policy as his principal achievement in politics.[43]

Whitlam, then, was more than capable of dealing with "religion" when it intruded directly into politics. But on two occasions as Prime Minister he did himself harm.

The first occasion is all but forgotten today. Not long into his first term, Whitlam altered the official title of Queen Elizabeth II as regards Australia. Previously there had been a reference to Her Majesty as "Defender of the Faith" – a description apt in the United Kingdom, where she is the formal head of the established church (the Church of England), but never applicable to Australia. At a meeting with the Queen at Windsor Castle on – exquisitely – Good Friday 1973, Whitlam secured Her Majesty's agreement to the deletion of this reference. However, the words "by the Grace of God" were retained.[44] At the time, all this annoyed some die-hard Anglicans. It may not have helped with some of them that, shortly afterwards, the Whitlams were received by Pope Paul VI.[45]

The second episode – while it ought to have been trivial – proved momentous. One of the Whitlam Government's most virulent critics was the Queensland Premier Joh Bjelke-Petersen, a Country Party populist, and a Lutheran by faith. In early September 1975, Bjelke-Petersen procured the appointment of an anti-Whitlam cipher, Albert Patrick Field, to fill a casual Senate vacancy in Queensland caused by the death of a Labor Senator. This gave the Coalition the numbers in the Senate to block supply, and ultimately led to Whitlam's dismissal as Prime Minister on November 11, 1975 by the Governor-General, Sir John Kerr.

Of course, Whitlam was outraged at the appointment of Field. But his antagonism towards Bjelke-Petersen went back further in time. In two separate outbursts in 1974, he had publicly mocked him as "an ostentatiously religious man who has taken a vow of poverty for Queensland" and a "Bible-bashing bastard". On the latter occasion Whitlam had added for good measure: "The man is a paranoiac, he's a fanatic, and he's a bigot." [46]

It seems probable that Bjelke-Petersen took offence at these remarks. It would be understandable if he had. Perhaps he harboured a personal grudge. (Albert Field certainly did – he said so on the record.) It may well be, therefore, that the conduct of both Bjelke-Petersen and Field in

1975 – while completely unscrupulous – was caused in no small part by Whitlam's loose tongue. His intemperate remarks came back to haunt him. (Compare James 3:5-12.)

Labor was annihilated at the election of December 13, 1975. For months afterwards Whitlam was "a divided soul" in "a terrible state". His life's ambition had been shattered, and he could not derive comfort from a living faith. He, did, however, have Margaret.[47] Ultimately he stayed on as Opposition Leader, but he suffered a second big defeat at the early election of December 1977 and stood down as Labor leader for Bill Hayden. He resigned from Parliament on July 31, 1978.[48]

It says much for Whitlam that he was eventually reconciled with Malcolm Fraser. They found common cause on a number of public issues – Fraser traversed them proudly in his Gough Whitlam Oration of June 6, 2012. But they also became friends.* Whitlam even made peace with Bjelke-Petersen, revealing in 1990 that he held no grudges against his former adversary: "I get along with Joh."[49] The person he never forgave was Sir John Kerr.

After politics Whitlam lived a rich life, and evidence of his continuing fascination with religion is not hard to find. From 1983-86 he served a three-year term as Australia's Ambassador to UNESCO. Interviewed one day in 1984 by a journalist in Paris, he was asked this leading question: "But being lapsed you wouldn't go to church often?" Whitlam fired back: "I don't go to church, but I always go to cathedrals".

This was both a joke against himself and a statement of fact. Church architecture was one of his passions. At UNESCO he took a special interest in a dispute over cultural property in Jerusalem. He was alive to, and impressed by, the seriousness with which European countries take such matters. "[Disputes] arise," he observed, "from conflicting priorities for preserving or restoring edifices dating from Solomon, Herod the Great, Constantine the Great and the First Crusade".[50]

On October 17, 1992, Whitlam represented the Australian Government at a ceremony at the Reichstag in Berlin. He took note – as only he would or

---

* Whitlam enjoyed other friendships which crossed party lines. John Howard told me when I interviewed him that he had recently visited "Gough" and considered him "a good bloke".

could – of a mosaic depicting "the settlement of Europe at the Congress of Berlin in 1878 by the Orthodox Emperor of Russia, the Lutheran Emperor of Germany, the Catholic Emperor of Austria, the Anglican Queen of England and the Ottoman Sultan, who was also the Caliph of Islam."[51]

At the time of writing, Whitlam is still alive – though very frail. Only he knows his current relationship with God. Will he rediscover his boyhood faith? It is never too late for anyone, of course. And in Whitlam's case there are unusual grounds for optimism. This is a man who refers to "*the* three books".[52] Two of them are the *Complete Works of Shakespeare* and his own massive tome, *The Whitlam Government*. The third is the Bible.

JOHN MALCOLM FRASER (B. 1930)
LIBERAL: 1975-83

Fraser came to office in November 1975 in uniquely divisive circumstances and when he left it, after heavy defeat at the March 1983 election, few Australians mourned. As Prime Minister he was vilified by the Left and defended by the Right; today he is vilified by the Right and defended by the Left. Yet Fraser insists that his basic beliefs have never changed. I am inclined to agree, with the rider added by Wallace Brown: what has changed is that "in his later and mellower years [Fraser] has bothered to *explain*".[1]

Sir Garfield Barwick once sneered (ungrammatically): "Fraser, like wealthy sons very often are, feel they've got to be doing something for the deprived."[2] To be so accused should be a badge of honour. Fraser built the best record on human rights of any Prime Minister in Australian history – his response to the "problem" of Vietnamese refugees in the late 1970s was a model of principled, constructive charity, a million miles from *Tampa*, the Pacific Solution, children overboard, "Stop the boats!", the Malaysia Solution, the "no-advantage" test, and other cruel expediencies since 2001. Fraser behaved like the Good Samaritan. Instead of asking "How can we avoid these people?" he asked "How can we help them?"

But it is not clear that Fraser is a Christian. His religious beliefs are hard to pinpoint: over the course of a long life he has said different things. While usually categorised as a Presbyterian[3], he was married in an Anglican church.* The charity and international aid organisation with which he became associated in 1987, CARE Australia, has no religious affiliations.

Fraser's religious background was an unusual hybrid. His father Neville was from a long line of Scotch Presbyterians, but his mother Una had both Anglican and Jewish antecedents. She identified as Anglican until her marriage, but then adopted her husband's denomination.[4]

Theirs was a fairly dour strain of Presbyterianism: "disciplined, stern and elitist ... with the emphasis on man's sinfulness".[5] It was also stridently anti-Catholic, a fact Malcolm Fraser has always lamented. As a boy, he frequently overheard conversations about Catholics – "how they were not to be trusted". In his memoirs he recalled asking his father: "What's the problem? What's the matter with Catholics?" The reply was curt: "Well, they are different; they owe their loyalty to the Pope." Fraser speculated that "if my sister [Lorri] had wanted to marry a Catholic, my father would have just cut the traces. He really would have. He felt very strongly. On other things he was very reasonable, but this was a common prejudice at the time."[6]

A more attractive feature of the Frasers' faith was the emphasis on charity – of a *noblesse oblige* sort. During the Depression Fraser's paternal grandmother, Lady (Bertha) Fraser, would be driven around Melbourne by her chauffeur, distributing food to the unemployed.[7]

Fraser attended three schools – all private, exclusive and (interestingly), Anglican rather than Presbyterian. The first, in 1938-39, was Glamorgan Preparatory School in Toorak, run by a Miss McComas. (Later taken over by Geelong Grammar, it is now known as Toorak Campus.[8]) Then, primarily for health reasons, Fraser's parents decided he should board at Tudor House, a preparatory school in Moss Vale in the southern highlands of NSW. He was there for four years (1940-43).

One of the stated priorities of Tudor House was the "spiritual growth" of its pupils. On the evidence of Fraser's letters back home this was not one

---

* Tamie Fraser (née Beggs) is an Anglican. She married Malcolm Fraser in 1956 in the small Victorian town of Willaura, near her family home, at the Anglican Church of All Saints. The Rev. Phillip Burgess performed the ceremony. In 2007 Tamie was asked by Susan Mitchell whether she believed in God. She replied: "I do. A very strong belief ever since I was a child. But it's a relationship between God and me. It doesn't have a lot to do with the institution of the church. I am C of E, which stands for Christmas and Easter."

of his own priorities.[9] Even so, Christianity was always in the background. In 1943 Fraser was in Common Room, and occasionally it was his duty to read the lesson at the daily chapel service or to say grace at meals.[10]

His next school (1944-48) was Melbourne Grammar. The headmaster during Fraser's time, J. R. (Joe) Sutcliffe, described his overriding aim as follows:

> I want it to be a recognised fact that, to say that a man has been educated at Melbourne Grammar School is the same thing as to say that he is a Christian gentleman.[11]

Malcolm Fraser won a Scripture prize in 1946.[12] But the school did not inspire him to a phase of religiosity, and overall he retained no great love for it.[13] Biographer Philip Ayres' conclusion in 1987 was that Fraser's time at Melbourne Grammar "seems to have contributed nothing in particular towards [his] qualities and resources".[14]

In summary, by the time Fraser left school his religious beliefs were undeveloped. He knew the rudiments of Christianity but little more. His mother's Jewish ancestry had been concealed from him. At Melbourne Grammar, he recalled in his memoirs, he "needed to have it explained to him what a Jew was, and why the Jewish students did not go to chapel".[15]

In 1949 Fraser was sent to Oxford University to study politics, philosophy and economics (a course known as Modern Greats). By his own admission he came ill-prepared[16], and, to try to catch up, he read widely. While never distinguishing himself as a student, by the end of his time at Oxford he had digested the works of, among others, Machiavelli, John Locke, Thomas Hobbes, Descartes, Rousseau, Bertrand Russell, Arnold Toynbee, A.J.P. Taylor and John Maynard Keynes.

Fraser's time at Oxford pushed him toward unbelief. At Magdalen College he was influenced by his tutor, Thomas Dewar (Harry) Weldon, a winner of the Military Cross in World War I and a notable man at Oxford. Fraser admired him.[17] Weldon did not get on with several more traditionalist Oxford dons, including the legendary Christian apologist C.S. Lewis. Lewis regarded Weldon as "the most hard-boiled atheist he had ever known".[18]

Fraser also admired one of his philosophy lecturers, Gilbert Ryle (1900-76). Ryle was an atheist who defined religion as "the protest of man against the non-existence of God".[19] He had written an influential book, *The Concept of Mind*, which was required reading for his students. From close study of Ryle's book, the impressionable Fraser concluded that certain metaphysical assumptions were unsafe. In one essay, while confirming the reality of free will ("otherwise morality goes out the door"), he denied the existence of the human soul as distinct from the body. "As Ryle puts it, there is no machine within the machine."[20]

It appears that, during this Oxford period, Fraser was grappling with the religious teachings of his boyhood. In a marginal note in one of his exercise books, he wrote: "Is there anything to be said for metaphysics? The idea that God exists is a nonsense."[21] The influence of Ryle and Weldon here seems obvious.

Perhaps this was a fleeting phase. Back in Australia in mid-1952, Fraser soon decided to enter politics rather than make his career on the land. Over 30 years later, in 1985, he explained that decision in metaphysical terms:

> I believe that there is something in the essential nature of men and women which cannot be explained by the scientist, something which is essentially metaphysical and therefore religious in its content and which, in my view, underlines and reinforces belief in God. *If I did not have that attitude to belief I would not have wanted to go into politics.*[22]

Let us now tackle the central issue: what were Fraser's religious beliefs in the critical years leading up to, and during, his Prime Ministership?

On July 20, 1971 he delivered the fifth Alfred Deakin lecture, entitled "Towards 2000: Challenge to Australia". He wrote it at a time when he believed his political career had been wrecked and that he would never become the nation's leader.[23]

This lecture contained Fraser's most famous utterance, "Life wasn't meant to be easy". But the words are almost always taken out of context. The full sentence was: "There is within me some part of the metaphysic, and thus I would say that life was not *meant* to be easy" (my emphasis). This in turn was an adaptation of a line from George Bernard Shaw's play *Back to Methuselah*: "Life is not meant to be easy, my child; but take courage; it can be delightful".[24]

As I read it, the basic point of Fraser's speech was that suffering is an unavoidable feature of human life. At Oxford he had decided that it is pointless in politics to "strive for a mythical end ... to imagine a society where all men are equal in every sense".[25] Financial incentive must play a role, and, more generally, it is up to individuals and nations to rise to the challenges which will certainly confront them. Indeed, that is the most satisfying and meaningful part of life.

Fraser credited the historian Arnold Toynbee for this insight[26], but it is, of course, a recurring theme of the Bible. Fraser seems to have understood this: he did not say that "life is not easy" – a bare statement of incontestable fact – but that "life was not *meant* to be easy". It is the word "meant" which conveys the critical metaphysical aspect of Fraser's message: only a Being which created human life can have intended ("meant") that suffering and struggle should be an essential part of it.

This is not to say that, at least in the 1970s, Fraser was an especially religious man. Here it is hard to be categorical. In 1971 he struck up a cordial working relationship with B.A. Santamaria, who approved of Fraser's vocal anti-Communism, his "agrarianism", and his criticisms of the "permissive society".[27] But there is no evidence that they discussed theological matters, which never appeared terribly important to Santamaria himself, let alone Fraser. Asked by John Edwards in 1972 whether religion was important to him, Fraser replied that it was, but added that "I really don't know how to rate it in terms of importance".[28] In June 1975 he described himself to the *Catholic Weekly* as a Christian.[29] Yet only two years later Edwards would aver flatly that Fraser, while very comfortable in the company of Christians*, was not one himself. "He trusts in those who trust the Lord," Edwards contended, but "spares us the pieties of his predecessor as Liberal Prime Minister, Bill McMahon".[30]

---

* Wallace Brown told a funny anecdote about Fraser's visit in 1981 to the University of South Carolina, where he spoke. The university chaplain said a prayer in his honour: "Lord God, who doth raise up leaders among nations, we acknowledge Thy wisdom in setting apart the Australian Prime Minister, Malcolm Fraser. Thou hast endowed him with the qualities extended to his office and Thou dost walk with him both among his own people and throughout the international community. Lord God, we thank Thee for giving us, and the world ... John ... Malcolm ... Fraser."

(It is true that in his public speeches as Prime Minister Fraser rarely invoked God. A rare exception was in his speech on March 23, 1981 at the opening of the 25th Anniversary Congress of the International Booksellers Federation. He quoted the poet John Milton: "Who destroys a good book kills reason itself, kills the image of God, as it were in the eye."[31])

What of Fraser's *conduct* during this period? There are two things to consider, to the extent that they shed light on his religious beliefs. First, the means by which he came to office in November 1975. Second, his record in office thereafter.

As to the former, my personal view is that Fraser's conduct throughout 1975 was unnecessarily ruthless. In at least one respect it was plainly immoral. I refer to his reliance in the Senate upon the tainted vote of Albert Patrick Field.

Field was an implacable opponent of the Whitlam Government. Yet, for a few vital months, he filled a casual vacancy in the Senate caused by the death of a *Labor* Senator. Queensland's Bert Milliner died on June 30 and Field was appointed to replace him on September 9. Admittedly it was the Country Party Premier of Queensland, Joh Bjelke-Petersen, who procured the appointment.* Bjelke-Petersen was, as it were, the primary sinner. But Fraser ate the forbidden fruit.

But for Field's appointment the Coalition would not have had the numbers to block supply. Sir John Kerr would not have had a crisis to resolve. It is as simple as that. In the words of Steele Hall, an Independent Senator and former Liberal Party premier of South Australia, Fraser and

---

* Strictly speaking the appointment of Field was made by a vote of the Queensland Parliament, which was controlled by the Coalition parties which Bjelke-Petersen led. Bert Milliner had died two months earlier. In procuring Field's appointment as his replacement, Bjelke-Petersen defied a long-standing convention that casual vacancies resulting from the death of a senator should always be filled by a nominee of the same party. Field was a member of the ALP but openly hostile to the Whitlam Government. And the breaches of convention did not stop there. The ALP challenged Field's appointment in the High Court, and, as a result, Field was on leave from the Senate, unable to exercise a vote, from October 1, 1975. According to another long-standing convention, Fraser's opposition parties should have provided Labor with a "pair" to maintain the relative positions of the Government and Opposition. They did not. In May 1977 Fraser's own government supported a referendum to amend the Constitution to ensure there could never be a repeat of the Field episode. The proposal gained 73.3 per cent support from the Australian people.

his colleagues "marched on the sleazy road to power over a dead man's corpse".[32] Morally it is irrelevant that the Coalition won the subsequent election in December. Fraser acted as and when he did precisely because the Whitlam Government was unpopular – but beginning to pick up its longer-term act. The reliable Labor MP Bill Hayden had been appointed Treasurer and, mid-year, he delivered a responsible budget.

Had Fraser won office in mid-1977 at a conventional election, his reputation today would be much more distinguished than it is. All he needed was patience. It is inconceivable to me that a committed Christian man – a Fisher, say, or a Scullin or a Lyons or a Chifley – would have acted as Fraser did. It is true that Robert Menzies supported Fraser in 1975. Yet Menzies had privately castigated Liberal leader Bill Snedden in 1974 for similar Senate tactics[33], and the other two former Liberal Prime Ministers who were still alive – John Gorton and Billy McMahon – disapproved heartily of the course Fraser took.[34] So did Paul Hasluck, Kerr's predecessor as Governor-General. John Howard, a backbencher in 1975, admitted to me that the appointment of Field "was hard, it was impossible in a way to defend".*

All that said, a man must be judged by the entirety of his life. Faith and works are not the same thing, and redemption is always possible.

What of Fraser's record in office – not only as Prime Minister but as a senior minister in various Coalition governments before his? What light does that record cast on his religious convictions?

Let us start with the positive. I have mentioned Fraser's sterling commitment to human rights. Fraser himself has often drawn a link between religious tolerance and human rights more generally. The anti-Catholic prejudice that he witnessed during his childhood scarred him, and he drew *political* lessons from it. In the words of the co-author of Fraser's memoirs, Margaret Simons:

> [Billy] Hughes' actions in encouraging sectarianism, says Fraser today, were the worst of any Prime Minister in Australian history.

---

* Howard added a qualification. He believed that "in retrospect" Whitlam should have complied with Bjelke-Petersen's request that he (Whitlam) submit a list of three names from which Bjelke-Petersen would select one.

They could have led to armed conflict, he believes, had there not been a settlement of the Irish question in 1922. The scars lasted for fifty years… Fraser has several times made the comparison between his father's generation's anti-Catholicism and the things that are said in present-day Australia about Muslims. Today, anti-Catholic prejudices look silly; it is hard to understand the hatred and suspicion that inspired them. So too, he says, will future Australians look back on the prejudice against Muslims as silly and ignorant. Reflecting on the reasons for his father's prejudice was to guide him during his own Prime Ministership. Racism is always present in society, ready to be stirred up, but political leadership can make a difference.[35]

Consistently with these sentiments, Fraser became a firm champion of State aid to Catholic schools. He had two stints as the Minister for Education and Science (February 1968-November 1969 and August 1971-December 1972), when the issue loomed large. Unlike several of his Coalition predecessors, Fraser got on well with the Catholic hierarchy in Australia, including, as I have said, B.A. Santamaria himself.[36] Fraser backed the cause of *all* independent schools – Catholic and Protestant, poor and wealthy – and presided over a huge increase in their funding.

It is interesting to note that during this period Fraser opposed a strictly needs-based approach (the Whitlam model). A needs-based approach would have resulted in a greater share of government money flowing to Catholic and State schools, which in the main were less well-resourced than Protestant schools. The Whitlam Government followed a needs-based approach from 1973-75. Fraser always favoured a per-capita approach, or at any rate one not based quite so strictly on pure financial need. There were obvious political advantages in doing so for the Coalition. But Fraser has since claimed that he was at least partially motivated by fear – the grave risk, as he saw it, of re-igniting sectarianism. He understood, better than most people, that anti-Catholic sentiment ran deep within the Coalition parties: "It was still alive. I could see it in Cabinet."[37]

What else? Fraser's economic policies were of the middle-of-the-road Keynesian variety – neither enlightened nor imaginative nor draconian. His record was mediocre. There is not much to be gleaned there.

Foreign policy is more interesting. At the height of the Vietnam War, Fraser served as Minister for the Army (January 1966-February 1968) and Minister for Defence (November 1969-March 1971).[38] He strongly supported Australian involvement, couching it as a "defence of the right of small nations to run their own affairs without interference."[39]

He also supported conscription. In a lengthy article for the University of Melbourne's *Ad Lib* magazine in 1967, entitled 'Liberalism as a Liberal MHR Sees it Today', Fraser sought to justify his position on philosophical grounds:

> Even in our society some sacrifices, great and small, must be demanded of individuals for the benefit of all citizens. There is no inconsistency in this; people could not live together in the most primitive of tribes without rules and they cannot live together in a modern state without them... *I believe our generation will be judged not on whether we were able to reach some perfect state of man, but on the way we acquitted ourselves in the great human adventure.*[40]

(The highlighted sentence is very Christian in sentiment – the ends do not justify the means. But to my mind this is the clinching argument *against* conscription.)

Fraser has subsequently recanted as to Vietnam. In 2010 he remarked wistfully that "those were innocent days, when I believed what the United States said ... It is easy to say, with the beautiful clarity of hindsight, that perhaps Australia should never have gone to Vietnam. *It probably was a wrong decision.* But at the time decisions were made, things looked very different."[41] In Fraser's view, the West's worst mistake was its failure to distinguish between genuinely nationalist movements and those inspired at core by Communist ideology.

These arguments are strictly pragmatic. Fraser has never been a pacifist, on religious or any other grounds. Throughout his career in politics, he was something of a hawk. As Prime Minister he strengthened the ANZUS alliance and endorsed the Reagan administration's hardline policies against the Soviet Union. He supported Israel's right to enforce "secure and safe borders", including its 1982 incursion into Lebanon, "because of the long history of the Jewish people, because of their courage and determination, because of their absolute right to a homeland".[42]

Fraser was never a militarist. He did not believe in vast spending on arms as a permanent state of affairs, in the manner of the military-industrial complex in the United States. Indeed, he came to disappoint people such as B.A. Santamaria, because he did not to any significant degree increase defence spending in real terms.[43] Nor did Fraser believe in pre-emptive (aggressive) war. He expressed grave reservations about the invasion of Iraq in 2003.

Nevertheless, in office, he was no peacenik. But it is crucial to understand that he came of age during the Cold War. And during the early 1980s, when Fraser was Prime Minister, the Cold War had entered another very dangerous phase.

Fraser was respectful towards citizens who held different views from his own on religious or ethical grounds, especially the young. In July 1976 he said publicly that "people's ultimate obligations are to their own consciences".[44] And during a thoughtful speech in New York in May 1982, delivered in the presence of President Ronald Reagan, he said this:

> If the advocacy of pacifism or unilateral disarmament increases rather than decreases the risk of war, it is even more important to be aware of it now. Pacifism genuinely based on conscience is, of course, a valid moral option for an individual, but in a world of nation states, of power politics, it can never provide the basis for a country's foreign policy, certainly not in a world in which the most powerful military force is a totalitarian, expansionist state.[45]

Fraser sincerely believed in the need for the West to maintain peace by deterrence, through military strength. In Christian terms, he saw himself as a peacemaker. And it must be said that, a few years later, this approach bore fruit. During his second term, Reagan overruled militarists in his own administration and responded to Michael Gorbachev's overtures for peace. Bilateral disarmament began. The Cold War ended in 1989.

The case of Malcolm Fraser is further complicated by an unpublished essay which he wrote in 1985, after leaving politics. It contained thoughtful, deeply personal musings. The general theme was that a spiritual view of life – in particular, belief in a personal God – shapes one's political ideals. In Fraser's own case, "policies were bound to be based on the individual and on a construction of society which would enhance each person's place in it".[46]

He elaborated:

> Belief in political freedom, in economic freedom, in equality before the law, and personal responsibility have significant implications for many aspects of public policy. They are the hallmark of a truly free society.
>
> Such beliefs will be held most strongly by those who believe in God's law, and that men and women are his creation.[47

Throughout his adult life, Fraser has clearly believed in the principles stated in the first paragraph of the above quotation. It is less clear that he has ever taken Soren Kierkegaard's "leap" to faith in God – let alone the Christian God.

Fraser seems to regret his prevarication. In 2010 he told Margaret Simons:

> I would probably like to be less logical and, you know, really able to believe there is a god, whether it is Allah, or the Christian god, or some other... But I think I studied too much philosophy. You can never know.[48]

Strictly speaking, then, Fraser is a thoughtful agnostic – or was in 2010. That was Margaret Simons' verdict on her co-author: "Fraser is not religious, and yet thinks religion is a necessary thing."[49] Alternatively, he might be categorised as an unconscious Christian. For, in the wise words of Warwick Fairfax, "highly intelligent people can deny strenuously with their reason a faith which the whole course of their nature shows that they are really following".[50]

ROBERT JAMES LEE (BOB) HAWKE (B. 1929)

LABOR: 1983-91

awke, famously, was a "son of the manse". His father, the Reverend Clem Hawke (1897-1989), was a Congregationalist minister at churches in New Zealand, South Australia and Perth. Clem was also a chaplain in the Australian Imperial Forces during World War II, and, by all accounts, a true gentleman. His sermons were "carefully prepared, thoughtful, and delivered with conviction".[1] Edith (Ellie) Hawke, Clem's wife, was also extremely pious. She met Clem when he visited her girlhood home as a Methodist home missionary, before they both converted to Congregationalism. Her own father, a stern self-made man named Will Lee, had been a lay preacher.[2]

Bob Hawke, then, grew up in a thoroughly Christian home. Yet he lost his personal faith in his early twenties and has described himself ever since as an agnostic. Even so, he wrote in his memoirs that it was his parents' "basic Christian principles of brotherhood and compassion" that drove his public life. "[They] fostered in me," he explained, "beliefs and precepts which were to guide me in my future career."[3]

Hawke's elder daughter, Sue Pieters-Hawke, has noted an additional influence – her mother, Hazel Hawke, Bob's much-admired first wife. Bob and Hazel were married for almost 40 years, and, according to Sue, both of them lived their lives according to a "progressive humanitarian ethic instilled by their Congregationalist upbringing". This ethic, she insisted, remained "unabated by the loss of their firm belief in God".[4] (The qualifying word "firm" is interesting, but it appears that Pieters-Hawke had in mind her mother rather than her father. She has also written of Hazel's gradual loss of "a vivid sense of God" and of Hazel still speaking occasionally of "Huey, up there".[5])

If a single word best describes Bob Hawke, it is charismatic. Australians from all walks of life used it about him frequently, and with good cause. The man could be inspiring. He led his party to outright victory in four Federal elections (1983, 1984, 1987 and 1990) and lost none. He could make a virtue even of his sins – among them serial unfaithfulness to Hazel and (before he gave up alcohol in May 1980) a vicious tongue when drunk. [6] In the words of Neal Blewett, a senior member of his cabinet, part of Hawke's public appeal was his image as a "repentant prodigal".[7]

Charisma is a Biblical concept. While the word itself has both Greek and Hebrew roots, it was first popularised by Paul of Tarsus. The key texts are Romans and Corinthians, written in or about 55–65 AD. In Paul's usage, the *charismata* were special qualities with which God had blessed certain individuals, for the benefit of the community-at-large.[8]

How important was Christianity in Hawke's journey?

He was born in 1929 in Bordertown, a small rural settlement in South Australia where Clem had been posted by his church. As a boy, Bob briefly imagined that he might emulate his father and devote his life to the pulpit. He practised sermons on an invalid who lived in the manse![9] Their content is unrecorded, but can perhaps be imagined.

Ellie Hawke (née Lee) was a different personality from Clem. She had been a country schoolteacher before her marriage and was, in Bob's words, "a woman of passionate commitments".[10] One of them was to the work of the Women's Christian Temperance Union.[11] She was a disciplined person, and a discipline-dispensing mother who commanded respect. She read the Bible daily.

Ellie always swore that, when she was pregnant with Bob, the book would often fall open at Isaiah 9:6: "For unto us a child is born, unto us a son is given; and the government shall fall upon his shoulders" (KJV).[12] Apocryphal or not, this anecdote resonates.

Many commentators have attributed Bob Hawke's sense of destiny to the all-encompassing love of his parents. They were devoted to him, certainly, but he was also the object of their own lofty ambitions – especially after the death from meningitis, in February 1939, of his older brother Neil. For one excruciating week the nine-year-old Bob witnessed his parents praying "day and night" by Neil's bedside.[13]

Ellie Hawke believed strongly in the importance of education. She taught her sons to read before they started primary school.[14] According to Bob, his mother's commitment to education was theologically and spiritually motivated. "It was an integral part of her religious faith that we each have a responsibility to develop to the limit the talents with which we are endowed".[15]

One of Jesus' immortal aphorisms comes to mind: "For everyone to whom much is given, from him much will be required" (Luke 12:48).

Reading from an early age is one of the keys to education. Hawke's first memory is of his parents reading to him as a little boy. He recalls "dramatic biblical tales"[16], of which a favourite was the story of Samson (see Judges 13-16). According to one biographer, Robert Pullan, young Bob was fascinated by this tale: he would often ask Clem *why* Samson was so strong.[17] Another favourite story was David and Goliath (1 Samuel 17). "The good winning against the odds appealed to me from the beginning," Hawke confessed in his memoirs.[18]

Commitment to the social Gospel ran deep in the family. In his sermons Clem Hawke eschewed "fire and brimstone" tirades; his emphasis was on "the human side of Christ's ministry"[19] and God's infinite capacity for mercy in both this world and the next.[20] He once told his son that "belief in the fatherhood of God necessarily involves believing in the brotherhood of man".[21] Albert (Bert) Hawke, Clem's younger brother, shared the same creed. A Methodist and self-described "Christian socialist", Bert Hawke served as the Labor premier of Western Australia from 1953-59.[22] He was a mentor to his nephew.

In early 1947 Bob Hawke enrolled at the University of Western Australia, choosing to take a degree in law. He played various competitive sports and was active in the Labor Club and the Australian Student Christian Movement, but devoted little time to his academic studies. Then came a pivotal event in his life. In August 1947 he blacked out while riding his Panther motorbike through King's Park in Perth. The bike crashed and Hawke ruptured his spleen.

Hawke hovered close to death for some days, aware of the presence of his parents by his bedside.[23] His survival was understood by his mother as a gift *of* God and as a sign *from* God. Hawke himself drew these lessons:

> While I did not embrace [Ellie's] esoteric visions, I firmly believed that God had spared my life. I felt the force of the Parable of the Talents* and saw in my attitude to school and university studies the bad servant's waste of his talent. I determined to live life to the full extent of my abilities, to live life to the limit.[24]

Hawke has admitted that campus life at UWA "made me more uncertain and inclined to quest after the truth". He had long discussions with both Christian and non-Christian students and was introduced to the tenets of Buddhism and Hinduism. The steadfastness of several Catholic friends was impressive but not persuasive: "against the laxness, almost ambivalence of the Congregational creed, I found the certitude of Catholic doctrine fascinating but intellectually unacceptable".[25]

It was around this time that he became close to Hazel Masterton. Hazel had first noticed Bob when she was nine, while participating in a church play directed by his mother Ellie. (Hazel played Esther and Bob a servant.)[26] As teenagers in Perth they attended an annual Easter camp and were involved in the Western Australian Congregational Youth Fellowship. For a period Bob was chairman and Hazel the state secretary.[27] They began seeing each other seriously in 1948 and got engaged in early 1950.[28] In church circles they were regarded as a "golden couple" but they could not get married if Bob was to remain eligible for a Rhodes scholarship.[29]

It is a matter of public record that they enjoyed an intensely sexual relationship, notwithstanding then-prevailing social and religious taboos against sex before marriage. Hazel, however, reasoned a different way. "We were engaged and in love, committed to each other for ever... Hadn't God given us these wondrous bodies?"[30]

---

* Matthew 25:14-30. It is interesting that both Bob Hawke and John Howard have placed reliance over the years upon the Parable of the Talents. In my view, Hawke has a better feeling for the essential thrust of Jesus' message. I doubt He had in mind free-market economics.

The watershed year for Hawke, in terms of his Christian faith, was 1952. There were two fateful events.

First, early in the year, Hazel fell pregnant. After many prayers and discussions with Bob, she decided to have an abortion. The experience was traumatic and she harboured "a nagging fear of retribution, of unearthly punishment".[31] But she did not feel resentment towards her fiancé, who was "very supportive throughout".[32]

Later in 1952 Bob Hawke attended the Third World Conference of Christian Youth. It was held in India, at Kottayam in the southern state of Travancore-Kochin (now Kerala). Kottayam was a major centre for Indian Christianity – the Mar Thoma Church – but, to put it mildly, Hawke was unimpressed. He witnessed first-hand some truly dreadful poverty and apparent indifference towards it on the part of conference delegates and local dignitaries. Years later Hawke recalled them all singing a Christmas carol at a banquet: "Christ to the world we bring/ The world to Christ we bring".[33]

Hawke has since pointed to this Indian visit as "the beginning of the end of my belief in the organised Christian religion".[34] It gave rise to "an enormous sense of the irrelevance of religion to the needs of people".[35]

No doubt these feelings were sincere – and, to an extent, well-founded. But it appears they were underpinned by a system of personal belief that was already faltering. The myriad (human) failings of the churches down the centuries are undeniable, but they do not disprove the existence of God.

Hawke, a Rhodes scholar, should have grasped this – if only as a matter of logic. At all events, he surely does now. He could have launched into a study of theodicy (theological explanations for suffering and evil), starting with the Chapters 38-42 of Job. He could have worked from within the Church to improve conditions in the Third World, as others at the Conference later did. Hawke did neither.[36]

I suggest it was because he had *already* lost his faith before going to India, even if he had not yet consciously realised the fact. According to his biographer and second wife, Blanche D'Alpuget, his pre-India brand of Christianity had never been fulfilling. It was "dull, worthy and teetotal … untouched by ecstasy".[37]

Perhaps the most revealing sentence in Hawke's memoirs, as regards Christianity, is this one:

Under Judaeo-Christian doctrine an individual's eternal eggs are all in the one basket of a single fleeting existence in the infinity of time, which is tough on the unredeemed sinner and a real dud hand for those who go through life without ever hearing God's message.[38]

With due respect to Hawke, and those Christians who may believe something similar, this is a shallow caricature. It is premised on several assumptions about God's justice which are, at the least, highly debatable.[39] Clem Hawke would not, I wager, have accepted them (though Ellie might have). If this was Hawke's understanding of Christianity at the time he visited India then it is no wonder he was disillusioned.

Back in Australia, he reported on his trip to the Congregational Church conference in Morialta, South Australia – Hazel was there and "was moved at his courage in questioning publicly what his parents had raised him to be".[40] Yet it has been contended by another biographer, John Hurst, that Hawke kept his agnosticism a secret from Clem for some years. According to Hurst, Clem "would have liked to tell his son that he could not blame God for what he had seen in India".[41]

Yet another of Hawke's biographers, Stan Anson, proffered a tenuous psychological explanation for his loss of faith. Anson's argument was that Ellie's frequent undermining of Clem within their family home in turn undermined Hawke's hero-worship of his father. "There is obviously a connection," Anson claimed, "between faith and doubt in God and faith and doubt in Dad."[42] I am unconvinced.

Hawke did not abandon religion straight away. On May 23, 1953, back in his familiar home city of Perth, he attended a non-denominational service commemorating Empire Youth Sunday.*[43] He still went to church sometimes, but his attendance became increasingly irregular.[44] It appears that his views may also have influenced Hazel's. In her memoirs she revealed that she lost her faith reluctantly. "I agonised more and more

---

* Sharing the speakers' stage with Hawke on that occasion was a 33 year-old Ronald Wilson (later Sir Ronald Wilson, a justice of the High Court of Australia from 1979-89 and the author of the *Bringing Them Home* report on the Stolen Generation). Wilson, too, had been at the World Youth Conference in India in 1952. But he remained a staunch Christian until his death in 2005. He was a Presbyterian who joined the Uniting Church in Australia after its formation in 1977.

about why some of us should be given access to the love of God through the church, while others would never know it. It didn't make sense. I became confused, then agnostic."[45]

It was at Oxford University, where he studied from 1953-56, that religion faded more or less completely from Hawke's life. Although he made friends with the Minister of the North Oxford Congregational Church, Rev. Geoffrey Beck[46], it appears this was a strictly a human relationship. Hawke's relationship with God waned. He became wholly immersed in things secular: above all, his thesis about the Australian industrial relations system. For the first time in his life, study became "pure joy".[47] Despite his loss of faith, Hawke interpreted this happy turn of events as being in some manner providential. "It would be an exaggeration to speak in terms of feeling some guiding force, but in a vague, indefinable way I had a sense that my past had prepared me for this task and that my future was being inexorably shaped."[48]

In March 1956, shortly after returning to Australia, he married Hazel. Clem Hawke and the Rev. Johnny Bryant presided at their wedding ceremony at Perth's Trinity Church.[49] By this stage Hawke was an agnostic. He "did not know whether he believed in God or not, and had rejected all Christian dogma".[50]

But there was a yearning in Hawke which needed to be satisfied. He soon found his calling at the Australian Council of Trade Unions, in advocacy work at which he excelled. According to Blanche D'Alpuget "Christian principles were in Hawke's bones", but from the late 1950s onwards "he found their expression not in lifeless Sunday ritual but in the vibrant, communal, morally cohesive and uplifting labour movement. As for many others, this was his new and true religion."[51]

Hawke had a brilliant career at the ACTU. He started as a research officer in 1958 – "the pivotal decision in his life".[52] Basing his family in Melbourne, he quickly became a formidable industrial advocate, beginning with the 1959 Basic Wage case. In court he was a dynamic, aggressive performer. In his personal relations he was gregarious, a good mixer in all company, and, in the main, fondly regarded by those who dealt with him. His reputation grew steadily and by the late 1960s he was "the best known figure in the industrial labour movement".[53]

To get that far, Hawke needed to draw upon copious resources of energy and skill. The Melbourne to which he came in the late 1950s was, in his words, "a cauldron of hatred, a witches' brew of loaded labels, mindless epithets and raw sectarianism".[54] As we have seen in earlier chapters, the creation of the DLP in the mid-1950s – ostensibly to fight communist influence within the union movement and to force the ALP to become a "true" party of the workers once more – had splintered Labor's traditional Catholic vote. That situation continued throughout the 1960s.

Hawke was dismayed by the religious aspect of the problem:

> Families were split, with brother set against brother or father, officials within the same union regarding each other as mortal enemies, worshippers in the same church treated by their co-religionists as lepers, while to be a Mason [that is, Protestant] was to wear a badge of honour in the Victorian ALP.[55]

In this atmosphere, it probably helped Hawke that he was an agnostic, unaligned to any of the religiously-based factions. At some stage in the 1960s he and Hazel had ceased to be churchgoers.[56]

At any rate, Hawke's rise was inexorable. On September 10, 1969 he was elected as president of the ACTU over the "conservative" candidate from the Right, Harold Souter.[57] He now had a national bully pulpit and he did not confine himself to traditional blue-collar concerns. He persuaded important white-collar umbrella groups to affiliate with the ACTU and took public stands on a range of topical issues including pensions, the Vietnam War and Apartheid.[58]

Another cause close to Hawke's heart was the State of Israel. He once said: "If I were to have my life again, I would want to be born a Jew."[59] He became a staunch and outspoken supporter of Israel, and in late 1976 a forest there was dedicated to him at Kerem Maharal. He and Hazel travelled there for the ceremony and took Hawke's parents with them. In her memoirs Hazel recorded with a note of wistfulness that Clem and Ellie Hawke felt a strong sense of identification with "the historic, Biblical places". They visited the Garden of Gethsemane, the Holy Sepulchre in Bethlehem and the Mount of Olives.[60] It is unclear from Hazel's account whether she or Bob, or both, went along too.

All this time, Hawke forged ahead. He never neglected his central responsibilities as a trade union leader. He earned a reputation as a "resolver, not an instigator" of industrial conflicts and was dubbed "the Fireman".[61] While some hard-nosed unionists used this moniker with derision, Hawke's approach resonated with the Australian people. He was perceived, deservedly, as a peacemaker. In his Boyer Lectures of 1979, he stated his belief that "in most people there is ... ultimately a desire for harmony rather than conflict".[62]

Hawke made this a central theme of the February/March 1983 election campaign, his first as Labor leader. His official slogan was "Bringing Australia Together"* – and it resonated. On March 5, 1983, the Fraser Government was ousted in a landslide. The Rev. Clem Hawke turned 85 that same day – there was a chocolate birthday cake for him in the hotel room in Canberra where the family watched the count.[63] Stan Anson has intimated that this night, for Clem, had truly Biblical significance. Clem's favourite chapter of the Bible concerned the building of the Temple – "David planned it, but it was his son, Solomon, who executed it".[64]

The Hawke Government of 1983-91 transformed Australia. For better or worse we joined the global economy and embraced multiculturalism. The tariff wall was brought down, Medicare was entrenched, and important progressive taxes (capital gains tax, fringe benefits tax) were imposed. On any view, Hawke's leadership was *effective*. He was "probably the greatest electioneering Prime Minister Australia has yet seen"[65] and he presided with skill and charm over a very talented ministry. Political journalist and author George Megalogenis hit the nail on the head: "Hawke, the vote magnet, secured permission from the Australian people for [Paul] Keating and other ministers to change the nation".[66]

---

* The wily NSW premier Neville Wran was sceptical of such attitudes. Earlier in 1983 he had good-naturedly mocked what he saw as Hawke's messianic pretensions, cautioning that "it's all very well to go on with all this spiritual stuff, but if the greedy bastards out there wanted spiritualism they'd join the f___g Hare Krishna". Wran, incidentally, is an agnostic. So too is Bill Hayden (a lapsed Catholic), the man whom Hawke replaced as Labor leader on February 3, 1983. Hayden's famous quip that day – also a dig at Hawke – was that a drover's dog could lead Labor to victory in the upcoming election, such was the state of the country. In my opinion, both Wran and Hayden were wrong: deep down the Australian people did want "spiritual stuff" and, in the circumstances of March 1983, Hawke was easily the best person to give it to them.

What was the secret of Hawke's success? In my opinion: his capacity to get on amicably with all sorts of people, both here and overseas. If he had a narcissistic streak, he also had bucket loads of empathy and compassion – and intelligence. He could usually see the other person's point of view. In this regard, his falling out with Keating was exceptional.

There is a beautiful example of Hawke's capacity for empathy. The subject-matter is right on point.

One evening in 1976, while he was president of the ACTU, Hawke participated in a "phone in" segment on This Day Tonight, a current affairs programme on ABC television.[67] A young boy came onto the line and told Hawke he was seven years old. The boy then asked: "Um, is there a real God?"

Hawke's off-the-cuff response was, in all the circumstances, a model of fairness:

> Ben, I hope you can understand this answer. It's a very complicated question which men and women have been trying to answer for thousands of years.
>
> Those who say there is a God are what we call theists or religionists. They believe in God and they say definitely there is one. Those who say there is not a God are what we call atheists, who just assert there isn't any God. Now I can't bring myself to say that.
>
> I haven't got any evidence which is compelling to me, Ben, which says 'yes there is' or 'yes there isn't'. What they call me is an agnostic, which is perhaps a pretty difficult sounding word to you, but what it really means is that I don't know whether there is a God or not.
>
> There are a lot of people I respect who believe there is, including my father, who has been a minister of religion all his life. We are good mates, Dad and I, and we agree to differ – he says there is a God and I say I don't know. Until I get some evidence one way or the other which is compelling to me, I am going to have to remain an agnostic, Ben.

Hawke has remained an agnostic – and, for the most part, a respectful one. On one occasion in 1988, however, as Prime Minister, he was angered by some over-zealous disparagement of Aboriginal spiritual beliefs. He returned serve at the Christians concerned in, perhaps, excessively hostile fashion. But Hawke was unrepentant in his memoirs: "The monumental hypocrisy of this position is mind-boggling. The same people who denigrate blacks in this way can easily accommodate and embrace the bundle of mysteries that make up their white Christian beliefs: the virgin birth, the Holy Trinity, God in His heaven – where is He?"[68]

Perhaps, one day soon, Hawke will resume searching – if he is not doing so already. There is a precedent. Hawke has often said that the Prime Minister he most admires is John Curtin, and there are obvious parallels between them at the political, personal and spiritual levels. As we have seen, Curtin kept searching for God until the day he died.

PAUL JOHN KEATING (B. 1945)

LABOR: 1991-96

In October 2011 I wrote a short piece for *The Drum* about the Bible and Australian politics. It evoked an indignant response from several bloggers, most of whom were scornful of Christianity. One post was especially revealing: "It's hard to accept that Keating is a Christian – I prefer my heroes to be thinking people."

Yet Catholicism is one of the keys to understanding Keating – perhaps *the* key. He remains the only Australian Prime Minister to have been educated by the Josephites.[1] As a teenager he adhered to what were, in his milieu, the "three imperatives" of a Catholic upbringing in Australia: go to mass, join the union, support Labor.[2] He might never have got his start in federal politics but for the backing of his family's parish church. In his own private life his reputation was as "the best family man in politics".[3]

Yet Keating was always much more than a "tribal" Catholic, in my estimation at least. True, many of his public and private statements down the years reveal an "Us versus Them" mindset, variously defensive and nostalgic. I am acutely conscious, also, of not having had the opportunity to interview him. My request was politely declined, and word filtered back that Keating regards his faith as "too private" a thing for public discussion. Don Watson has written of Keating's need for "the refuge of the inner life".[4]

Nevertheless, there is a surprising amount of material on the record. Keating has referred on occasion to the spiritual and theological aspects of his faith as well as its role in his upbringing. Indeed, more than once, he has explicitly linked the basic tenets of Catholicism – as he understood them – with his political philosophy.

If I may hazard a generalisation, that philosophy has two main strands.* It combines economic liberalism with social conservatism. But there are two vital riders.

First, Keating's economic liberalism has always been tempered by a strong belief in State-sponsored charity for the helpless and deserving. At the beginning of his career this was very much his emphasis (he had imbibed Thomist teachings about distributive justice), but by the late 1970s his views had evolved. Increasingly his focus was on economic growth as "the engine of everything"[5], *including* social justice. In this respect he was a Labor innovator and – perhaps unknowingly – a convert to a more broadly Protestant view of political economy. For this he earned the hatred of his fellow-Catholic B.A. Santamaria, who was still rooted in old age to a romantic medieval vision of an agrarian, church-centred society.[6]

It is true that Keating's enthusiasm for economic rationalism and globalisation bordered, at times, on the zealous. It was hard to reconcile with *Rerum Novarum* – the encyclical on labour and capital – but not, I would submit, impossible. For Keating (and for Bob Hawke), economic growth was always a means to an end. The Coalition gives itself credit for providing bipartisan support for Labor's deregulation of the economy during the 1980s and 1990s – and that is fair enough. What is not usually mentioned is that the Coalition opposed almost all of Labor's "balancing" measures. In the mid-1980s it opposed the introduction of new progressive taxes (Fringe Benefits Tax, Capital Gains Tax, etc). At the 1987 election it advocated the dismantling of Medicare. In 1992 it opposed the introduction of compulsory employer-funded superannuation, now regarded as the single most important factor in the mitigation of wealth inequality in Australia. Examples could be multiplied.

---

* I put to one side Keating's views about matters military – they are well-informed and nuanced. He is neither a pacifist nor a spoiler for every fight that the United States might seek to draw Australia into. Interestingly, Bob Hawke wrote in his memoirs that Keating initially expressed "grave reservations" about the First Gulf War of 1990-91. Hawke intended this as a criticism, but, assuming his account to be accurate, it might also be regarded as a point in Keating's favour.

It must be doubtful whether deregulation would have been socially or politically feasible – let alone just, in any Christian sense of the word – without the retention of a generous social safety net. The trade unions were drawn into the process, through the Accord, rather than being demonised and sidelined. Australia did not become the United States or Margaret Thatcher's Britain.

The second of my riders is even more important. While in most things Keating has always been a social conservative (in 1997 he lamented the fact that "today there seem to be no certainties or absolutes"[7]), his views became increasingly progressive on issues of race. As Prime Minister, he was bold. If, as the prominent British Rabbi Jonathan Sacks has argued, humanity's "supreme challenge ... is to see God's image in one who is not in our image"[8], then Keating met that challenge admirably. I will come in due course to the Redfern speech of 1992, but would stress at the outset the vital link between, on the one hand, Keating's record as an economic reformer, and, on the other hand, his liberal views on issues of race. In this respect he was well ahead of many economic "hardheads" on the Coalition side of politics, whose views in the 1980s and 90s were too frequently infected by snobbery and xenophobia. He was also well ahead of the left of the ALP, which never fully appreciated the link between racial tolerance and a strong economy.

In order to create and maintain economic growth, Keating insisted, Australia could not remain "a little European enclave in the Pacific". Rather, it had to "trade its way into the south-east Asian community" – to, if you like, make disciples of all nations. This became the central theme of his political career.[9] It never made him popular – and he felt the visceral backlash at the 1996 election – but he was right. His vision is now conventional wisdom on both sides of politics.

Speaking in 2009, Keating recalled that by the early 1990s he "had in my mind that by thought and cooperation, we could make the East Asian hemisphere a better, safer and more cooperative place altogether. And by we, I mean Australia."[10] China, of course, is now a superpower. I wonder what Keating makes of the fact that Christianity is growing faster there than in any other country of the world.

Keating grew up in south-western Sydney in the 1950s and 1960s in a large and close-knit family. He had two younger sisters (Lyn and Anne), and one younger brother (Greg). The head of the household, Matt Keating, seems by all accounts to have been a kind and likeable bloke. He was also a small businessman of some enterprise – a boilermaker and union official who made good – and an active member of the local branch of the ALP. He died at 60, in 1978, but had already made his mark. According to John Edwards, the importance of Matt Keating in his son's political career "is hard to overestimate".[11]

Matt's wife, Min Keating (née Chapman), was a full-time homemaker of considerable strength of character. "My mother had views about how everyone should behave," Keating once recalled, "and if you didn't behave that way she'd give you a clip over the ear, simple as that."[12] But as tough as she was, Min cherished her older son, and they always remained close. Even as Prime Minister, Keating often began phone calls to her with a humble greeting: "It's only me, Mum." [13] As an old woman, Min could recollect only one boyhood misdemeanour on Paul's part: he once grabbed the hat off a Protestant boy's head and tossed it into a tree![14]

Both Matt and Min Keating were practising Catholics, "good, honest souls"[15] who inculcated in their four children a firm sense of right and wrong. Matt, especially, was a man of "lively faith".[16] He did voluntary work for the Society of St Vincent de Paul and listened on Sunday evenings to 2SM, a Sydney radio station established by the Catholic Church. Matt enjoyed a talkback show hosted by a priest, Dr Leslie Rumble, who fielded questions on theology.[17]

For several years the Keating family worshipped at St Felix de Valois church in Bankstown. Then, in the early 1950s, part of that congregation was hived off to a new parish and St Brendan's church (also in Bankstown) became the centre of their religious life. Matt and Min were hard-working members, generous with their time, and Paul went with them to mass every Sunday.[18] At one stage he was an altar boy.[19] Later he joined the Catholic Youth Organisation – it was the centre of his innocent social life.*

---

* Keating's social life really was remarkably innocent. It is true that he once managed a band. It was called the Ramrods but regrettably went hitless before breaking up in 1966: Keating later quipped that he took it "from nowhere to obscurity". It should not be assumed that young Keating harboured impure motives when he ventured into the milieu of rock-and-roll. To the contrary, he was a square: sex and drugs were never remotely on his radar. The furthest he went with girls was "to squire young debutantes to the annual CYO ball". One of the Ramrods later testified that "his morals were as high as anybody I've ever known".

Keating's formal education was almost exclusively in the Catholic system. As a small boy he attended St Jerome's at Punchbowl; from third class onwards, the parish school attached to St Brendan's. "It was," Keating recalled over forty years later, "converted from a school to a church each weekend and back again for the following Monday". He added wistfully: "I can still see exactly the way those benches and pews were".[20]

The sisters who ran these schools made a lasting impression on Keating. He came to admire them for having taken their vows of poverty and celibacy – and for their "love, devotion and commitment".[21] At St Jerome's, a Sister Inez was in charge. She still remembered Keating after 45 years, and, even when he was Prime Minister, had no qualms about grabbing him by the arm and telling him what to do.[22] Young Paul – believe it or not – had been regarded by the nuns as "a docile little chap".[23]

Speaking on February 18, 1997 at the launch of a book about the religious order founded by St Mary MacKillop, the Sisters of St Joseph, Keating sought to explain why he admired the nuns so much.[24] He quoted St John of the Cross (from the section headed "Obedience"):

What does it profit you to give God one thing if he asks of you another? Consider what it is that God wants and then do it. You will as a result satisfy your heart better than with something toward which you yourself are inclined.

These words, Keating said, "are still as valid today as ever".[25] Furthermore, in his view, the sisters of St Joseph were inspiring because they genuinely tried to live by this ethos. Their prime focus was "fidelity to the poor, and the belief in God's interest in them, Christ's interest in them, and their intrinsic importance as his children".[26]

This same ethos was also prevalent at De La Salle College, Bankstown, where Keating went to secondary school. In those days, it was still staffed mainly by the brothers. A priest close to the Keating family in the 1960s, Father Michael McCarthy, explained to John Edwards that "the whole basis of a Catholic formation [was] to give people a strong sense of why they are here, the fact that they are created by God and destined for heaven".[27]

In 1959, aged 15, Keating left school. In those days this was not an uncommon thing. He had coasted to his Intermediate Certificate and found a job as a pay clerk for the Sydney County Council, in its electricity division. He worked there for seven years, contentedly enough, and rose slowly through the ranks – but it was during this period that he got his first serious taste of sectarianism. A fellow worker also named Keating, a Freemason, taunted that he was "one of the Keatings dragged up by the Catholics".[28]

This is all very well, I can hear sceptics saying. But who cares? How much of this endured beyond Keating's childhood and adolescence? My answer: a great deal.

For a start, Keating's Catholicism inspired and facilitated his entry into politics. One day in early November 1960, as a 16 year-old, he read a newspaper article about John F. Kennedy's recent victory over Richard Nixon in the US presidential election. "If a Catholic like Kennedy could become President of the United States," Keating thought to himself, "why should a Catholic like Paul Keating not become Prime Minister of Australia?"[29]

(Of course, the comparison was not really apt – though it is understandable why, late in the era of Menzies, a 16 year-old who self-identified as a "tyke" would feel that way. For demographic reasons the electoral barriers faced by a Catholic in the United States were far, far greater than they ever were in Australia. By 1960, we had already had three practising Catholics as Prime Minister – Scullin, Lyons and Chifley. To this day, JFK is the only Catholic to have been US President.)

By the mid-1960s Keating had developed a sense of mission. He took the view that "if God has given you the capacity to handle and grapple with politics and to be articulate you have a duty to serve your own class".[30] The ALP's values were in tune with the spiritual values instilled in him by the Sisters of St Joseph: "the whole ethos of a fair go or our sense of justice and social inclusion".[31] Despite their staunch Catholicism neither Matt nor Paul Keating ever flirted with the DLP. Matt shared plenty of its concerns about Communist infiltration of the unions, and had been a member of the Industrial Groups before they were proscribed by the ALP in 1955.[32] But at no stage did he contemplate defection.[33] Both he and Paul were ambivalent about the Vietnam War – it was a cause which presented difficult issues for conservative Catholics – but ultimately they came down against it. Paul was not personally threatened by the prospect of conscription. When Menzies introduced the birthday ballot, in late 1964, he was just 12 months too old to be eligible.

In 1966 he took a new job as a researcher and advocate with the Federated Municipal and Shire Council Employees' Union.[34] It was a good career move, for by then he had set his sights on the Federal seat of Blaxland, based around Bankstown.

We now come to a little-known fact about Keating. The Labor pre-selection battle in Blaxland of 1967-68 hung by a thread, and Keating would not have won but for the church. He owed his hard-fought victory (146 votes to 125), to the numbers he and his father accumulated through a network of contacts at St Brendan's and in the Catholic Youth Organisation. (He also benefited from intervention by Gough Whitlam in a subsequent dispute about the count – at the height of the ALP's internal debate on State aid, Whitlam wanted a right-wing Catholic.)[35]

Elected to parliament in October 1969, Keating identified himself straightaway as a social conservative. His Catholicism was central. In his maiden speech to Parliament, on March 17, 1970, he expressed views that would be regarded by many people today as weird or even scandalous:

> Young mothers have been forced out of their homes by economic pressure ... Family life is the very basis of our nationhood. In the last couple of years the [Coalition] government has boasted about the increasing number of women in the workforce. Rather than something to be proud of, I feel that it is something of which we should be ashamed.[36]

Two-income families are now the norm in Australia and across the West. Contemporary criticism of this phenomenon, while not unknown, is generally seen as aberrant. Yet Keating's personal views on this subject – as to the critical societal importance of full-time mothers – seem never to have substantially changed.[37] His own wife, Annita, gave up her career for him and their four children.

In 1975 the Whitlam Government introduced its seminal Family Law Bill. The prospect of no-fault divorce made Keating uneasy; he spoke in the House about the need to protect "faithful conscientious wives".[38]

But he also saw the writing on the wall. Like Malcolm Fraser and John Howard, he favoured a compromise position on the Bill's key provision – an amendment which would have required a period of two years' separation rather than one, as a prerequisite for the grant of a "no-fault" divorce.[39] (John Gorton and Billy McMahon – and, of course, Whitlam – supported one year.) Keating himself has been separated from his wife Annita* since 1998, but they have never divorced. He said in 1999: "When you're married for 25 years, you never really get unmarried."[40]

Abortion may be the quintessential moral-political issue. Rightly or wrongly, defence of "the right to life" has become in some circles – and especially in the United States – one of the litmus tests of Christian belief. The Second Vatican Council declared in 1965: "Life must be protected with the utmost care from the moment of conception: abortion and infanticide are abominable crimes."[41]

During the 1970s Keating won the approval of Christians within the parliamentary ALP for getting to his feet one morning at Sunday mass in Bankstown and interrupting the homily. The priest had alleged that Labor was "in favour of abortion". In fact, the party's official position – then and now – was to permit a conscience vote. Keating set things straight.[42]

In March 1979, during a debate in Parliament, Keating stated his personal position.

"Abortion," he said, "threatens the nation through the destruction of its children".[43] He elaborated:

> I do not approve of abortion for contraceptive or convenience
> reasons. In fact, there are very few grounds on which I
> would approve of abortion taking place. I do not believe that
> governments in Australia should approve of convenience
> abortions.[44]

---

* Keating met Anna Johanna Maria van Iersel in mid-1973, on an Alitalia jet flying from Sydney to Bangkok. Annita was Dutch, beautiful, informed, multi-lingual - and Catholic. Keating pursued her around the world for the best part of 18 months; finally, in Buenos Aires, she accepted his proposal. They were married on January 17, 1975 in the village of Oisterwijk in Holland, in the local Catholic church. The reasons for their estrangement remain obscure and Keating, properly, has steadfastly refused to comment.

In 1996, in response to a direct question from biographer Michael Gordon, Keating stood by this position. On what he termed the "essential point", he affirmed his belief that "life begins at conception and if it's terminated, it's finished".[45]

What of theology more broadly? Writing in 1996, Gordon averred flatly that Keating "has remained faithful to the tenets of the Catholic church, though he attends mass irregularly".[46] Don Watson described him in 2002 as a "pre-Vatican II Bankstown tyke"[47] and as a man of "old-fashioned Catholicism ... [who] ... believed in core values in education, commonsense environmentalism, multiculturalism without the pieties, the virtues of community and family, a capacious safety net but plenty of standing on your own two feet".[48]

Does Keating believe in the Resurrection? The Final Judgment? Is he still a "seeker" as regards such matters? To some extent I must speculate, but the answers appear to be yes. Keating took several chances afforded him as a parliamentarian to broaden his religious horizons and to give voice to his beliefs. I will mention five episodes (four from his Prime Ministership) and readers can make of them what they will.

In April 1979 Keating spoke on a condolence motion for the late Frank Stewart, a Catholic Labor member from the inner-west of Sydney to whom he had been close:

> He died after Easter Sunday and those of us who shared some of his view like to think that he died in a state of grace and will live an eternal life with Christ. Our most fervent wish is that his family will join him in a life with Christ after death.[49]

On a visit to Ireland in late 1993, during a speech in Tynagh, Keating enunciated the principle which, he said, had guided him in politics:

> Catholicism gives you the view that we were born equally and die equally and that no one of us is intrinsically worth more than the other.[50]

In January 1995 Pope John Paul II visited Australia. Keating gave speeches of arrival and farewell. According to Don Watson, the Prime Minister's mood lifted markedly in the presence of His Holiness and a group of

Catholic priests: "he experienced a rare glow of personal approval".[51]

In February 1995 Keating made a speech to Parliament upon the beatification of Mary MacKillop:

> The beatification of Mary MacKillop rings with significance for all Australians. The qualities she embodied – openness and tolerance, courage, persistence, faith and care for others are qualities for individuals, communities and nations to live by. We will serve Australia well if we allow the values which inspired and guided Mary MacKillop's work to inspire and guide our own.[52]

The final anecdote (also from 1995) is my personal favourite. When Keating flew to Israel for the funeral of assassinated Prime Minister Yitzhak Rabin he took time to visit Jerusalem, and the experience moved him profoundly. He spoke in unguarded terms of wonder: "You know you can see where Christ walked on the way to the Crucifixion."[53]

I come now to Keating's Redfern speech of December 10, 1992. Paul Kelly has referred to it as the "atonement" speech[54] – and the label is apt. The following part is the best-known; it was during this passage that the crowd began to stir:

> The starting point might be to recognise that the problem starts with us non-Aboriginal Australians.
>
> It begins, I think, with the act of recognition. Recognition that it was we who did the dispossessing. We took the traditional lands and smashed the traditional way of life. We brought the disasters. The alcohol. We committed the murders. We took the children from their mothers. We practised discrimination and exclusion.
>
> It was our ignorance and our prejudice. And our failure to imagine these things being done to us. With some noble exceptions, we failed to make the most basic human response and enter into their hearts and minds. *We failed to ask – how would I feel if this were done to me?*

That last sentence, of course, was a reworking of the neighbour principle. ("Do unto others as you would have them do unto you." (cf. Luke 6:31)).

Later in the speech, Keating elaborated:

As I said, it might help us if we non-Aboriginal Australians imagined ourselves dispossessed of land we have lived on for 50,000 years – and then imagined ourselves told that it had never been ours. Imagine if ours was the oldest culture in the world and we were told that it was worthless.

Imagine if we had resisted this settlement, suffered and died in the defence of our land, and then were told in history books that we had given up without a fight. Imagine if non-Aboriginal Australians had served their country in peace and war and were then ignored in history books. Imagine if our feats on sporting fields had inspired admiration and patriotism and yet did nothing to diminish prejudice.

Most crucially, for present purposes, Keating also framed the issue in terms of religious tolerance: "Imagine if our spiritual life was denied and ridiculed."

Keating suggested a way forward – a system of land rights, based upon the principles laid down by the High Court in its (then) recent decision in the *Mabo* case.

The Redfern speech – and Keating's subsequent achievement, the Native Title Act of 1993 – were not well-received by the majority of white Australians. Some in rural areas had pragmatic concerns about the security of their land holdings, and this was understandable. But most such concerns were dealt with competently. The real problem was much more deep-seated: many people seemed driven by nebulous feelings of resentment, sometimes tinged with racism. Some complained of "Aboriginal industries", of "political correctness", of being held *personally* responsible for sins (real or imagined) committed by their forebears in the distant past. *Mabo* and *Wik* and the Native Title Act were products of "the guilt industry" and of "black armband" Australian history.

Yet Keating had expressly stated in the Redfern speech, and in a subsequent national address, that feelings of guilt should *not* be the prime motivation for making an act of atonement. Guilt was not, he suggested, "a useful emotion".[55]

From a Christian perspective, two things might be said. First (the Old Testament lesson), the sins of the fathers may, in certain circumstances, justly be visited upon their children. Second (the New Testament lesson), an act of atonement does not depend on an assuagement of *personal* guilt. Christians believe that the purpose of Christ's death on the Cross was to atone for mankind's individual and collective sins, past, present and future. Christ was in no way personally responsible for the sins of mankind: the essence of God's plan was that an *innocent* man should take it upon himself to "correct" the injustices caused by those sins. That is what made it a sacred sacrifice.

I would like to think that Keating had these notions in mind. At all events, following the passage of the Native Title Act, he acknowledged that most (white) Australians opposed it. But, he said – a profoundly Christian sentiment – "more of them felt better about themselves".[56] Who today would argue with that? We all have our crosses to bear, both as individuals and as blessed Australians citizens.

The Redfern speech may well have been an expression of "impossible idealism"[57] but that was one reason for its greatness. The same could be said of the Sermon on the Mount. It should also be remembered that the themes of the Redfern speech had been enunciated before – by Pope John Paul II, no less, on a visit to Alice Springs on November 29, 1986.[58] His Holiness acknowledged the sincerely-motivated work of Christian missionaries, and of countless other white people who had sought to understand and help Indigenous peoples since 1788. But he squarely recognised the myriad sins committed against them and advocated atonement for those sins:

> From the earliest times men like Archbishop Polding of Sydney
> opposed the legal fiction adopted by European settlers that this
> land was terra nullius – nobody's country. He strongly pleaded
> for the rights of the Aboriginal inhabitants to keep the traditional
> lands on which their whole society depended. The Church still
> supports you today.
>
> Let it not be said that the fair and equitable recognition
> of Aboriginal rights to land is discrimination. To call for the
> acknowledgment of the land rights of people who have never
> surrendered those rights is not discrimination. Certainly, what

has been done cannot be undone. But what can now be done to remedy the deeds of yesterday must not be put off till tomorrow.

These arguments reflected a strain of Catholic "natural rights" thinking that went back more than three hundred years, to Hugo Grotius's seminal work *The Rights of War and Peace* (1645). Grotius argued that colonial powers could not unilaterally extinguish the rights of native peoples to their land. God's justice prevails over "the brand of justice made in the image of the majority".[59]

If that is the Christian case "for" Keating, what of the case against? The vice most frequently attributed to him is pride – what C.S. Lewis called the Great Sin.

One aspect of this charge can be dismissed outright: Keating's propensity to tell it straight. He did not sugar-coat the truth ("Banana republic" etc.) or kowtow to the base or ignorant voices in the community. Consider this exchange in 1993 with a talkback-radio caller on the show hosted in Sydney by John Laws. Such candour would be unimaginable today.

CALLER: Good morning.

LAWS: Okay, the Prime Minister is here.

CALLER: Yes, good morning. Just a very broad question, Mr Keating, is: why does your government see the Aboriginal people as a much more equal people than the average white Australian?

KEATING: We don't. We see them as equal.

CALLER: Well, you might say that, but all the indications are that you don't.

KEATING: But what's implied in your question is that *you* don't; you think that non-Aboriginal Australians, there ought to be discrimination in their favour against blacks.

CALLER: Not... whatsoever. I... I don't say that at all. But my... myself and every person I talk to – and I'm not racist – but every person I talk to...

KEATING: But that's what they all say, don't they? They put these questions – they always say, "I'm not racist, but, you know, I don't believe that Aboriginal Australians ought to have a basis in equality with non-Aboriginal Australians." Well, of course, that's part of the problem.

CALLER: Aren't they more equal than us at the moment, with the preferences they get?

KEATING: More equal? They were... I mean, it's not for me to be giving you a history lesson – they were largely dispossessed of the land they held.

CALLER: There's a question over that. I think a lot of people will tell you that. You're telling us one thing...

KEATING: Well, if you're sitting on the title of any block of land in NSW, you can bet an Aboriginal person at some stage was dispossessed of it.

CALLER: You know that for sure, do you?

KEATING: Of course we know it for sure!

CALLER: Yeah, [inaudible].

KEATING: You're challenging the High Court decision, are you? You're saying the High Court got this all wrong?

CALLER: No, I'm not saying that at all! I wouldn't know who was on the High Court.

KEATING: Well, why don't you sign off, if you don't know anything about it and you're not interested. Good bye!

CALLER: Yeah, well, that's your ...

KEATING: No, I mean, you can't challenge these things and then say, "I don't know about them".

LAWS: Oh well, he's gone.

This was admirable counterpunching on Keating's part – in a worthy cause. More questionable was his public skiting ("the Placido Domingo of Australian politics"), and his penchant for bitchy abuse of rivals and opponents. Jesus' counsel of perfection was that we turn the other cheek in the face of provocation. "Everyone should be quick to listen, slow to speak and slow to become angry, for man's anger does not bring about the righteous life that God desires" (James 1:19-20, 26). Even so, it is fair to point out that Jesus Himself used terms of abuse when sincerely angry. He did so to warn and correct. On one occasion He denounced the scribes and Pharisees as "hypocrites", "blind guides", "snakes" and "the brood of vipers" (Matthew 23:13-33).

Keating's invective* had a number of saving graces. It was often truly funny. It was darkly Australian in character. Most importantly, it was rarely specific: he usually employed the "corporate slur" rather than concrete defamatory allegations.[60] But he lost his temper too often, and, since his defeat at the 1996 election, he has exhibited in public an unseemly level of bitterness. There seems to be a good deal of hatred in his heart – in sharp contrast to Ben Chifley, whom Keating dismissed as a mere "plodder" in his "Placido Domingo" speech in 1990.

But there are other considerations which militate in Keating's favour. Perhaps I will be accused of special pleading. But pride – and its counterpart, humility – manifest themselves in many ways.

The younger Keating faced up squarely to his limitations. He educated himself in economics and other pertinent areas of public policy, and was not afraid to seek counsel from wiser heads.[61] He also took pains to expand his mind via reading and music and the fine arts. As John Edwards observed in 1996, Keating came to realise that immersion in the world of politics can be narrowing, a barrier to proper understanding of life's wider

---

* Keating's repertoire of insults is now the stuff of legend: entire websites are devoted to the subject, as was a song in *Keating! The Musical*. It is worth noting that, not infrequently, he employed words and phrases of a religious flavour. Perhaps, when he was Prime Minister, this ought not to have been surprising: his principal speechwriter, Don Watson, once remarked that "if you take away the New Testament and the Old, what is there left for oratory?" Even so, most of Keating's sharpest "religious" lines – "wear like a crown of thorns", "shocking Philistines", "pre-Copernican obscurantist" etc. – were not scripted.

purposes.[62] He did not allow himself to be corrupted by the world (cf. James 1:27).

As regards Keating's personal conduct while Prime Minister, two other things might be said. First, his manner inside his own office was collegiate and unpretentious: he knew and used everyone's first name, sought their opinions, gave them a fair degree of freedom, and thanked and encouraged them routinely. They called him Paul, or "mate", and he expected nothing else.[63]

Secondly, Keating was not a healthy man. Indeed, he was "exhausted from the first day he took the job".[64] According to insiders "he got by on willpower rather than energy or a strong constitution"[65]; by the mid-1990s he was physically spent and given to bouts of melancholy.[66] That he persevered for so long was to his credit: he did not enjoy the job but he believed passionately in the cause (cf. 2 Corinthians 11:16-31). When his eight-year stint as Bob Hawke's treasurer is taken into account, Keating can lay claim to having been, with Alfred Deakin, one of the two most important Prime Ministers in Australian peacetime history. Indeed, because Keating was primarily responsible for the final dismantling of Deakin's Australian settlement, I would rate him as the most important.

What, then, is the final verdict? Keating is a far from faultless man, of course. But he was a visionary Prime Minister and no mere nominal Christian. Indeed, as Greg Barns has justly observed, he devoted his last few years in politics to a battle for "Australia's independent soul". That is why Keating was a much greater threat to the Liberal Party's long-term national hegemony than Bob Hawke ever was.[67] Today Hawke (the lapsed Protestant) gets on fairly well with John Howard (the mild Protestant), but their antipathy towards Keating is notorious. So is Keating's for them.

Deeply-felt Catholicism defined Keating, and still does. He said it best himself, in late 1992, over lunch with Don Watson at the Lodge:

> He [Keating] asks me if I am a tyke. I say I'm not. I'm Presbyterian, can't you tell? He says, it doesn't matter: 'You think like a tyke. You've that view of the world. It's different'.[68]

JOHN WINSTON HOWARD (B. 1939)

LIBERAL: 1996-2007

Howard was the second-longest serving Prime Minister in Australian history. He is still held in esteem by a sizable percentage of his fellow citizens and is known among intimates as a courteous and measured person, thoughtful in his personal conduct. He is a devoted husband and father: in the mid-1990s he contemplated leaving politics when Janette, his wife, was diagnosed with cervical cancer. In many ways he has lived a worthy, industrious life. He is a practising Christian. Why, then, do a good many fellow-believers regard him with ambivalence?

Party politics has a lot to do with it, of course. To this day Howard is detested by left-wing partisans. He was pilloried for 20 years by some influential figures in the commentariat – several made it a kind of art-form. But such people, however sincerely motivated, usually played straight into Howard's hands. Part of his appeal to Coalition voters was that he seemed unperturbed by their criticism. Too much of it was indiscriminate and intemperate; at times it had an ugly anti-Christian subtext or was couched in unhelpfully crude language. Coalition supporters made a virtue of bemoaning the "Howard-haters".

Nevertheless, as I shall argue, some of this criticism had substance. Howard's record as Prime Minister is vulnerable to challenge on a number of Christian grounds. In one respect (human rights) it is badly tainted.

In certain other respects, however, it merits high praise. And as far as Howard's personal faith is concerned, there is no basis for questioning its genuineness. A few critics have done so, most notably Marion Maddox* in her 2005 book *God Under Howard*.[1] She has continued to lambast him in subsequent writings. Some of Maddox's arguments have merit, and her research into Howard's early life in Earlwood is invaluable. But her real beefs are political and theological: to put it mildly, Howard is not her sort of Christian. She has even held his ecumenism against him, as being somehow indicative of insincerity.

Paul Kelly has gone to another extreme:

> There was a bizarre … idea that gained traction among his critics – that Howard was driven mainly by religion. The truth is that he wasn't interested in religion, never talked religion and saw it as a strictly private domain.[2]

It is true that, unlike several of his Coalition colleagues, Howard did not purport to run an overtly "Christian" party or administration. He was happy to attend the annual National Prayer Breakfasts at Parliament House, and, three or four times a year, went on morning walks with people who had made large donations to religious charities.[3] Occasionally he lauded "Judaeo-Christian values". He opened the Hillsong Church's new $25 million complex in Sydney in 2002.[4] But he rarely invoked God or discussed his own faith. In his public comments he was generally respectful of Islam and other non-Christian religions.[5] He encouraged inter-faith dialogue in the aftermath of the Bali bombing.[6] He did not belong to the Lyons Forum (a group of conservative Christians active in the Coalition in the 1990s) nor the cross-party prayer group which met at Parliament House on Monday nights.[7]

Perhaps this was cagy politics. "Even religious people [in Australia] are secular in their political tradition," Howard once observed. "Australians

---

* At page 292 of *God Under Howard*, Maddox wrote of John and Janette Howard: "He refused and she did not reply to interview requests for this book." During my interview of Howard he surprised me by saying (unprompted), that Maddox "may have consulted the other person mentioned in the title but she didn't consult me." When I told him that Maddox had claimed that he had refused her an interview, Howard said: "I don't recall her approaching me, I really don't. She may have approached somebody who presumed to speak on my behalf. I didn't read the book."

are more sceptical [than Americans] of politicians who frequently invoke Christian beliefs to justify policy."[8]

But of course Howard was *interested* in religion. Paul Kelly's suggestion to the contrary was, he thought, "ridiculous" – and I agree. Howard's innovative policies as regards non-government schools demonstrated his interest clearly. So too the National School Chaplaincy Programme and his insistence that the proposed Preamble to the Constitution (rejected at the 1999 referendum) contain a reference to God. In any event, a man does not attend church more or less regularly for 70 years unless he is – to some extent – interested. Only in early middle age does Howard seem to have attended church less than regularly. He has used the word "occasionally".

Until the age of 30, Howard belonged to the Methodist Church. Indeed, he described himself as a "communicant member" as late as 1975.[9] No doubt there was a "crossover" period, at least in Howard's mind, but in point of fact he had been drifting away from the Methodists since 1971. In that year, upon marrying Janette*, he followed her into the Church of England. After buying a unit in Wollstonecraft, they began attending St Giles Anglican Church in Greenwich, and stayed there for many years.[10]

Howard told me that he remembered St Giles this way:

> It was quite a strong congregation. The local minister John Henderson and his wife Roberta were both activists in the community and it was quite a community, Greenwich, and as often happens when you have children you get to know a lot of the parents and you become friends and we've retained

---

* Janette Parker and her mother were members of the congregation at St Peter's, Watson's Bay (in Sydney). It was their local parish church, and the venue for John and Janette's wedding ceremony on April 4, 1971. I asked Howard if he could recall the hymns and readings that day. He replied promptly that "we had 'All Praise to my Redeeming Lord', and Handel's Water Music, the Trumpet Voluntary and the prayer of St Francis of Assisi." Subsequently all three of the Howard children (Melanie, Tim and Richard), were baptised at St Peter's, but their confirmations were at St Giles in Greenwich. I also asked Howard why he and Janette gravitated to the Anglican Church. It was entirely understandable that they wished to worship together, but why the Anglicans rather than the Methodists? He replied with a glint in his eye: "I suppose it was a view that maybe in something like that I should defer to my wife." He then added: "But on top of that I had, prior to my meeting Janette in the '60s, occasionally attended services at St James in the city … and when I was in England I occasionally went to Anglican services."

those friendships. But it was what I would call 'in the Anglican tradition' which I don't pretend to be an expert on because I didn't grow up in the Anglican church, but it was certainly closer to the evangelical norm of Sydney rather than the opposite direction, it was middle to low rather than middle to high.

More recently, Howard has worshipped at the Anglican church at Lavender Bay. "I go there once a month," he told me. "That's my church attendance, once a month."

What are Howard's core theological beliefs? He wrote in his memoirs that "the fundamentals of Christian belief and practice which I learned [as a child] have stayed with me to this day, although I would not pretend to be other than an imperfect adherent to them".[11] When I asked him to specify "the fundamentals" his reply was exemplary: "The fundamentals are the divinity of Christ and the sacrificial nature of His death. They're the fundamentals. There are a lot of others but that's the core of Christian belief which separates it out from other Abrahamic religions."

In his memoirs, he explained his faith in these terms:

Any religious belief requires a large act of faith. To many people, believing in something that cannot be proved is simply a step too far. To me, by contrast, human life seems so complex and hard to explain yet so extraordinary that the existence of God has always seemed to offer a better explanation of its meaning than any other.[12]

For some Christians these sentiments might appear timid and vague. There was no mention of Jesus. But Howard's lack of dogmatism is, in a way, disarming. He does not claim a stronger faith than he really has. "One of the great things about the Anglican church," he said to me, "some people see it as a weakness, is you're required to give general assent to the Thirty-Nine Articles. It's a wonderful expression; it accommodates a whole range of beliefs." As we have seen, Alfred Deakin came to much the same opinion.

Howard's parents, Lyall and Mona Howard, were his role models. According to biographers Wayne Errington and Peter van Onselen, Lyall and Mona "saw the Methodist Church as more a social than a theological institution."[13] Neither was a demonstrative person and Lyall (a garage proprietor by occupation) attended church "very infrequently".[14] Mona went more often, especially once her boys got older. After Lyall's death she went frequently with John.

It is revealing that, while Lyall Howard was notionally a Methodist[15], and Mona an Anglican, they were married in a Presbyterian church.[16] In their family home they did not require the saying of grace at meals[17], and matters theological and spiritual were not often discussed.[18] Nonetheless, both of them were buried from the Earlwood Methodist Church opposite their house in William Street[19] – the church at which their four sons had worshipped on Sundays while growing up.

According to members of the Earlwood congregation who remember them, "the Howard boys took up the back pew because the family's red setter dog insisted on coming".[20] John was the youngest of the brothers, and, it seems, the one who took church the most seriously. He participated with enthusiasm in inter-church cricket and soccer competitions on Saturday afternoons.[21] He developed "a wonderful Methodist hymn-singing voice".[22] He was also a regular prize-winner at Sunday school and chose to sit state-wide exams, in which he performed well. In the 1950s and 1960s Sunday school was a much bigger deal than it is now. Earlwood Methodist employed the services of dozens of staff to educate several hundred children.[23] As a teenager Howard taught Sunday school for a while at a church in Hurlstone Park; as a young adult, from 1961-63, he served as Secretary of the Earlwood Methodist Sunday school.[24]

Via this hotch-potch of influences he developed a Christian consciousness. Moreover, although he attended State schools – Earlwood Primary and Canterbury Boys High – they were not in those days as determinedly secular as they are today. The verities of hard work, frugality and respect for authority were drummed into Howard at school, and, even more vigorously, at home. "What you would generally call the Protestant work ethic* was very strong in our family," he recalled years later.[25]

---

* Howard has said elsewhere that "the idea of working and expecting some reward ... I regard as part of the Protestant work ethic: that work has its own reward". In fact, the original idea which emerged from the Reformation was rather different: that God may be worshipped through ordinary daily life, so that any form of work (remunerated or not) becomes a form of spiritual activity.

My overall impression is that the Howards were Old Testament rather than New Testament Christians. Their emphasis was upon diligence and righteousness, not joy or charity – let alone evangelism. It is noteworthy that the family did not care for the official magazine of the Methodist Church. It was never seen in their house, and the reason is obvious. This was the era of a champion of social justice, one of the most passionate and effective in Australia's history, the Rev Alan Walker (1911-2003).[26]

Under Walker's influence, the *Methodist* was pacifist in orientation. It ran progressive "crusades" on Aboriginal issues and Apartheid in South Africa. It was frequently disapproving of consumerism and big business.[27] To a degree, these messages were reflected in the Sunday school curriculum at Earlwood, but they were hammered home to young Methodists more forcefully at Crusader camps and youth festivals. John Howard rarely attended these events. According to his brother Bob, "our parents weren't into the Alan Walker aspect of Methodism at all – in fact, they were strongly against it."[28]

Howard's Christian faith is real, but it is limited. As the journalist and author Craig McGregor observed back in 1987, Howard "doesn't seem to be disturbed by any internal conflicts ... the distance between his interior and his exterior is nil".[29] There is little evidence his faith his evolved since 1987, or, indeed, since the early 1960s. There is also little evidence that he enjoys discussing it. In all my dealings with Howard he was impeccably polite, but his tone and body language betrayed a certain defensiveness.

During our interview I tried to approach the matter tangentially by reference to his friendship with US President George W. Bush:

JH: I go to Dallas quite a bit, because we have a son who lives there, and more often than not the four of us will have a meal together.

RW: Do you, for example, say grace at those meals?

JH: No, they are usually in a restaurant. George Bush is a practising churchgoer; he doesn't ram his religion down your throat.

RW: Do you ever talk Christianity?

JH: In very general terms. We're just not the type that ...

RW: I sense you aren't but I thought he might be.

JH: No, neither was Blair. You talk about the influence of religion and you talk about the role of the church and the impact of religious belief on particular issues but we never have personal exchanges about faith.

This sort of Christianity made Howard a comforting figure for Christians of like temperament (especially the affluent elderly), but a disappointing and even infuriating one for those with different priorities.

It is not sufficiently well-remembered – by the Left or the Right – that many of the Howard Government's more contentious policies were opposed by the mainline churches. A good deal of this opposition was voiced in a measured way by clerics of high stature, men who could not lightly be dismissed as "chardonnay socialists" or "moral relativists". Cardinal George Pell, Archbishop Peter Jensen and Bishop Tom Frame are names that spring to mind. Yet the record shows that Howard almost never changed tack as a result of rebuke by the churches.

He ignored the Christian Left, in particular the Uniting Church (the successor body to the Methodist Church of his childhood).[30] He had little time for prominent "progressive" clerics – Anglican Archbishop Peter Carnley, the Rev. Tim Costello and Father Frank Brennan, among others – and permitted Coalition colleagues to attack them. Alexander Downer's Sir Thomas Playford lecture of August 27, 2003 was a prime example. Howard was never so vehement, but sometimes he appeared to bristle at ecclesiastical criticism. His standard suggestion was that they focus upon "spiritual" or "moral" issues, not "political" ones.[31]

Of course, there is no clear, bright line. War is just as much a moral issue as, say, euthanasia or abortion. Likewise poverty and human rights. Since the early 19th century there has been a "venerable tradition" in Australia of churches speaking bluntly on all manner of subjects.[32]

Occasionally Howard tried to deflect Christian criticism away. But he rarely gave signs of having considered the arguments on their theological merits. It was more a case of taking sides: are you with us or against us?

In 2003 his government floated a proposal to disqualify from charitable status any body engaged in "attempting to change the law or government policy". It was a preposterous idea, opposed by the National Council of Churches in Australia, and not pursued.[33]

Once Howard proffered this advice:

> I know something about the composition of church congregations. There are a range of political views and you can offend. Particularly [when] some of the church leaders have been particularly critical of our side of politics, they end up offending a large number of their patrons.[34]

However well-meant, this was a mistaken view. Christians can disagree amongst themselves and at an interpersonal level it may often be desirable to "agree to disagree". Certainly debate must be respectful (see 1 Peter 3:15). But it is a positively good thing that, from time to time, every Christian's conscience is challenged. Christians are members of a church, drawn to what St Paul termed a "calling". They are not "patrons" (Howard's word) of a club or a business. Pope John Paul II did not become one of the great world leaders of the 20th century because he worried about giving "offence" on matters political.

That said, there is such a thing as tact. Howard expressed himself better during our interview, when he made this just and thoughtful observation:

> The struggle between belief and non-belief is so challenging in the modern world that I don't like to see church leaders gratuitously alienating people of good faith just because they disagree with their attitude on a particular issue.

In the remainder of this section I will look at four aspects of Howard's record in office. Two stand up well to Christian analysis; two do not.

First, schools policy. In 1998 the Howard Government instituted a major, if unheralded, reform, which has since facilitated the teaching of Christianity (and other religions) throughout the country. In his memoirs Howard declared himself "intensely proud" of this measure, and he has every right to be.[35]

The so-called New Schools policy was enacted with the support of Tasmania's independent (former Labor) Senator Brian Harradine – a staunch Catholic. The point of the initiative, the brainchild in or around 1995 of the-then Anglican Archbishop of Sydney, R.H. (Harry) Goodhew, was to make it easier for new independent schools to be started up in geographical areas already serviced by a state school and a Catholic parish school. Critically, these new schools would charge low or moderate fees. Protestant parents of modest means would have another viable option for their children's education. Since 1998 there has been a rapid increase throughout Australia in the number of such schools. They stay afloat because federal government assistance is available to them, irrespective of religious affiliation (or none).[36]

Labor speechwriter Graham Freudenberg has argued that Howard's education funding policies constituted, in effect, a revival of the State aid debate. In his view, "Howard, the erstwhile Methodist, resurrected the issue in order to create a new Liberal party constituency, exploiting the so-called 'faith-based' drive for political influence and public money."[37] It is true that the Howard Government pitched for the "religious" vote, but I do not believe its school funding policies were an attempt to exploit lingering sectarianism. Howard has never harboured anti-Catholic views. In the early 1960s, as a Young Liberal, his was a voice *against* sectarianism – at a time when the Coalition was still riven by it. He visited B.A. Santamaria on his deathbed in 1998.

Howard's social conservatism also attracted the ire of the secular left. But the complaints against him were largely misconceived. I believe he was true to his own conscience. His positions on these issues were all legitimately Christian – even if, in some cases, Christians themselves are far from unanimous in their views.

Within the limits of Commonwealth power, Howard stood against the legalisation of drugs, euthanasia and same-sex marriage.[38] He questioned the "right" of gay couples to adopt children or to receive IVF treatment.[39] He frowned upon abortion* and de facto relationships. He favoured

---

* At a public meeting of the Women's Electoral Lobby at Lane Cove Town Hall in 1974, Howard was asked for his views on abortion. "Not surprisingly," he recalled in his memoirs, "my rather conservative response caused an audible intake of breath from most of those in the audience". In 2006 Howard voted against RU-486. (See further the chapter on Julia Gillard.)

stricter censorship of pornography.[40] He instituted work for the dole. He was tough on violent crime in a *practical* way: the national gun laws of 1996 still stand as one of his finest achievements.

Howard has also expressed misgivings about the Family Law Act of 1975: "More than 30 years later," he wrote in his memoirs, "it is hard to dispute the fact that marriage has been weakened as the bedrock institution of our society."[41] His government left no-fault divorce untouched, but did introduce tax incentives for families with stay-at-home mothers[42] and enacted amendments to the Family Law Act bolstering the custody rights of fathers.

As to homosexuality, Howard once described himself as being a "liberal".[43] Yet he has also said that he would be "disappointed, even upset", if one of his children were gay.[44] (None of them are.) He never attended or supported the Sydney Gay and Lesbian Mardi Gras, so as not to "endorse" homosexuality.[45]

His critics maintained that he used his social conservatism as a kind of counterweight or bargaining chip, to try to appease "the battlers". He once said himself:

> People want a bit of constancy in their lives. If you've got a lot of rapid economic change, you want a bit of anchorage in ordinary life. The one, in a sense, reinforces and complements the other.[46]

But perhaps the opposite is true: rapid economic change undermines ordinary family life.[47] So does the 24/7 economy: working hours are unpredictable and constant pressure is applied to managers at all levels to maximise "shareholder return". For employees there is reduced job security. Sundays have long since ceased to be sacred.

In 1996 Howard may have created false expectations by promising a more "relaxed and comfortable" Australia. While politically astute, and not an unreasonable goal, it appears in retrospect to have been a cynical thing to have said. At no time did Howard reverse any of the Hawke-Keating economic reforms which, however desirable, had been a major cause of the battlers' unease. His inclination was to accelerate the pace of neo-liberal change, not slow it down. On issues such as taxation, privatisation of basic services, and industrial relations, some of Howard's positions as

Prime Minister failed the test of simple fairness. (It may be noted here that Tony Abbott and Kevin Andrews – the staunchest Catholics in Howard's Cabinet – opposed WorkChoices behind the scenes.)

I put to Howard the view of many Christians that economic justice and social conservatism should go hand in hand. He said:

> It's the argument of a lot of Christians but it's not in my opinion a Christian argument because the Christian argument can equally be that the economic order that produces the maximum economic benefit for the whole community is one that takes pressure off family life and creates greater wellbeing and greater order and greater opportunity for families. … I can understand why people on the left and socialists would invoke the Bible in defence but I [have] always quoted the parable of the talents as [supportive of] the free market.

That is a tenable point of view. I will leave it there and focus on the two aspects of Howard's record which are, in my opinion, the hardest to defend – that is to say, on any coherent *Christian* basis. Electoral and other worldly considerations are a different matter.

One was the invasion of Iraq in March 2003. To many it appeared unwise from the start even on legal, military and geo-political grounds. Ultimately it proved calamitous: hundreds of thousands dead, infrastructure ruined, Islamic terrorism and sectarian violence exacerbated, trust in America undermined, trillions of dollars wasted. It soon transpired that Saddam Hussein's (secular) regime did not possess *any* weapons of mass destruction (let alone an imminent nuclear weapons "capability"), the stated pretext for the invasion. Yet those who raised sensible questions in 2002-03 were at best ignored, and at worse traduced, by the government and its supporters.

Many qualified commentators have covered this territory – my point here is a different one. Simply put, Christians should not *start* wars. In the Sermon on the Mount, Jesus said: "Blessed are the peacemakers, for they will be called Sons of God" (Matthew 5:9). On any fair interpretation, that pronouncement requires every country, every leader, every soldier and every citizen to strive to avoid war if there is any tolerable alternative.[48] There were plenty of alternatives worth trying in March 2003 – and hundreds of millions of people were urging them upon the West.

Howard insists that he waged war in good conscience. He accepted the Bush administration's assurances about WMD, and took into account the possibility that a cornered and desperate Saddam might use them. His diary entry on February 19, 2003 read as follows:

> Anyone who thinks that I'm a warmonger should understand how I feel. I think about it all the time, have broken sleep and hope that a late capitulation (very unlikely) or assassination of Saddam [Hussein] will remove the need for military action.[49]

It seems to me that Howard was not thinking as a Christian. He was thinking as a politician, forced to juggle the competing pressures of the American alliance, his rapport with Bush, party politics, military and intelligence advice, and domestic opinion. Thinking along similar lines, if at all, were his fellow Christians in the Liberal Party. According to Howard there was no Christian dissent within caucus: "No, I don't recall any," he told me, "*none whatsoever.*" The only two Liberals who expressed reservations to him did not mention Christianity.

This is in equal parts surprising and disturbing. Put to one side what we now know as regards the mendacity and incompetence of the Bush-Cheney administration.[50] Across the West, most mainline church bodies opposed the invasion before it was launched.[51] Both Pope John Paul II and the Archbishop of Canterbury voiced strong opposition. So did the Catholic Bishops Conferences of the United States and Australia. On February 21, 2003, the executive committee of the World Council of Churches declared that "war against Iraq would be immoral, unwise, and in breach of the principles of the United Nations Charter."[52] In Australia, very few mainline church bodies were in favour. Some individuals hedged their bets: Cardinal Pell and Archbishop Jensen were equivocal. Nevertheless, shortly after hostilities began, Jensen said that he "remained unpersuaded".[53] Pell waited longer to clarify his position, but later insisted that "I never publicly endorsed the Iraq war".[54]

Howard is an Anglican. The only prominent Anglican in Australia who publicly endorsed the invasion of Iraq was Bishop Tom Frame, then senior Anglican Chaplain to the Australian Defence Force. Frame justified his stance on Christian principles of just war, and Howard was quick to praise his analysis as "very thoughtful".[55]

Fifteen months later, Frame recanted and apologised. He made a formal announcement on Palm Sunday 2004[56] and later published an article in the *Melbourne Anglican* entitled "Forgive me, I was wrong on Iraq". The article, which should be read in full, concluded as follows:

> On March 18 last year – two days before the war began – I addressed students in the united faculty of theology at the University of Melbourne. In reply to the question: "Is the proposed war against Iraq just, or just another war?" I said: "We are, as yet, unable to say with complete confidence. The final determination cannot be made until we are acquainted with the information now known by the Government, when we have seen the extent of the WMD that the 'coalition of the willing' alleges Iraq maintains, and when the full human cost of war has been calculated." I am now able to answer that question: it was just another war.
>
> Looking back on the events of the past 18 months I continue to seek God's forgiveness for my complicity in creating a world in which this sort of action was ever considered by anyone to be necessary. Even so, come Lord Jesus.

Howard's record on human rights was also subjected to strong criticism by the Australian churches.[57] As in the case of Iraq, many Christians here found common ground with the secular Left (Green voters and the progressive wing of the ALP). But these unlikely allies, even in combination, represented barely a quarter of the voting population. Ranged against them were most Coalition voters and a majority of Labor voters.

Countless words have been written about the issues in question: the rise of Pauline Hanson and her One Nation Party in the 1990s, the Hindmarsh Island Bridge affair ("secret women's business"), multiculturalism, the legislative response to the High Court's decision in the *Wik* case, the apology to the Stolen Generation, *Tampa*, "Children overboard", the sinking of the SIEV X, offshore processing of asylum-seekers, mandatory detention of asylum-seekers, and conditions in the detention centres. Most of the relevant facts are available on the public record.[58]

Let us take a closer look at the vexed question of asylum-seekers. It is instructive and illuminating for the light it casts upon Howard's Christianity and the attitudes of many Australians (Christian and non-Christian) to issues of race and nationality. At the outset, for the avoidance of doubt, I would make two key points.

First: the widespread use of the term "illegals", as a pejorative synonym for "asylum-seekers", is simply wrong. It is not illegal to *seek* asylum in Australia. The right to do so is entrenched in national and international law. Of course, an asylum claim may later be rejected. But even that does not render the initial request illegal, and most asylum claims heard in Australian courts succeed. These facts cannot be emphasised enough. When I discussed them with Howard he agreed to use the correct word, "asylum-seekers". Considering that he is a lawyer I did not think it a pedantic thing to insist upon.

My second overriding point is this. I believe Howard when he insists he acted at all times in good faith. He told me that, as regards the treatment of asylum-seekers generally, he remembered "having discussions with a couple of leading churchmen who in fairness to them I won't disclose". On November 8, 2001, just two days before the *Tampa*/"Children Overboard" election, he attended a church service at the Royal Military College, Duntroon. (He read the first lesson, from Ecclesiastes 3.)[59] Later that day, at the National Press Club, he said his conscience was clear: "I examine criticisms of my behaviour that have moral strictures contained in it like other strictures but I am satisfied within myself that what we are doing is in the national interest."[60]

Was all this window dressing? The Rev. Tim Costello, then Chairman of the Baptist Union of Australia, was one of several Christian spokespersons who appeared to think so. On November 7, 2001 he lamented that he did not "remember a time when there has been an election with such a clear moral issue but treated by the major parties with such clear amoral electioneering."[61]

Much as I admire the Rev. Costello, I think he was being too harsh *if* he was accusing Howard of acting in bad faith – pursuing a policy which he personally knew to be immoral in order to win votes. I broached the issue with Howard:

RW: There's no question that you had vast majority support.

JH: But a lot of Christians would say no, what you should say is we will take anybody who wants to come to this country.

RW: No, I don't think they'd say that, I think what they would say is that we should listen to the story of anybody that wants to come to this country and decide what the fair thing is in relation to ...

JH: The real problem with that, though, is that if you don't have a process for listening to and adjudicating on the story before they arrive, in reality you can't send them back.

RW: Because they're all genuine refugees?

JH: No, because it becomes impossible. Once someone has been here for a significant period of time, it becomes very difficult to send them back.

RW: That's because our legal system is a just one.

JH: I don't think any legal system can handle the volume of people who would come. The system is under enormous strain now.

RW: It will just mean that the system somewhere else will come under strain...

JH: I accept that, but if you are a political leader in this country your first responsibility is to maintain a sense of order and fairness within our society. One of the things that I noticed is that whenever we looked as though we were losing control of the borders, support for orthodox immigration fell.

RW: Did you really keep track of that, polling ...

JH: Yes, and after 2001 support for immigration began to rise again. I can understand the feeling of people ...

RW: Can you understand the bleeding heart Christian attitude to this?

JH: Well I never used that expression.

RW: No, I'm using it against myself.

JH: No, I understand it. I didn't agree with it, I mean I respectfully disagreed with it.

I put it to Howard that his own views had not always been so rigid. On August 18, 2001 – just 11 days before SAS troops boarded the *Tampa* – he gave an interview to Melbourne radio announcer Neil Mitchell. The context was a recent boat arrival at Christmas Island:

MITCHELL: What do you do now?

HOWARD: We are a humanitarian country. We don't turn people back into the sea, we don't turn unseaworthy boats which are likely to capsize and the people on them be drowned. We can't behave in that manner. People say well send them back from where they came, the country from which they came won't [will?] have them back. Many of them are frightened to go back to those countries and we are faced with this awful dilemma of on the one hand trying to behave like a humanitarian decent country, on the other hand making certain that we don't become just an easy touch for illegal immigrants.

MITCHELL: The strategies are not working are they?

HOWARD: Well when you say the strategies are not working what is the alternative? You see the only alternative strategy I hear is really the strategy of using our armed forces to stop the people coming and turning them back. *Now for a humanitarian country that really is not an option.*[62]

Howard admitted to me that he had changed his mind. I took a breath and said: "I suppose all I'd say is that, with the greatest respect, your first Christian instinct was correct." He replied evenly: "Well, you may say that. I don't accept what's implicit in that, that my subsequent conduct was unChristian … I tried to reach an accommodation between a proper Christian concern for the interests of people seeking to come here, but an equally Christian concern for the long-term interests and stability of the country that I was sworn to serve and protect."

I turned then to a discrete question – the treatment of asylum-seekers once they had reached Australia. Howard did not invent the mandatory detention system; it was instituted during the Hawke-Keating years. But Howard presided over a marked "toughening" of the system – notably the introduction of temporary protection visas in 1999, a measure first proposed by Pauline Hanson and initially denounced by the Coalition as "highly unconscionable".[63] For several years Howard also resisted impassioned pleas to release children from detention centres and to improve conditions at the centres to a level less dangerous to the inmates' physical and mental health.

In her confronting book *Blind Conscience* (2008), Margot O'Neill demonstrated beyond reasonable doubt that the primary reason Howard eventually made concessions on these matters (during his fourth and last term) was to prevent four dissenters within the federal parliamentary Liberal Party from going public. They threatened a private members' bill which would have attracted support from Labor, and, possibly, from other Coalition members hitherto afraid to break ranks. The dissenters were Petro Georgiou (the leader), Judi Moylan, Bruce Baird and Russell Broadbent.

Baird had been visiting detention centres since 2001 and he couched his position in explicitly Christian terms. "I couldn't believe what I saw. I couldn't believe the despair and the terrible conditions. I'm a practising Christian. This is where the rubber hits the road for me."[64] Broadbent, a marginal seat-holder in Victoria, was backed by the Catholic Church.[65]

Howard and I had this exchange:

JH: I agreed to a whole lot of changes.

RW: You did. But according to the account in this book ...

JH: I haven't read Margot.

RW: I realise you can't read everything. But the gist of it is this: that Georgiou, Bruce Baird, Judi Moylan, they dragged you kicking and screaming towards ...

JH: That is wrong. I spent hours and hours ...

[pause]

JH: Well, look, I had meetings with them and once again I don't remember her [Margot O'Neill] talking to me about this.

RW: She didn't.

JH: She did a lot of stories on this issue and they always from what I recollect were highly critical of the government. I spent hours and hours with this group; they weren't ignored and I agreed …

At that point I asked Howard to read an extract from O'Neill's book relating to one of his meetings with the Liberal dissidents, in June 2005:

'That's it,' Petro [Georgiou] says sharply, rising to leave. 'I'm introducing my bill tomorrow'.

'Let me be clear about this Petro,' John Howard replies just as sharply. 'If you do this, you will embarrass your government and you will embarrass your party.'

The intensity and directness of what comes next surprises even Petro's three colleagues.

'I'll tell you what's embarrassing, John,' says Petro. 'Three years ago you agreed to let out a three-month-old baby who'd been born in detention. She's now three years old and she's smashing her head against a wall inside Villawood. That's an embarrassment to the party, John. We've got patients I went to you about, who should have been released for treatment … That's what I call an embarrassment to the party. And we've got 140 people locked up for three years or more with no convictions and no evidence they pose a threat to anyone. Let me tell you John, *that's* an embarrassment! I'm introducing the bill tomorrow.'

John Howard tries to defuse the confrontation. 'Petro let's all back up here a bit.'[66]

Howard read this passage carefully and our discussion continued:

JH: He [Georgiou] could well have said that, I just don't recall it but, look, we did ameliorate the conditions and they were difficult, but then you have a lot of circumstances in society where if you have any kind of detention system it creates difficulties for people. And how many people in detention when I was defeated?

RW: On Nauru? Not many.

JH: Three.

RW: That was Nauru. But this was about [Australia] …

JH: I remember when they first raised the thing and I had a long discussion with Peter Shergold, who was the head of my department, and he spent a lot of time talking to me and we agreed to an easier system of detention and people say, well, he had to do that in order to avoid … well I didn't have to, a lot of people in my party thought I was too generous to them.

RW: Indeed, I read that, and they were ostracised by many. But what I'm trying to understand, Mr Howard, is why you or anyone else would be reluctant to grant those sorts of concessions to ameliorate the conditions for …

JH: I don't know that I was so reluctant to do so. I mean, I accepted that the process of detention inevitably resulted in some young children being in detention. I also accepted that if you took them away from their parents outside the detention centre that would be very harmful to them as well.

RW: Separating …

JH: Breaking up families. I mean, you've got to ask yourself the question, is it better to have a family intact in detention or to have a family split up with very young vulnerable children outside detention but away from their parents? If the answer to that is at all costs you've got to keep the family unit together, then the inevitable result is that the detention system is compromised. That's obviously one of the things I had to take into account. You may think that's very hard-hearted, but on the other hand when you've got the sort of position I had it's a judgment you've got to make. And given that I held the view that detention conditions in Australia, whilst unpleasant and anything but ideal, but not inhumane in the context in which most Australians understand it. And knowing something about the detention conditions that operated in Nauru compared with the detention conditions that operate in many refugee camps in south-east Asia, I was encouraged to the view that people were not being treated in an inhumane fashion.

What conclusions should be drawn from all this? That Howard and all who voted for him are racists? Of course not. Howard told me he was "taught [that] everyone is equal irrespective of the colour of their skin", and his sincerity was plain. But in the final days of the 2007 election campaign he made an interesting concession. The context was Indigenous policy, but I think the remark is relevant more broadly:

> There have been low points, when dialogue between me as Prime Minister and many Indigenous leaders dwindled almost to the point of non-existence. I accept my share of blame for that. The challenge I have faced around indigenous identity politics is in part an artefact of who I am and the time in which I grew up.[67]

What was he alluding to? I will try to describe it. It is a cast of thinking which has been prevalent in Australia since Federation and which was encouraged by both sides of politics until the early 1970s. It has been called "monoculturalism"[68] and goes something like this. We (white Australians) are a good people. We deserve what we have. We built a fine civilisation and most of us obeyed the rules. We do not say we are superior as human beings but our (Anglo-Celtic) culture is superior to other cultures. Our religion (Christianity) is superior to other religions (Islam, say, or Hinduism, or Aboriginal spirituality). Yet we have plenty of troubles of our own and we must attend to them.

These are the premises; and most of them are valid or at least defensible. Yet the conclusion that white Australians are wont to draw from those premises is inconsistent with the letter and the spirit of the New Testament. That is why Howard received so much criticism from the mainline churches.

Jesus spoke out boldly against tribalism and commanded us to help people in distress – regardless of where they come from. Consider the Parable of the Good Samaritan and His speech at the Last Supper about the Final Judgment. St Paul, too, said things directly in point. (See Ephesians 2:14, Galatians 3:28 and like passages.) In the early fourth century, in his *Divine Institutions*, the philosopher/theologian Lactantius gave voice to the *political* precept that "what is due to other people ... still equally relates to God, since humanity is the image of God".[69] What this means for Christians is that "the national interest" (an amorphous concept in any event) must never trump the dictates of the Gospels. We live in the age of the church.[70]

In 2008 Tony Abbott suggested that "detention in Nauru never sat very easily with refined consciences".[71] If Abbott was alluding to Christian colleagues within the Coalition, then I am bound to say that they masked their unease well. John Anderson, Howard's Deputy Prime Minister, and Peter Costello, his Treasurer, were two who had the opportunity after leaving politics to address these issues from a considered Biblical perspective. Both followed the party-political line.[72]

Of course, only a small minority of Australians are practising Christians. And even some of those who are practising Christians would disagree with their church leaders as to the dictates of the Gospels concerning issues of race and charity. The blunt fact is that most Australians (including most immigrants) are deeply suspicious of *all* asylum-seekers. They cannot picture themselves or their families in a like predicament. Like Howard himself, they lack "that special quality of imaginative empathy that would allow [them] to enter into the minds of souls of those whose experience is totally outside [their] own".[73]

Howard's instinct was never to challenge such people but to defend them to the hilt. "I don't find people behaving in an irrational, racist fashion," he said in November 2001. "Quite frankly, on their behalf, I resent the suggestion being made that anybody who supports the Government's policy is in some way supportive of racism."[74]

But in making comments such as these Howard set up a false choice. There were, and still are, plenty of shades of opinion between out-and-out racism and indifference to those in need. Howard once insisted that he sought to strike a balance between "the guilt merchants and the insensitive rednecks".[75] But an appropriate rhetorical balance was rarely if ever struck. He repeatedly declined to criticise – effectively or at all – people who were, patently, rednecks and bigots. Even after the Cronulla riots of December 2005 he chose to soft-pedal: "I do not accept that there is underlying racism in this country."[76] Perhaps some Jesus-style invective was called for. Or an appeal to the better angels of our nature.

At times Howard seemed much angrier at people who spoke against racism and xenophobia than at people who exhibited those attitudes. Does this matter? It should, I think, especially to those who care about the Liberal Party. The party of Howard and Tony Abbott draws its support from a rather different pool of voters than did the party of Menzies or Holt or Gorton or Fraser. Or even Billy McMahon. The cohort of affluent, well-educated Australians dubbed by political historian Judith Brett as "the moral middle class" – many of them Christians – were part of its core constituency until the early 1980s. Now they are derided as the "chattering classes". Many of them are former Methodists who now worship in the Uniting Church. Not a few of them, I would wager, sat the same Sunday school exams as John Howard.

KEVIN MICHAEL RUDD (B. 1957)

LABOR: 2007-10

In 2007 Kevin Rudd did for the ALP what Joe Lyons did in 1931 for the conservative side of politics: he brought into his party's fold hundreds of thousands of voters who had previously been estranged on religious grounds. In Lyons' case, the voters in question were middle-class Catholics. In Rudd's case they were lower-income Christians of all denominations – but especially Protestants.

The idea is scoffed at in secular left-wing circles, but, in my view, one of *the* key reasons for Labor's electoral decline since June 2010 has been the re-alienation of this important demographic, especially in Rudd's home state of Queensland. (John Harrison, a lecturer in the School of Journalism and Communications at the University of Queensland, has also proffered this theory: he refers to "the Bonhoeffer effect".[1]) It is hard to prove empirically; my judgment is based in no small measure on private discussions with Christians throughout Australia. But for three years – from late 2006 to late 2009 – Rudd was the most consistently popular politician in Australian history as measured in opinion polls. He enjoyed a personal approval rating in the 60s – or higher.[2] I have little doubt he got the extra 10 per cent or so from Protestant Christians normally suspicious of any Labor Prime Minister. Not all of them voted Labor, but they could live contentedly with Rudd. He is still immensely popular in the Australian community, if not in the federal Labor caucus or the Canberra press gallery.

A huge amount has been written about Rudd's faith. In terms of digesting information and opinion, he presented, for me, the second-biggest challenge after Deakin. For a start there are his own writings: those interested should begin with his October 2006 essay for *The Monthly*, "Faith in Politics", and a paper he presented at Parliament House in August 2006 to the National Forum on Australia's Christian Heritage, entitled "Christianity, the Australian Labor Party and Current Challenges in Australian Politics". Rudd also gave numerous television and radio interviews on religious topics. His biographers have delved into the territory, as have journalists of all shades of belief and political affiliation. Opinions vary widely, but too often they have seemed driven by political ideology rather than religious principles. Balanced, informed critiques have been rare, but there are examples to be found.[3]

Rudd was often derided as a God-botherer.[4] An anecdote from 1995 bears mention because it illustrates – at an early date – the distrust and dislike of him within certain Labor circles. In late August 1995 a Queensland Liberal Senator, Ian Macdonald, made mischievous mention of Rudd in federal Parliament. Macdonald's aim was not to criticise Rudd on religious grounds (it was before Rudd came to Canberra), but to highlight factional divisions within the Queensland ALP. He quoted an attack on Rudd in the newspaper *Keep Left*, in which Rudd was described as "an extreme right-wing fundamentalist Christian with no understanding of fundamental Labor principles."[5] Of course, both aspects of that charge were absurd.

For some time the right-wing commentariat seemed in a quandary about Rudd. But when he became Opposition Leader in late 2006, their attacks began. Partly from sincere conviction, partly because they realised the massive electoral threat he posed to the Coalition, several columnists denounced him as a "cafeteria Christian" – selective and shallow.[6] Admittedly, Rudd had levelled that charge himself against political opponents.

The position is further complicated by the fact that, since June 2010, Rudd's reputation has been sullied in public by many of his Labor colleagues. A majority in the Federal caucus would appear to prefer opposition or unemployment to serving under Rudd again. Stories of his bad temper, profane language and overweening pride have become legion. Not all of the stories can be baseless, but I would guess that the truth has been exaggerated for political purposes. Jealousy, laziness and thwarted ambition must also have played a part. So too Rudd's non-blokey manner. The visceral animosity of a few key people would appear to date back to the period 1988-95, when Rudd ran the office of Queensland Labor leader Wayne Goss.

Yet on every major count, Rudd has been defended by people who should command respect – colleagues, political opponents, journalists, speech-writers, staffers.[7] When I interviewed him in November 2012, at his office in Parliament House, he was friendly and forthcoming.

As Prime Minister Rudd was undoubtedly a workaholic who drove his colleagues hard. He had a nasty side, and made the mistake of surrounding himself with inexperienced "advisers". They were smart and idealistic young men, but their loyalties were exclusively to Rudd rather than the Government as a whole. They lacked gravitas, and, in some cases, good manners.

Policy-wise, Rudd blundered on climate change. He has since admitted this himself. First, in February 2010, he declined the chance to call a double dissolution election on Labor's proposed Emissions Trading Scheme, which had been twice rejected in the Senate. (Fecklessly, in my view, the Greens had refused to support it.) In April 2010, at the urging of Julia Gillard and Wayne Swan, he postponed the ETS indefinitely – it was put over for further discussion in 2013.[8]

Climate change had been one of Rudd's trump cards and his record to that point entirely honourable. Despite the disappointing outcome of the Copenhagen Summit in December 2009, no political leader in the world was better-placed than Rudd to continue to make the *Christian* case for action. "The earth is the Lord's, and everything in it" (Psalm 24:1)[9]. Rudd's backdowns were made at the first signs of political trouble. To be sure, they were inconsequential in the overall scheme of the problem; indeed, it may well be that the problem – though real – is politically and scientifically insoluble. (That is my personal view: mankind is just too lazy and selfish to act upon it seriously, and, accordingly, our fate is in God's hands.) Be that as it may, Rudd looked gutless. He undermined his own hard-won credibility.

Courage is a treasured Christian virtue. Rudd himself had said so publicly, in 2006, during an interview at a Scripture Union fundraising dinner with Pastor Matt Prater of New Hope Church in Brisbane. (A transcript was published in May 2009 in the Salvation Army's magazine, *War Cry*.) "It's written in Scripture*," Rudd had then observed, "that God did not give us a spirit of fear, but of love, power and self-discipline". He had even made this bold claim: "On a personal level, as well as the social one and the national one, I spend most of my life choosing to do this".[10]

My most significant reservation about Rudd prior to November 2007 related to the Iraq War. The events of 2002-03 – which I have addressed in some detail in the section on John Howard – had been a test of his commitment to Christian principles.

It seemed to me that, as Shadow Foreign Minister, he tripped a very fine line. As Howard often points out, Rudd said in an address to the State Zionist Council of Victoria on October 15, 2002 that it was "an empirical fact" that Saddam Hussein possessed weapons of mass destruction.[11] No doubt Rudd believed this to be true: like Howard, his sin was sedulous gullibility rather than deliberate deceitfulness. And, unlike Howard, Rudd still had doubts about the strategic wisdom of invasion. He never denounced sceptics as "weak" or "appeasers", as the Coalition did. Nor did he indulge in crude rhetoric about "Islamic fundamentalism".

But, equally, the prospect of war *per se* did not seem greatly to faze him. Whereas millions of Australian citizens were appalled by the very notion of pre-emptive (that is, aggressive) war, Rudd left all options open. He hoped for a United Nations Security Council resolution (none was forthcoming), or a diplomatic deal which would not displease the Bush administration.[12]

In the end, it was Opposition Leader Simon Crean who decided that Labor would formally oppose Australian involvement. But Crean's public explanations were convoluted. Ironically enough, it was future Opposition Leader Mark Latham – outspoken agnostic and Rudd-hater – who got it absolutely right on the WMD issue. Writing in his private diary on February 3, 2003, Latham referred to the excessive confidence of the likes of Rudd as to the existence of WMD. "But where is the hard evidence, other than the assertion of the foreign policy establishment?" [13]

---

*   2 Timothy 1:7. In the NIV translation, Paul's admonition is against "timidity".

But all this was history by November 2007. Rudd had long since become a fierce critic of the Iraq occupation. He had defeated John Howard at the polls. Here, it seemed, was a bright, educated, moderate, hard-working Christian* man. He leaned to the left on economic issues and to the right on social issues. He tried to stand apart from Labor's corrupt faction system. He was a bilingual internationalist, pro-American but not aligned to the religious Right or the neo-conservatives. He was steeped in Christian theology, but rejected the view that "the only relevance of Christianity is an individualised salvation experience".[14] He had nominated Dietrich Bonhoeffer – the great Lutheran pastor executed in 1945 for resisting the Nazis – as "the man I admire most in the history of the 20th century" [15]

Rudd's term as Prime Minister ended in tears. But his achievements were considerable and – the ETS aside – he was mostly true to his principles. Having scoured the record and sized the man up in person, I would reject out of hand any suggestion that his faith is contrived. I may not fully understand his determined ecumenism – as we shall see, he refuses to identify with any denomination – but in the essentials his theology is orthodox.

He attends church weekly and has done so for most of his life. In his home town of Brisbane he has worshipped for many years at St John the Baptist Anglican church in Bulimba. In Canberra he usually goes to St John the Baptist's in Reid. During his diplomatic postings in Sweden (1981-84) and China (1984-87) he took the trouble to involve himself actively in local congregations. (In China, he was a lay preacher.) As a backbencher and Shadow Minister (from 1998-2006), he was a mainstay of the cross-party Christian fellowship group which met on Monday nights at Parliament House.[16] The group's convenor, Jock Cameron, holds Rudd in high regard.

Rudd's knowledge of Christian doctrine and history is extensive, and his everyday speech is littered with religious phraseology.[17] When I spoke with

---

* In an interview in February 2003 with *The Australian Financial Review*, Rudd described himself as an "old-fashioned Christian socialist". The use of the bogey-word "socialist" may have been unwise; the term "*Christian* socialist" needed to be understood in historical context and in the light of Rudd's admiration for Andrew Fisher and the Scottish Labour leader Keir Hardie. At all events, the comment pleased me. One knew where Rudd's sympathies lay.

him, he told me he had just embarked on a project to study Luke's Gospel in its original Greek, so as better to understand the nuances of the Third Evangelist's message. I take him at his word that he exults in Mozart's Requiem at Easter; that his favourite novel is Dostoevsky's *The Brothers Karamazov*; and that his favourite painters are the Pre-Raphaelites, because their work is imbued with Christian overtones.[18]

When I met Rudd, my primary aim was to explore his theology. Was it Catholic or Protestant? Sophisticated or shallow? Without appearing too zealous I wanted him to explain the foundations upon which it is based. We had this exchange:

> **RW:** I'm sorry if I'm labouring the absolute obvious here, but you believe in the Resurrection as an actual supernatural event?

> **KR:** Yes. And the reason for believing ...

> **RW:** Yes. It sounds like an obvious question, but go on.

> **KR:** No, if you're dealing with Anglicans it's a perfectly valid question. The Bishop of Durham was never quite sure of that one. Remember those debates? Remember *Yes Minister*? My god, we can't have an Archbishop of Canterbury who believes in God; that would be rather radical.

> **RW:** Have you read N.T. Wright's book about ...

> **KR:** Yes, I've got all three volumes of Wright.* The Resurrection tome is a very good tome. But no, my view about that is in part my own personal experience of a living God and part the mind of an historian which is, whatever you say

---

* N.T. (Tom) Wright (b. 1948) is an Anglican bishop. In my opinion he is one of the world's best living New Testament scholars – indeed, one of the best ever. The "three volumes" to which Rudd referred constitute Wright's magnum opus: *The New Testament and the People of God: Christian Origins and the Question of God* (1992) (vol 1); *Jesus and the Victory of God: Christian Origins and the Question of God* (1996) (vol 2); and *The Resurrection of the Son of God: Christian Origins and the Question of God* (2003) (vol 3). Anyone with a serious interest in Christianity – especially educated sophisticates trapped in the mindset that the New Testament is fiction – should read Wright.

about this minor sect of Judaism as it was then, something explosive happened then demonstrably by virtue of it uniquely becoming a wildfire across the known world within, really, a generation. And it is difficult to conclude that all that was simply based on a flight of fancy.

RW: Or a hopeful myth created *ex post facto*.

KR: That's true, and quite apart from the record of post-resurrection appearances and the multiple accounts in the synoptic gospels and elsewhere. I'm a keen student of Luke and I read Luke a lot because of the co-authorship of the Gospel and the Acts, and what I like in particular about Luke is that if he is a non-Jewish author, which is possible …

RW: Probable.

KR: … yes, and his Greek is certainly better than everyone else's who was in the New Testament, it's certainly much more classical than Paul's Greek, and if you look at the first four verses of the first chapter of Luke, what you find is him using the expression that *many accounts have been written but because I have been following these events from the beginning and because I have dealt with many of the eyewitnesses, and because the time has come to lay down a systematic and orderly account of these things.* And he uses a quite defined Greek term to [say] that but it's not even a matter of synoptics; it's almost a term of contemporary Latin and Greek historiography. But it's actually a good text for historians to read …

RW: And lawyers. I agree with you. That is one of the two reasons I came to faith myself, by reading the Gospels and Acts. It's like when a lawyer sits down to take a statement from witnesses … you always get slightly different versions from everyone, even if they're telling the truth.

KR: But that's natural.

RW: That's natural. In fact it would be more suspicious if it wasn't.

KR: If it's perfectly synchronised it sounds like [the Soviet newspaper] *Pravda*. If it's not synchronised it's probably much closer to the truth because everyone sees a reality through a different prism.

RW: When was your first proper reading of Luke and Acts?

KR: I couldn't answer that question. I think when I started reading the New Testament as a believer I was attracted to the kingdom Gospel of Matthew, then in time to the simple Gospel of Mark as it's the earliest of the gospel texts and the earliest of the New Testament texts* and it's more common, as you know, to the other synoptics as was found with either Matthew or Luke. Luke I came to later, I think, maybe because of deeply entrenched views that because Luke was often the preferred gospel of Roman Catholics, because of the emphasis on the Virgin Mary, that I wanted to read more broadly than my upbringing had been. But as an historian myself I have just been brought back to Luke. So it may not be the oldest gospel, but if you look at its systemology …

RW: It appeals to you on a sort of rational, historical, logical basis.

KR: Very much so. And I think it is entirely fallacious for people in the 21st century to assume that someone in the 1st century who is educated in Greek, and presumably Latin – we don't know if he read Latin – but given the quality of his Greek he probably did.

---

* This is questionable. A few scholars date Mark's Gospel to the mid-40s AD, but that is very much a minority view. On the balance of probabilities, the earliest New Testament texts were the letter of James and Paul's first letter to the Thessalonians. Mark's is probably the earliest gospel though a case can be made for Matthew's.

RW: He was excellent at geography as well.

KR: Yes, you are correct. But it's arrogant of us to assume that this guy is simply going to be some 1st century supernaturalist. Remember the prevailing Greco-Roman order was not necessarily a deist or even a theist order. The orthodoxy is some form of pantheism: Greek or Roman. But the entire philosophic traditions which existed at the time: Platonic, Aristotelian and the rest, these were not necessarily given to basic religious belief about a whole bunch of other things.

RW: No, indeed. And even basic notions that we now take for granted like humility being a virtue. There's a great book by John Dickson, who's an Australian Christian author, about this subject. The very notion of humility being the greatest virtue is a result of Christianity. In the Classical world it was sort of seen as a sign of weakness.

KR: Certainly in the Classical Western world that's true. I'm a little more sceptical of its uniqueness vis-à-vis, say, Confucianism. Confucius wrote five centuries before the Gospels. Certainly in Confucianism there is an emphasis on self-effacing behaviour. But I think in the classical Western tradition you're right. The whole Jesus revolution in many respects is about the radical proposition of putting others first and yourself last. Not making yourself public but having yourself as a private human being who acts correctly but, like with the widow's mite, is not wishing to be seen with a great flourish of grandeur and glory. And this is entirely revolutionary within the Western tradition as it evolved until then.

How did a man like Rudd become the leader of the ALP in the 21st century? Let me sketch his story and, along the way, flesh out something more of his religious life – in theory and practice.

Kevin Rudd was born on September 21, 1957, in Eumundi, a small town in Queensland about 20 kilometres south-west of Noosa in the

Sunshine Coast hinterland. In the 1950s and 1960s, the dairy industry was one of the main sources of income in the district. Kevin's father, Albert (Bert) Rudd, had served in the Middle East and Borneo in World War II.[19] He seems to have been a phlegmatic sort of character. Whenever he was asked, "How are you, Bert?" his invariable response was, "I've been battling".[20] He eked out a modest living as a sharefarmer on 400 acres (about 160 hectares) of land owned by a prosperous local businessman. There were five mouths to feed aside from Bert's own: those of his wife Marge (née De Vere), youngest son Kevin, and three other children (Malcolm, Loree* and Greg).

Bert and Marge had a "mixed" marriage. Marge was a strict Catholic – righteous, teetotal and thrifty, but not sectarian. Her favourite book was *The Robe*, by Lloyd C. Douglas[21], a popular 1940s novel about the Crucifixion and its aftermath told through Roman eyes. She voted without fail for the DLP. Many years later, Rudd described his mother's worldview as "old-style Queensland Catholic Country Women's Association".[22] Need more be said?

Bert Rudd was of Protestant stock. Although much less religiously observant than his wife, he did not convert to Catholicism. Indeed, "he wanted no part of it".[23] He was a member of the local Masonic Lodge and a conservative politically, maintaining inactive membership of the Country Party.[24] When I asked Rudd about his father's faith, his answer was this:

> He died before I was really able to have anything approaching adult conversation with him so I really don't know. What I do know is that as he was dying in hospital he had a quite deep spiritual experience and was supported in that by a hospital chaplain. And so what his lifelong beliefs were, the extent to which he reflected those beliefs in the way he lived, I couldn't really comment; I was too much of a kid.

---

* In the late 1960s Loree Rudd was briefly a novice at a Sisters of Mercy convent. In December 2011 she resigned from the ALP when delegates to the National Conference voted to allow MPs a conscience vote on same sex marriage. "Gay marriage is not good for the community," she said. "Homosexuals should be loved and treated right and they should not be discriminated against. But to make that huge leap from their rights to breaking a commandment of Moses, to say homosexuals' relationships are marriage, is utter nonsense."

It was Marge's way which prevailed in the Rudd home. She and Bert were married in a Catholic Church (St Joseph's at Nambour[25]), and their children raised as Catholics. Indeed, the children were instilled with "a deep sense of the importance of faith".[26] They attended mass with their mother every Sunday at St Ita's church in Eumundi. Rudd described to me "a tiny wooden country Catholic church – you've seen a thousand of them in Australia – and … all four of us sitting in line next to Mother in descending order". There was also catechism every second Saturday. On Sunday nights they said the rosary.[27]

Everything changed for the Rudd family on the night of December 14, 1968. Driving home from a social event in Brisbane's Fortitude Valley, 100 kilometres to Eumundi's south, Bert crashed his car into a telegraph pole at about 2am. He had fallen asleep at the wheel and was not wearing a seatbelt. He suffered severe injuries to his pancreas, liver and stomach.[28]

In later life, Kevin Rudd would suggest that his father received "ropy" medical treatment. That was the impression he carried away as a boy. The Coroner's report is inconclusive on that score, but it must be a possibility that, with the best and most expensive doctors, Bert could have survived. His initial prognosis was good but his condition steadily deteriorated because infection set in. Eight weeks later he died of peritonitis at Royal Brisbane Hospital.[29]

Not long afterwards, the surviving Rudds were forced to vacate their Eumundi home. The small house on the farm had come with Bert's job, and, since Bert was dead, the owner had no legal obligation to allow the family to stay. The exact circumstances of their leaving the house are disputed[30], but as to one thing there can be no question whatever. For Kevin Rudd, a sensitive boy of 11, this whole sequence of events was a calamitous, scarifying experience.

Bert had left little money and his modest life insurance was slow in coming. Initially Marge Rudd had no choice but to accept Christian charity from her family and a few neighbours in Eumundi. But there were limits to any such arrangements: Marge soon accepted that she would have to earn a dignified living to support herself and her children. She had trained as a nurse during World War II and decided to resume that vocation, obtaining a temporary post in a nursing home at Scarborough. Then, for two years, she re-trained at the Mater Hospital in Brisbane. Eventually, in mid-1971, she found a job at the Selangor Private Hospital in Nambour and the family moved into a fibro cottage close by.[31]

Unquestionably, during this period, Marge Rudd's robust, practical faith served her well. This made a huge impression on her younger son. Later in life, he recalled his mother as "exceptionally stoic".[32]

In the meantime Kevin needed to get on with his education. For Marge this was critical – Kevin was an intelligent, knowledge-thirsty boy. In mid-1969, in deference to Marge's financial predicament – and her devout Catholicism – the powers-that-be at Marist College Ashgrove (in Brisbane) agreed to waive their fees and to accept Kevin as a boarder.[33]

To put it mildly, Kevin did not enjoy his two years with the Brothers. He once admitted that he preferred not to remember those days. "It's not that the school was in any sense a bad school," he told me. "I was just an unhappy kid. It's quite a different thing. I'd grown up on 400 acres with a horse, with a mum and a dad, a small country school where I was pretty happy as a kid. Then your life gets turned on its head. And so because my father had died I felt quite lonely, vulnerable – I was 11 years old – and then suddenly you're thrown into this whole world you know nothing about."

That world encompassed compulsory attendance at mass three mornings a week and regular prayers in the classroom.[34] The school's emphasis was on sport – its motto was *viriliter age* (act manfully)[35] – and for an academic boy such as Rudd the atmosphere must have been uncongenial. He told journalist Julia Baird in 2006 that "it was tough, harsh, unforgiving, institutional Catholicism of the old school".[36]

The family's move to Nambour in mid-1971 was another turning point in Rudd's life. Nambour was a proud, upright town. According to social historian Professor Michael Wesley, it was run by "sober men with stubborn jaws". Many were scions of the Methodist Church. In keeping with that creed's emphasis on hard work and civic virtue, tempered by private charity and social justice, Nambour was a place of contrasts. It boasted good schools and other public facilities, but was "stifled by its proprieties, snobbishness and low horizons".[37] Biographer Robert Macklin called it "the very buckle of the provincial Queensland Bible belt".[38]

Marge Rudd was a tough cookie. She expected a lot of her children.

One's God-given talents ought not to be wasted, and one's duties ought not to be shirked, she believed. To do so was sinful. Her favourite Biblical passage was from Christ's exhortation to the Disciples at the Last Supper:

> Every branch in me that beareth not fruit he taketh away: and every branch that beareth fruit, he purgeth it, that it may bring forth more fruit. … I am the vine, ye are the branches: He that abideth in me, and I in him, the same bringeth forth much fruit: for without me ye can do nothing. If a man abide not in me, he is cast forth as a branch, and is withered; and men gather them, and cast them into the fire, and they are burned. (John 15:2, 5-6 (KJV).)

Marge Rudd understood the critical importance of education. The Marist Brothers experiment had failed. In Nambour, Kevin was sent to the State high school, and, immediately, his scholastic performance improved. And it kept improving, exponentially. Moreover, his behaviour was impeccable – "he was," reminisced a fellow student, "the one with the halo".[39] By 1974, his final year, Kevin Rudd was the school's star student. He had pushed himself extremely hard and it had brought forth much fruit. He was dux of his year, and, much more significantly, he had acquired a ferocious appetite for higher learning and worldly success.[40]

On the other hand, Nambour High had killed his faith – ostensibly, at least. Journalist David Marr has suggested that, by 1974, Rudd was "a swaggering atheist".[41] I put this to Rudd; he smiled and said that he was "something close … an agnostic". Certainly he had rejected notions of Papal infallibility, priestly authority and other formal strictures of Catholicism[42], but, in all the circumstances of his life to that point, this was scarcely surprising. Indeed, it was almost certainly a blessing in disguise, God's grace in action. Unlike most Catholic (or Protestant) teenagers who abandon their slender childhood faith, and never return to Christianity at all, Rudd soon rethought his entire theological position.

He took a gap year in 1975 and knocked around doing various odd jobs, at first in Brisbane and later in Sydney. While in Sydney, he lodged for a time with the Freckleton family at their home in Bayview Avenue, Earlwood. Frank Freckleton, the head of the household, was an elder in the Church of Christ who "took his responsibilities seriously". Rudd attended services with Freckleton's congregation in Earlwood and at other Protestant churches in Sydney, including Wesley Mission and Scots Church in the city.[43] Although he did not formally renounce his childhood Catholicism – indeed, he never has – Rudd came to the belief that "denominationalism" was much less important to him than the basics of the Gospels.

He told Robert Macklin in 2007:

> I think there's only one essential question and that is, "Based the evidence that you're presented, do you believe or not in the existence of God?"
>
> I reached the decision [in late 1975] after a year's worth of reflection. The proofs available to me were no more remarkable than [those that] were available to people who have reflected on these things over the centuries; no more persuasive or unpersuasive depending on who is reflecting upon them. But that's the conclusion I reached and it's the conclusion that I've subsequently been comfortable with; but I've not, frankly, been all that engaged with matters denominational.[44]

By late 1975 Rudd had chosen a broadly ecumenical path. He was bound for the Australian National University in 1976, and he chose not to apply to the (then) male-only Catholic college on campus, John XXIII. Instead he obtained a place at the Protestant co-ed college, Burgmann. On his application form for Burgmann, he described his religion as, simply, "Christian".[45]

At ANU, Rudd was uninvolved in campus politics: they were of no interest to him. Mostly he concentrated on his coursework, and, in 1979, he graduated with a First Class Honours degree in Asian Studies.[46] His extra-curricular activities were based around the Student Christian Movement. He was known at Burgmann as a wowser – "the opposite of bohemian"[47] – and belonged to a group of Evangelicals called the Navigators.[48] It was at Burgmann College that he first read the works of Dietrich Bonhoeffer, starting with *Letters and Papers from Prison*.[49]

It was also at Burgmann – on the first day of Orientation Week 1976 – that he met Therese Rein, his future wife. Therese was from a well-to-do Melbourne family. She grew up in Beaumaris, on Port Phillip Bay, and attended Firbank Church of England Girls Grammar School where she excelled in most things she did.[50] There was instant mutual attraction. What Therese and Kevin Rudd had in common was a broad and idealistic interest in current affairs, determined ambition, and, above all, their Christian faith. They "fought like Kilkenny cats for the [first] year or two … in debates and discussions on the meaning of life and all the rest of it".[51] She was as earnest as he. At Firbank, Therese had nominated religious instruction as one of her outside interests.[52] At Burgmann she was asked by the Master of the college to establish "a series of solid Bible Studies on Christianity and Sexuality".[53]

Therese held similar views to Kevin on matters denominational. She too had been raised in a "mixed" household, but a tolerant one. She told Robert Macklin that her mother "thought of Anglicanism and Catholicism and Methodism or whatever as basically Christian, as did my father, so she was prepared to get married in a Catholic church". But the priests objected – explaining that her mother would have to be rebaptised and reconfirmed – and her father "was really deeply offended". They married in an Anglican church.[54]

Kevin and Therese were married on November 14, 1981 at the beautiful St John the Baptist Anglican church, in the Canberra suburb of Reid.[55] It was Therese's church rather than Kevin's; he had been worshipping at the Uniting Church in O'Connor. In opting for St John's for his wedding – and the Anglican Church thereafter – Rudd took the view that "families that pray together, stay together".[56]And the Rudd family *has* stayed together. Kevin and Therese both built stellar careers while raising three children: Jessica (born 1984), Nicholas (1986) and Marcus (1993). As far as I can ascertain, not even Rudd's worst enemies have questioned the loving stability of his family life, or accused him of anything sexually untoward.*

---

* There were revelations in August 2007 about Rudd's visit to a strip club in New York one night in 2003. He was drunk in the company of another Labor MP, Warren Snowden, and a journalist, Col Allan – and could remember little or nothing about the night. In the event the story did him no electoral harm. But it is noteworthy that Rudd feared in 2007 that the story might well do him great harm. The night before it broke, Rudd warned Julia Gillard in a deadly serious tone that "there's something we have to deal with in tomorrow's newspapers – it's a big problem for us". When told the details, Gillard burst out laughing. "Of all things, of all people!" she thought to herself. But she was judging things by the relaxed standards of the general community. Rudd, to his credit, was judging himself by Christian standards.

I will skip over the details of Rudd's time as a diplomat (1981-87), other than to remark that he finished it a convinced internationalist. Later he would write that this worldview gelled with his personal understanding of Christianity. I agree: God is no respecter of persons – or of countries. Dietrich Bonhoeffer, in Rudd's estimation, was "never a nationalist, always an internationalist".[57]

How, then, does Rudd's record as Prime Minister hold up – judged from a Christian perspective?

I have mentioned his key electoral achievement: making Labor respectable in the eyes of many more Christian voters. He did this concertedly from early 2005, when, in David Marr's phrase, he became "Labor's shadow minister for Christ".[58] And he did not let up when Labor was elected in November 2007. While some in positions of influence carped and sniped, many anonymous citizens were interested and impressed.

Take Rudd's interview with Matt Prater, mentioned earlier. Here was the Prime Minister of Australia talking openly about his book of daily devotional prayers (My Utmost for His Highest, by a Scottish evangelist named Oswald Chambers, who ministered to the Anzacs at Gallipoli as a YMCA chaplain). He also spoke of the value of church attendance:

> It's a very simple question of what is important and what's not, what's transient and what's eternal, what is meaningful and, in fact, what is of no meaning at all.[59]

These were fine words, I can hear some Christians muttering – but what did Rudd actually do? For a start, I would point to his continuation of the policies of the Howard Government for the funding of low-fee independent schools. He also retained Howard's National School Chaplaincy programme.[60] Correctly – for Australia enjoys freedom *of* religion, not freedom *from* religion – Rudd rejected suggestions that the programme violated the non-establishment clause in section 116 of the Constitution, or, more broadly, the principle of the separation of church and state.

On social issues, Rudd was usually but not always conservative. In Opposition he had voted against euthanasia and the cloning of human embryos.[61] But he voted reluctantly for stem cell research, and – less understandably from a Christian perspective – the "morning after" abortion drug RU-486. As Prime Minister he continued those stances, while taking a conservative position within the ALP on the issue of funding abortion services as part of foreign aid programmes [62]; he also maintained his opposition to same-sex marriage.[63] He favoured mandatory "filtering" of the internet for pornography.

I can now hear a different sort of Christian muttering – but what about public policy more broadly? I have mentioned climate change. What else?

There can be little doubt that the Rudd Government's most important achievement was to steer Australia through the Global Financial Crisis. Of course, it was helped by the solid state of the economy bequeathed to it by the Howard-Costello Government (which in turn owed a lot to the Hawke-Keating governments). Even so, there were critical decisions to be made when the crisis hit in September 2008. By most expert accounts Rudd made them boldly and correctly – after wide consultation, it is true, but in the face of vocal opposition from the Coalition.[64]

I am not an economist, but the results would seem to speak for themselves. Australia has emerged from the GFC in far better shape than most other OECD countries. Much human misery was averted. From a Christian perspective, the most important thing is that Rudd erred – if at all – on the side of *generosity*. He was accused of being profligate. But one is reminded of Franklin Roosevelt's wise words in 1936, uttered during the Great Depression, which I quoted in the Introduction:

> Governments can err, Presidents do make mistakes, but the immortal Dante tells us that divine justice weighs the sins of the cold-blooded and the sins of the warm-hearted in different scales. Better the occasional faults of a Government that lives in a spirit of charity than the consistent omissions of a Government frozen in the ice of its own indifference.

Rudd was not going to preside over mass unemployment, corporate collapses and/or runs on the banks, if there was anything he could possibly do about it. There would be no repeat of the nightmare endured by James Scullin in 1929-31.

What riled some on the political Right even more than Rudd's successful handling of the GFC was his analysis of its root causes. In an essay published in the February 2009 edition of *The Monthly*, he delivered a blistering attack on the West's "neo-liberal" economic policies over the previous 30 years. He denounced, among other things, excessive deregulation of the private sector (especially the financial sector), rising inequality, and corporate and individual greed.

Argument as to the root causes of the GFC continues. The issues are complex. But, on any fair-minded view, Rudd made some valid points. In broad sentiment his case was similar to that made by Pope Benedict XVI in the papal encyclical *Caritas in Veritae* (2009). It might also be pointed out that Rudd was not a Johnny-come-lately to this debate. In his maiden speech to the House of Representatives, on November 11, 1998, he quoted these prescient words:

> Given the bigger role for economic contagion, more and more people are asking whether the international financial system as it has operated for most of the 1990s is basically unstable... By now, I think the majority of observers have come to the conclusion that it is, and that sudden changes have to be made.[65]

Beyond responding to the GFC, Rudd's economic policies were in the tradition of all Australian Labor Prime Ministers. He abolished WorkChoices and increased the aged pension. He raised spending on education, health and other social services. He tried to do something about homelessness. He proposed a mining super profits tax.

More so than most of his predecessors, Rudd emphasised the *Christian* social justice angle. In his seminal essay of October 2006, "Faith in Politics", he had written that "Christianity must always take the side of the marginalised and the vulnerable and the oppressed". In a follow-up essay in November 2006 ("Howard's Brutopia"), he had elaborated the arguments in a contemporary Australian context. He continued to do so throughout his term as Prime Minister.

Rudd was harshly criticised for his government's home insulation and school building programmes, but much of this criticism struck me as mean-spirited. These were well-meaning measures, of necessity implemented in haste, and both achieved their primary purpose. They served to pump-prime the economy and to keep many people in work – to say nothing of insulating many homes and enhancing school facilities. The vast majority of school principals were happy.

Unquestionably there was rorting. In the case of the school building scheme, all that was lost was money – and what was lost on the swings was almost certainly made up on the roundabouts. But the home insulation scheme ("pink batts") was different. There were four tragic deaths and over 100 house fires. Tens of thousands of householders were inconvenienced when faulty insulation had to be removed. Who deserved the blame? Primarily, I would suggest, the shonky business operators (a small minority in the relevant industries), who saw the chance to make a quick buck. Rudd, however, does not escape scot-free. It is fair to point out that the Office of the Coordinator-General, located within the Prime Minister's Department, did a poor job of overseeing the programme – including key safety aspects.[66]

Beyond the economy, what else did Rudd do or not do? As I have said, he wrote in 2006 that "Christianity must always take the side of the marginalised, the vulnerable and the oppressed". Did he adhere to that precept?

In one memorable respect, he did. His "Sorry" speech of February 2008 was pitch-perfect in content, tone, delivery and length. He did not equivocate or seek to make party-political distinctions – the mistake made by the then-Opposition Leader, Brendan Nelson.* Rudd's best sequence was this one:

> We apologise for the laws and policies of successive parliaments and governments that have inflicted profound grief, suffering and loss on these our fellow Australians.

---

* Brendan Nelson's speech was booed by the crowd outside. One felt sorry for Nelson, a decent man, but his speech that day was a curious mixture of genuine eloquence, carefully-phrased fence-sitting, and sly racial politics. It was much longer than Rudd's and appeared to have been drafted in committee: all shades of opinion within the Coalition were represented. I doubt that Nelson agreed with everything he was required to say. For present purposes, it is notable that he referred several times to the good intentions of many people in the Christian churches who were involved in removing children from their mothers. That their intentions were good is incontestable and Rudd would be the first person to acknowledge it. I expect he would not have disagreed with a number of Nelson's other riders and digressions (though not with all of them). But Rudd had the grace and good sense to realise that the Apology had to be unequivocal. Nelson's jangled mish-mash of sentiments was inappropriate for an historic occasion.

We apologise especially for the removal of Aboriginal and Torres Strait Islander children from their families, their communities and their country.

For the pain, suffering and hurt of these stolen generations, their descendants and for their families left behind, we say sorry.

To the mothers and the fathers, the brothers and the sisters, for the breaking up of families and communities, we say sorry.

And for the indignity and degradation thus inflicted on a proud people and a proud culture, we say sorry.

We the parliament of Australia respectfully request that this apology be received in the spirit in which it is offered as part of the healing of the nation.

That was one of Rudd's finest days as a leader and a Christian. I wish that I could be so enthusiastic about his policies on asylum-seekers. In Opposition he had been forthright: he made sweeping promises to the Australian Christian Lobby in 2007.[67] In office, his record was mixed. While his approach was considerably more humane than that of his predecessor – and his successor – it still fell short in key respects. Mandatory on-shore detention was maintained, albeit in ameliorated form. More disquieting still was the shift in Rudd's rhetoric. Far too much of it came to be focused upon deterrence and the evil of people-smugglers ("the absolute scum of the earth"/"the vilest form of human life"/"they should rot in jail and … rot in hell", etc.) rather than consideration for those in need. That said, Rudd had inherited a ghastly moral-political problem. It was not of his making.

As regards foreign policy, Rudd fulfilled his 2007 election promise to withdraw Australian troops from Iraq. To that extent he was a peacemaker. But he kept Australian troops in Afghanistan and his Defence White Paper of 2009 struck several qualified commentators as an excessively bellicose document. (Some hawks loved it, which was of even more concern.) Overall, the record suggests that Rudd had a tendency to hedge his bets as regards "national security" issues. Such an approach may be no bad thing in the dark world of *Realpolitik*, but it is less easily defensible on Christian grounds.

Similarly, it was very disappointing that Rudd decided not to appoint a properly-empowered Royal Commission to investigate government and public service complicity in the activities of the Australian Wheat Board. No less than $290 million was paid by the AWB to Saddam Hussein's regime in Iraq – a regime against which Australia had seen fit to go to war. Yet the full truth has never been unearthed due to the proscribed terms of reference of the Cole Enquiry in 2006.[68] This was and remains a genuine scandal and Rudd, in Opposition, had quite rightly pursued it. As David Marr pointed out, it chimed neatly with his belief that Christianity is, or should be, "the religion of truth tellers".[69]

I asked Rudd about the AWB at the tail end of our interview. He had decided, he said, that as a newly-elected Prime Minister he ought not to be seen "to be exacting a retrospective retribution on a previous government". He added:

> And by that stage various referrals had been made to various legal entities, legal bodies, and the judgment that I took is that at best it would be allowed to take its course. Whether it has or not is a matter for historians, but I think it's a very uncomfortable chapter in the history of the Howard government.

Some would say that Rudd acted sagely – even magnanimously. For others, this was another instance of his lack of courage. The case for a proper Royal Commission had been laid out with admirable cogency in two books published in 2007, Caroline Overington's *Kickback* and Stephen Bartos's *Against the Grain*.[70] Some once-powerful people must still be sighing with relief.

Kevin Rudd's two and a half years as Prime Minister were in many respects admirable. He did much more good than bad. But his mistakes, and the circumstances of his downfall, serve as a cautionary tale. Contemporary politics is a vicious and murky game, and even the most conscientious of Christians can be buffeted by it.

It is a positively eerie thing that Rudd himself, in an interview with journalist Geraldine Doogue in May 2005, foresaw his own fate. Asked whether he had ever felt that he was being "taken over by his political beliefs" and that his faith was being "sidelined", he said:

I think … from time to time there's been a real danger of that. The sheer technology of politics for want of a better term is mind-boggling. The techniques of politics are mind-boggling. *And there's a danger that you see at the end of that the suffocation of the soul.*[71]

At the time of writing Kevin Rudd still sits on Labor's back bench, despised and rejected by at least half the Labor caucus. The leadership spill of March 21, 2013 proved a pitiful anti-climax. Yet Rudd's position is not nearly as hopeless-seeming as was Robert Menzies' in, say, early 1942. Or John Howard's on May 9, 1989, when he joked blackly about his prospects of becoming Liberal leader again ("That'd be like Lazarus with a triple bypass"). Rudd, at least, is still respected by the Australian people, who elected him in 2007 and rightly regard him as more sinned against than sinning.

Although he has ruled out a return to the leadership "in any circumstances", it remains possible that Rudd could yet do a Menzies or a Howard – learn some hard lessons, make peace with his colleagues, and come back a better man. We are all refined and tested in the furnace of affliction.

JULIA EILEEN GILLARD (B. 1961)
LABOR: 2010-

On June 29, 2010, just days after becoming Australia's first female Prime Minister, Julia Gillard was asked during an ABC radio interview whether she believed in God. Her reply was matter-of-fact: "No, I don't. I'm not a religious person."

She elaborated:

> I am not going to pretend a faith I don't feel, and for people of faith I think the greatest compliment I could pay to them is to respect their genuinely held beliefs and not to engage in some pretence about mine. I think it's not the right thing, and I'm not reflecting on past Prime Ministers here, I'm definitely not doing that, but I'm trying to answer your question as frankly as I can – I've never thought it was the right thing for me to go through religious rituals for the sake of appearance.[1]

These remarks were unusually candid. True, Gillard had said similar things before – in Jacqueline Kent's 2009 biography she had been quoted as saying "I'm not any kind of religious person".[2] However, coming from a new Prime Minister her remarks were bound to receive special attention. Many from the secular Left no doubt nodded in approval just as many Christians sighed in disappointment.

I would guess that, politically, Gillard's declared non-belief has been a handicap. There is some empirical evidence that it hurt Labor at the 2010 election.[3]

While her candour is admirable it is also, for a good many people, somewhat confronting. And Christians are wont to be irritated when, at times, she *does* go through religious rituals for the sake of appearances. On November 30, 2012, for instance, at a church service held in honour of Australia's most recent winner of the Victoria Cross, she quoted sonorously from Scripture. (It was John 15:13 – "Greater love hath no man than this, that a man lay down his life for his friends".)

In fairness to Gillard, it is necessary to understand: (i) that it is far from clear she is really an atheist, as too many people routinely claim or imply[4]; and (ii) how and why she lost any childhood faith she may have had.

As to (i), the position is this. Publicly*, so far as I have been able to ascertain, Gillard has never called herself an atheist or described a state of mind that amounts to atheism. Genuine atheism is a positive conviction that God does not exist. As the likes of Richard Dawkins have demonstrated it is a form of passionate quasi-faith, not of mere uncertainty or indifference. The most that can be said of Gillard is that she has not taken the trouble to refute the "atheist" label. For these reasons the editors of Wikipedia have thus far declined to label her as an atheist.[5] She is an unbeliever.

As to (ii), Gillard's Welsh heritage is well-known. Her parents, John and Moira Gillard, were archetypal "10 pound poms"[6], who arrived in Adelaide in February 1966. Julia and her older sister Alison had a stable, happy upbringing. They attended local state schools (Mitcham Demonstration School and Unley High).

What, then, during this formative period, were the Gillard family's "core values"? The work ethic was one. So too the importance of education. But another, equally important, was social justice.

John Gillard was not a member of the ALP but both he and Moira were strong and informed supporters of it. John, a psychiatric nurse, was also active in the affairs of his union. The whole family took a keen interest in current affairs in general and politics in particular. Not surprisingly,

---

* During a telephone conversation with US President Barack Obama in October 2012 Gillard claims to have quipped: "You think it's tough being African American. Try being an atheist, childless single woman as Prime Minister." That is scarcely conclusive even if she said it. She was talking about the stereotype of her.

given the time and place, they developed a special admiration for Gough Whitlam (known in the Gillard home as "The Colossus").[7]

Perhaps most revealing of all, John Gillard was a lifelong admirer of Aneurin ("Nye") Bevan (1897-1960), an icon of British Labour politics. As Minister for Health in the post-World War II administration of Clement Attlee, Bevan had the task of establishing the National Health Service, the linchpin – then and now – of Britain's modern welfare state.[8]

Bevan is a fascinating case-study, religiously as well as politically. Both his parents were steeped in Non-Conformism: his father was a Baptist and his mother a Methodist. But Bevan himself was not a religious man. A Christian colleague once wrote of him that "he had a burning faith in whatever seemed good to him at the time but, outside politics, had no personal faith at all". In other words, politics – Labour politics – *was* his religion. On one famous occasion Bevan as good as said so himself: "The language of priorities is the religion of Socialism." Another time he compared the House of Commons to a church.

The parallels with Julia Gillard are striking. She too has devoted her life to the cause of Labor politics – to the exclusion of almost everything else, including, in her case, marriage and children. And though her parents were not practising Christians, she, like Bevan, was exposed to Church teaching during childhood. She eschewed all theological and supernatural mumbo-jumbo while retaining respect for Christian principles of social justice – again, just like Bevan.

As a girl she went to Mitcham Baptist Church. Her attendance was an accident of geography: "We lived two doors down from the Reverend there, Ian Porter, and I was great friends with his daughter Helen. So I grew up going to Baptist youth group and all the rest."[9] John and Moira, it seems, had no objection. Indeed, during their early years in Adelaide, they welcomed chances to make friends and alleviate culture shock. According to Jacqueline Kent, "the Gillards were not a particularly religious family, but church membership did increase their social circle."[10]

Julia applied herself to Sunday school activities with characteristic diligence. As she told Parliament in March 2011: "I did have the benefit of a very rigorous grounding at the Mitcham Baptist Church, which included endless committing to memory of catechisms – I was actually a prize-winner at it." Even so, the Baptist faith was not for her. "I am steeped in that tradition but I've made decisions in my adult life about my own views," she said in 2010.[11]

Once at university, those views were set in stone. She became – much like John Curtin and Bob Hawke – a true believer in the labour movement.

Here it is important to distinguish between fact and fiction. Some of the distrust of Gillard in conservative Christian circles stems from a misconception that, during her student days, she was some kind of firebrand feminist.[12] True, she involved herself in student politics. But at least by campus standards she was a long way from the "far left".[13] Mostly it was bread and butter stuff.[14] Gillard was a pragmatic networker who never evinced the slightest interest in the fantasies of atheistic Communism. Her argument "was always that [student politicians] shouldn't bother with world issues [they] could not influence, but instead concentrate on matters that directly concerned students".[15]

Likewise, within the Victorian ALP, she was a moderate. This was not always to her advantage. In 1992, when she sought ALP pre-selection for the Federal seat of Melbourne, she was perceived as the most *conservative* of the three candidates who stood. (She lost to Lindsay Tanner, in part because the preselectors "felt she wasn't a feminist"![16])

Another prevalent myth is that Gillard climbed to the top in ruthless, dishonest ("unChristian") fashion. In fact, her conduct was rather less ruthless and dishonest than the norm. Kevin Rudd's overthrow aside, she earned her success. After entering parliament in 1998, she worked productively for 12 years with four Labor Opposition leaders – Kim Beazley, Simon Crean, Mark Latham and Rudd. She also co-existed with Rudd during most of his Prime Ministership, and, after the deadlocked 2010 election, it was her skill and charm that won the day in negotiations with the cross-benchers. While she can appear wooden and abrasive in public, she has a reputation for being polite and approachable in private. She treats her personal staff in a warm and considerate manner.[17]

There is a lovely anecdote in Jacqueline Kent's biography from Gillard's time as a solicitor at Slater and Gordon. She once acted in a pay dispute for a migrant with broken English. At a preparatory conference, when Gillard informed her client of the date of the trial, the lady said: "Oh, the case is on the 10th of April, that is my daughter ten birthday. I won't forget that day, Miss Julia." After the case was resolved Gillard handed the woman a birthday present for her daughter. "This will be good for your daughter to read," Gillard said. "I liked this book as a child." Her grateful client burst into tears.[18]

As regards the carbon tax she was not a "liar" but a run-of-the-mill political sinner. She did not knowingly deceive on August 16, 2010 ("There will be no carbon tax under the government I lead"). However, she did break a significant election promise for cynical reasons. As to whether the tax is good policy, views can reasonably differ.

It is salient to mention another factor in Gillard's rise. Throughout her parliamentary career – with one glaring exception – she has been respectful of religious people and religious issues.

First, she understands the key role of the churches in the provision of healthcare. When Gillard was a child her mother worked at an old people's home run by the Salvation Army, and she and Alison often went there after school. They witnessed the social Gospel at its most practical.[19] "I don't have any difficulty in the world with not-for-profit managers," Gillard told the ABC's Tony Jones in 2006. "[Where] I come from we are well served by the Werribee Mercy Hospital which is a public hospital run by the Sisters of Mercy and they do a very good job indeed."[20] In the lead-up to the 2004 election, as Shadow Health Minister, she worked closely with Catholic Health Australia in formulating Medicare Gold.

Second, from early 2005 onwards, she supported Kevin Rudd's attempts to re-connect the ALP with Christian voters.[21] In late 2006 she joined forces with Rudd to oust Kim Beazley as Labor leader. On his own, Rudd could never have mustered the numbers in caucus.[22] It is more than a little ironic that, but for the supposedly "irreligious" Julia Gillard, Australia would never have had a chance to elect Rudd – the most overtly Christian Prime Minister since Joe Lyons.

Third, as Minister for Education in Rudd's government, she gained respect from some noted commentators on the Right for her championing of "traditional" teaching methods and values. She conceived her role in moral terms: "Making a difference to disadvantaged children is much more than a question of economics."[23]

Fourth, as Prime Minister, she has treated most Christian groups with deference. In the lead-up to the 2010 election, she agreed to an interview with Jim Wallace of the Australian Christian Lobby.[24] Like Rudd, she has maintained John Howard's School Chaplaincy programme and the funding arrangements Howard put in place for low-fee church schools. In 2011 she intervened to appoint Monsignor David Cappo, Vicar-General of the Catholic Archdiocese of Adelaide, to head the Mental Health Commission (though he later resigned).[25] In announcing a Royal Commission into child sexual abuse in late 2012 she indicated – very wisely – that its remit would not be confined to the Catholic Church. That would have been a recipe for sectarianism.

And she continues to oppose same-sex marriage. This, it must be said, is puzzling. Rudd would have done the same, but his position is based on orthodox Christian grounds. Whether you agree with it or not, it is principled and comprehensible. Gillard's position seems unprincipled and incomprehensible. The most charitable interpretation of her behaviour is that she is fulfilling an election promise. When questioned by the ACL in August 2010, she pledged that under her government "the Marriage Act will remain unchanged".

These things, then, *should* be to the good. So too Gillard's championing of the National Disability Insurance Scheme, which now has bipartisan support. Why, then, is she so unpopular with Christian voters?

There are various factors at play: her unbelief might not have mattered so much in other circumstances. She replaced Kevin Rudd, a popularly-elected Christian Prime Minister, and is blamed by many for having "knifed" him. She formed an alliance with the Greens, a party deeply distrusted by many Australian Christians.* She and her partner since 2005, Tim Mathieson, have conducted the first-ever *de facto* relationship at the Lodge.[26] And she is childless: infamously, in May 2007, Liberal senator Bill Heffernan described her as "deliberately barren".[27]

---

* John Howard said to me: "God neither votes Labor nor Liberal and he certainly doesn't vote Green. That's my current add-on." The sentiment may be a trifle unfair – there are sincere Christians who vote Green, of course – but it is understandable. The Greens' hard-core secularist supporters in the media too often display their prejudice and their ignorance as regards theology and people of faith.

Pausing there, Gillard could justly take umbrage. By most accounts of the 2010 coup she was drafted at the eleventh hour by Rudd's many enemies in the party; she did not plan it herself. Her deal with the Greens was unwise and unnecessary (were Adam Bandt and the Green senators ever going to support the Coalition?), but it was struck in the chaotic circumstances of a hung parliament. Her relationship with Mathieson is her own business, and Heffernan's comments were offensive. Gillard is a loving aunt to her sister Alison's children, and friendly with children generally.[28] Her views on the perils of busy female politicians having children are nuanced and sensible.[29]

But Gillard has also done things that reveal a basic lack of judgement. In November 2011 she sacrificed a good and respected Labor man, Harry Jenkins, to make ex-Liberal MHR Peter Slipper* the Speaker of the House. (Temporarily, this gave Labor an extra vote.) Admittedly Slipper was a creature of the Coalition, and the (civil) sexual harassment suit later brought against him in the Federal Court was dismissed as an abuse of process in December 2012. But enough was already known of Slipper's past conduct and reputation to enable one quickly to form the view that he was an unsuitable choice for the important and impartial office of Speaker. He still faces criminal charges in relation to the alleged misuse of Cabcharge vouchers, to which at the time of writing a plea of "not guilty" has been entered.

Slipper resigned as Speaker on October 9, 2012. His position was untenable. Yet right until the end Gillard had gone out of her way to defend him – even after the publication of a slew of sexually-explicit texts which Slipper had sent to a male staffer.[30] (Some of them referred to the female genitalia in derogatory terms and were truly vile.) It is important to recall that Gillard's now-famous "misogyny" speech in Parliament on October 9, 2012[31] was made in the context of defending Slipper. On the same day, her government also announced cuts to welfare payments to vulnerable single mothers. The hypocrisy was disturbing.

It must be acknowledged that Gillard's speech struck a nerve with many women, both in Australia and around the world. In part this was

---

* It is sobering to have to record that, in 2008, Slipper was ordained as a priest of the Anglican Catholic Church in Australia.

understandable: misogyny and sexism (two very different things, by the way), are both far too prevalent in Western society. But to the extent that Gillard's speech was a direct personal attack on Tony Abbott, she was condemning the wrong man. Abbott can justly be criticised for many things – and on Christian grounds – but he is self-evidently *not* a misogynist (a hater of women). I am not convinced that he is even a sexist (a discriminator against women on invalid grounds), though he may have been one in earlier days, before he became a husband and a father to three accomplished daughters.

What Abbott truly is, is a social conservative and a practising Catholic. He began his career in the DLP. The spiteful *ad hominem* attacks on him by Gillard and the secular Left have annoyed many Christians and moral traditionalists – including a good number who disagree with Abbott and the Coalition on issues of public policy. The "Bonhoeffer effect" built up assiduously by Kevin Rudd has been completely eradicated and Labor will feel the backlash at the 2013 election, whenever it is held. An anti-Labor landslide seems in the offing.

There is one other area in which Gillard is genuinely vulnerable to Christian criticism. That is on the question of abortion. She will lose few votes here, because Christians in the West lost this argument long ago. But it may explain the depth of feeling against her in some sections of the community. The likes of Rudd and Keating never had to contend with hostility on this ground.

In 1996 Gillard helped to set up EMILY's List Australia, the local version of an influential American lobby group created in 1984. The American body has become associated with the extreme "pro-choice" side of the abortion debate. The Australian body supports female candidates for political office who have been pre-selected by the ALP *and* who are pro-choice. Gillard still supports the cause.[32]

It is one thing to be pro-choice – even many Christians who are repulsed by abortion would not necessarily advocate that it be re-criminalised, at least not in all circumstances. There is plenty of room for respectful debate, but the tendency of zealots on both sides is to demonise anybody who does not agree with them 100 per cent. Some of Gillard's public comments about abortion down the years have betrayed a shallow understanding of the real issues* and the nature of religious faith in general.

In February 2006 the House of Representatives took a conscience vote on the "morning after" drug RU-486. (I have referred to this issue already in the chapters on Howard and Rudd.) In the event there was clear bipartisan support for an amendment to the Therapeutic Goods Act to strip the federal Health Minister (then Tony Abbott) of the power to ban the drug's importation. That outcome was predictable – possibly even defensible – but the standard of debate was low. At the time Gillard was the Opposition spokesperson on health. She said of Abbott (who favoured a continuation of the ban):

> A minister's personal opinions should not influence policy decisions on this matter. The current Minister for Health has decided views and we have always said his personal opinions should not be what guides policy here, and we maintain that.[33]

This was specious cant, pure and simple. The opposition of Abbott and others to yet-speedier forms of abortion than are already available – a sincerely-held and religiously-based position – was dismissed as an irrelevant "opinion". On the other hand, the support of Gillard and others for the further liberalisation of abortion law was somehow more than an opinion. It was self-evident common sense. Such an argument, though sadly typical of many anti-religionists today, ought to have been beneath her.

---

* The core issue is whether a foetus is a human being. If the answer to that question is "yes", as many Christians believe, the implications are profound. So, too, if there is reasonable doubt about the matter. Even if the answer is a clear-cut "no" – and it is hard to see how anyone can be sure – a foetus is at least a potential human life. Valid medical, ethical and sociological questions arise as to whether the incidence of abortion ought to be reduced – for example, by encouraging the practice of adoption and/or (as suggested by Pope Francis I in one of his first public statements) by destigmatising young single mothers who have taken the decision to go to term. See generally Dr Megan Best's monumental book *Fearfully and Wonderfully Made: Ethics and the beginning of human life*, Matthias Media (2012).

CONCLUSIONS

I t is time to draw some threads together and to indulge in a little speculation. First, how many of Australia's 23 Prime Ministers were believers in God? By that I mean believers in God as at the time of their death, or, in the case of the still-living Prime Ministers, as at the present day. It is simplest to begin by excluding those who were or are – on the evidence available – almost certainly unbelievers. In this category I would place the two life-long agnostics (Edmund Barton and Harold Holt), as well as Chris Watson, Gough Whitlam, Bob Hawke and Julia Gillard. Malcolm Fraser is a more complicated study, though, on the basis of his 2010 memoirs, he also must be classed as an agnostic.

That is seven unbelievers. As I hope I have demonstrated, all seven still have a fascinating "religious" story to tell. Holt's is the only "open and shut" case of unbelief. The possibility of Barton or Watson having turned to God very late in life cannot be ruled out, and, of course, any or all of the other four may yet do so. Each of them – but most notably Whitlam and Hawke – has a substantial body of Christian knowledge upon which to call.

Turning to the remaining 16 Prime Ministers, I would not hesitate to class 12 of them as sincere believers: Alfred Deakin (though a Deist rather than a Christian), Andrew Fisher, Joseph Cook, Billy Hughes, Jim Scullin, Joe Lyons, Ben Chifley, Robert Menzies, Billy McMahon, Paul Keating, John Howard and Kevin Rudd. Of those 12, five were from the ALP and four from the various non-Labor parties. Cook, Hughes and Lyons all began their careers in the ALP and ended them on the other side. Labor true believers would call them rats or defectors. Conservatives would say that they saw the light.

That leaves the four trickiest cases: George Reid, S.M. Bruce, John

Curtin and John Gorton. My personal opinion is that Reid and Curtin were late converts. Bruce and Gorton were more enigmatic, but, on balance, I am inclined to think that each would have called himself a Christian in his twilight years. Each was certainly a fellow-traveller. Bruce underwent a substantial ideological journey in his middle to late years, and Gorton was always an iconoclast. Nothing would surprise me in relation to either of them.

The overall score, then? Sixteen believers to seven unbelievers. And 20 to seven if one counts Page, Fadden, Forde and McEwen.

Turning to the 12 clear-cut believers, a further question arises. To what extent were each of these men faithful to Christian principles – while in office, and more generally throughout their lives? Who, in short, were the "best" Christians? Everything depends on the criteria to be applied, and views will differ between Protestants and Catholics, liberals and conservatives, Labor supporters and Coalition supporters. Speaking for myself, eight factors loomed largest:

First, orthodox theology – above all, belief in the divinity of Jesus Christ. Deakin must be marked down here, despite his genius and his rectitude.

Second, a contribution to evangelism. A number of our past leaders did a good deal to promote Christianity, whether in their private lives (Fisher, Cook, Rudd), and/or in their public statements – Hughes, Lyons (though mainly through his wife), Menzies, McMahon, Keating, Rudd. Those who played a part in minimising sectarianism or in resolving the State aid debate also merit high praise. Lyons and Menzies (and Whitlam), were by far the most important figures, but Scullin, Howard and Rudd also played noble roles. So did Gorton and Fraser.

Third, the quality of moral courage – the determination to believe in yourself and your own principles in the face of populist opposition and internal doubts. As Paul Keating once said, effective political leadership "always involves, in some sense, a leap of faith"*.[1] In recent times Kevin Rudd lost his nerve on climate change – and, in the opinion of some, by

---

* The expression "leap of faith" was coined in the 19th century by Soren Kierkegaard (1813-55), the great Danish philosopher-theologian. He was referring to the moment when a person's intellectual convictions about God are transformed by a mysterious act of will into genuine faith in God.

not running on the day of the ALP leadership spill (March 21, 2013). He declined to take a leap of faith.

Two other mostly admirable men – Fisher and Scullin – can also be faulted on this ground. Fisher ought to have followed his gut instinct as regards the evil insanity of World War I. Even if he had merely stayed in politics for a couple more years (he was only 53 when he quit in 1915), the country would have been spared Billy Hughes and the conscription plebiscites and Labor's first disastrous split. Likewise, Scullin ought to have called a double dissolution election in 1930, as some of his colleagues urged at the time, once it was clear that the Senate and the banks would obstruct most of Labor's programme to deal with the Great Depression.

Our bravest Christian leaders were Lyons (for his rejection of easy militarism in the late 1930s), and Keating. Keating was brave on two fronts: his proactive commitment to racial tolerance, and his implementation of tough but fair – and far-sighted – economic reform. He also had the courage to challenge Bob Hawke a second time for the Labor leadership, in December 1991, when even a narrow loss could have been fatal to his life-long dreams. He eked out a five-vote win.

Fourth, an abhorrence of war, or, at the very least, a marked disinclination to wage war except as an absolute last resort on rock-solid grounds. On this criteria several of our leaders come out badly – Cook, Hughes, Menzies (as regards World War I and Vietnam, less so World War II) and Howard. Only Scullin and Lyons score notably well. Apart from them, the Prime Ministers with the strongest anti-war instincts were, not coincidentally, those had had actually seen serious combat as young men – Bruce, Gorton and Whitlam.

Fifth, economic policies principally aimed at helping the less fortunate members of society, or, at any rate, not aimed at making the rich any richer *at their expense*. As discussed in the Introduction, most of our Prime Ministers had a good record in this respect, though the stand-outs among the Christians were Fisher, Chifley and Keating.

Sixth, social conservatism and a righteous private life (in terms of sexual conduct, scrupulous honesty, financial probity and so on). In the latter respect it is dangerous to be judgmental, because all the relevant facts can rarely if ever be known. But it seems not unfair to say that – putting aside the unbelievers – Reid, Hughes, Chifley, Gorton and McMahon are those most vulnerable to criticism, on the various grounds I have outlined. By contrast, Fisher, Cook and Scullin seem to have been above reproach. Nobody *tried* to smear them, presumably because there were no charges about them to repeat, let alone any with even a hint of credibility. Each of the other Christian Prime Ministers was the subject of certain rumours and allegations. But these appear to me to have been either too trivial to warrant mention (that is, even if they were well-founded) or largely if not entirely baseless.

Seventh, the respect of one's peers. All politicians can expect to be denounced by their political opponents, at least on questions of policy and ideology. But it is a worrying sign if they are disliked and distrusted by many in their own party – as Hughes, the young Menzies, McMahon and Rudd all were. On the other hand, it is a very positive sign if a man's character is praised, even revered, by colleagues and opponents alike. Chifley was remarkable in this respect. Fisher and Scullin also rate highly, as do Lyons and the latter-day Bruce. Keating had some enemies, but he is adored by most Labor partisans and even among many conservatives he commands admiration (if little affection).

Eighth, an absence of bigotry on racial grounds – and, ideally, a commitment to eradicating racism and xenophobia from Australian society. In this respect most of our leaders – even progressive icons such as Deakin, Fisher and Chifley – had a blind spot. Some (such as Cook and Hughes) were much worse than others (such as Reid and Lyons), but nobody emerged with honour until Harold Holt. The White Australia Policy was enforced by every Prime Minister from Barton to Menzies, and few took more than a passing interest in Aboriginal affairs. (Curtin had a lamentable record on such issues: he race-baited shamelessly during the 1943 election campaign.[2]) It is true that at the time of Federation, and for some decades thereafter, there were genuine economic factors at play. The White Australia Policy was in part designed to protect the jobs and the wages of local workers from cheap foreign labour. But it cannot be denied that plain bigotry was also a major motive.

It easier to forgive the earlier leaders than the later ones. After World War II, bigotry in any form becomes much harder to explain or excuse. Menzies was not personally a racist ("absolutely the opposite!" his daughter insisted to me in a spirited tone) but he did little or nothing to challenge the White Australia Policy. Gorton had a xenophobic streak and McMahon raised the spectre of Asian immigration during the 1972 election campaign. Even Whitlam (in 1975) made his notorious comment in Cabinet about "f_____g Vietnamese Balts". Bob Hawke, in 1977, was an early adopter of the term "illegal immigrants" to describe refugees arriving by boat, and, as Prime Minister, he resorted to another misleading and pejorative label, "queue jumpers".[3] I have discussed Howard's problematic record on these matters.

Somewhat disturbingly, from a Christian perspective, two of the four Prime Ministers with the best records on racial issues – Holt and Fraser – were unbelievers. That leaves Keating and Rudd. Neither was flawless – Keating presided over a system of mandatory detention of (mostly Cambodian) asylum-seekers which he inherited from Hawke, and, as discussed, Rudd resorted to some dubious rhetoric late in his term. But, for the most part, both strived to do the decent thing.

Who comes out best overall? There is a good case for Jim Scullin, for whom "Christ and Labor were one"[4], but it is incontestable that he was a political failure. The best Christian man is not the same thing as the best Christian Prime Minister. And I must not fall into the trap of lauding most highly the men with whom, theologically, I feel the closest affinity – Menzies and Rudd. They were (are) cerebral ecumenicists, university-educated and in love with the written word. In that sense they were atypical Australians and both of them, as politicians, did things which are hard to defend.

Two Prime Ministers stand out. Among those who served before World War II, I would plump for Joe Lyons – a choice unlikely to be controversial among Christians. Of the Prime Ministers who followed Lyons, the decision is harder. The field is chequered. Too many have dark stains on their record. But, all things considered, including his record as treasurer, I would submit that Paul Keating comes out best.

Despite his mean streak, and an unattractive propensity for sulking, the quality of moral courage tips the scales in his favour. One must also take account of his sheer hard-nosed effectiveness in advancing worthy though unpopular causes. As Menzies said of St Paul – and St Paul of himself! – Keating got things done in the face of the odds. When the big picture is considered, his legacy looms over 21st century Australia like a city on a hill. And I can hear the cries of outrage already.

ENDNOTES

INTRODUCTION

1. Ryan Westmore, 'Faith-based initiatives deserve a place in the public sphere', *The Australian*, October 22, 2012, p. 12.
2. John Warhurst, 'The Faith of Australian Prime Ministers 1901-2010', paper presented to the Australian Political Studies Association, APSA Conference, Melbourne, 27-29 September 2010, p. 16.
3. Marion Maddox, 'Best of 2011: God under Gillard', *ABC Religion and Ethics*, 16 January 2012, p. 2.
4. Warhurst, 'The Faith of Australian Prime Ministers', p. 5 (re Billy Hughes).
5. Kim E. Beazley, *Father of the House: The memoirs of Kim E. Beazley*, Fremantle Press (2009), p. 73.
6. Hugh Ross Mackintosh, *Types of Modern Theology: Schliermacher to Barth*, Nisbet and Co. Ltd. (1937), p. 292. See also Phyllis Tickle, *The Great Emergence: How Christianity Is Changing and Why*, Baker Books (2008), pp. 90-91; Brian McLaren, *A New Kind of Christianity*, Hodder & Stoughton (2010), pp. 91-92.
7. Alfred Deakin, quoted in C.M.H. (Manning) Clark, *A History of Australia*, Volume V, Melbourne University Press (1987), p. 245.
8. Manning Clark, *A Short History of Australia*, first published 1963, fourth revised edition, Penguin Books Australia (1995), p. 198.
9. I.M. Cumpston, *Lord Bruce of Melbourne*, Longman Cheshire (1989), p. 22.
10. Manning Clark, *A History of Australia*, Volume VI, p. 313.
11. Quoted in Manning Clark, *A History of Australia*, Volume VI, p. 316.
12. Michelle Grattan, 'John Winston Howard' in *Australian Prime Ministers*, ed. by Michelle Grattan, New Holland (2000), p. 442.
13. John Douglas Pringle, *Australian Accent*, Chatto and Windus (1958), p. 86.
14. Quoted in Ross Fitzgerald, *The Pope's Battalions: Santamaria, Catholicism and the Labor Split*, University of Queensland Press (2003), pp. 33-34.
15. Robert Macklin, *Kevin Rudd: The Biography*, Viking (2007), p. 209.
16. Quoted in Barry Donovan, *Mark Latham: The Circuitbreaker*, The Five Mile Press (2004), p. 255. Donovan quoted some other interesting observations of Latham's in relation to Christianity. Latham revealed that he had read "half a dozen" books about Jesus. "I've got no doubt he lived as an historical figure. If he was the Son of God or not is a different issue... I'm in no position to judge."
17. See generally Tom Frame, *Losing My Religion: Unbelief in Australia*, UNSW Press (2009).
18. Sir George Houstoun Reid, *My Reminiscences*, first published by Cassell and Company, Ltd 1917, Hardpress Publishing Edition, p..286.
19. Quoted in Deane Wells, *The Wit of Whitlam*, Outback Press (1976), pp. 47-48.

EDMUND BARTON

1. Martha Rutledge, 'Barton, Sir Edmund (Toby) (1849-1920)', Australian Dictionary of Biography, National Centre of Biography, Australian National University, http://adb.anu.edu.au/biography/barton-sir-edmund-71/text8629, accessed 21 December 2012, p. 2.
2. Sir Adrian Knox, quoted in Rutledge, p. 8.
3. J.A. Barton, quoted in John Reynolds, *Edmund Barton*, first published by Angus & Robertson 1948, Bookman Press (1999), p. 72.
4. Reynolds, pp. 15, 75; see also Rutledge, p. 2.
5. A.B. Piddington, quoted in Geoffrey Bolton, *Edmund Barton: The one man for the job*, Allen & Unwin (2000), p. 58.
6. Bolton, p. 110.

7. Ibid, p. 59.
8. Ibid, p. 161.
9. Ibid, pp. 205-14ff.
10. Rutledge, p. 8.
11. Reynolds, p. 72.
12. Bolton, pp. 270-71.
13. Quoted in Reynolds, p. 204; see also McMinn, *George Reid*, p. 193.
14. Graham Fricke, *Profiles of Power: The Prime Ministers of Australia*, Houghton Mifflin (1990), p. 19.
15. Quoted in Fricke, p. 18.
16. Quoted in Bolton, p. 343.
17. Manning Clark, *A History of Australia*, Volume V, p. 73. See also p. 229.
18. Reynolds, p. 72.
19. Manning Clark, *A History of Australia*, Volume V, p. 219.
20. Rutledge, p. 8.
21. J.A. La Nauze, *Alfred Deakin: A Biography*, first published by Melbourne University Press 1965, Angus & Robertson edition (1979), p. 66.
22. Al Gabay, *The Mystic Life of Alfred Deakin*, Cambridge University Press (1992), p. 198.
23. Stuart Macintyre, *A Concise History of Australia*, Cambridge University Press, first published 1999, third edition (2009), p. 138.
24. Manning Clark, *A History of Australia*, Volume VI, p. 165.
25. Bolton, p. 16.
26. Ibid, p. 8.
27. Ibid, p. 21.
28. Ibid, p. 13.
29. Ibid, p. 21.
30. Reynolds, pp. 31-32.
31. Bolton, p. 27; Reynolds, pp. 40-42.
32. Michael Page, *The Prime Ministers of Australia*, Robertsbridge (1988), p. 28.

ALFRED DEAKIN

1. John Warhurst, 'The religious beliefs of Australia's prime ministers', 11 November 2010, published online at www.eurekastreet.com.au
2. Gabay, *The Mystic Life of Alfred Deakin*, p. 66 (see note 22 to the section on Edmund Barton).
3. Manning Clark, *A History of Australia*, Volume VI, p. 280.

4. Quoted in Warhurst, 'The Faith of Australian Prime Ministers', p. 3, note 10.
5. Gabay, p. 197.
6. For two rather different perspectives see generally David Walker, *Anxious Nation: Australia and the rise of Asia, 1850-1939*, University of Queensland Press (1999); Keith Windschuttle, *The White Australia Policy: Race and Shame in the History Wars*, Macleay Press (2004). For a short overview of the various factors at play see Manning Clark, *A Short History of Australia*, pp. 216-19; Mungo MacCallum, 'Australian Story: Kevin Rudd and the Lucky Country', *Quarterly Essay* 36, 2009, pp. 24-25.
7. Fricke, *Profiles of Power*, p. 33 (see note 14 to the section on Edmund Barton).
8. Quoted in Gabay, p. 41, note 20; see also p. 183
9. Quoted in La Nauze, *Alfred Deakin*, p. 70 (see note 21 to the section on Edmund Barton).
10. Bolton, *Edmund Barton*, p. 241 (see note 5 to the section on Edmund Barton).
11. Quoted in Gabay, p. 40.
12. Gabay, pp. 117-20
13. Ibid, pp. 101, 145, 152, 197
14. Ibid, p. 155
15. La Nauze, p. 69.
16. Gabay, pp. 27-28, 39.
17. Quoted in La Nauze, p. 70
18. Quoted in Gabay, p. 39
19. Gabay, p. 145.
20. Quoted in La Nauze, p. 74.
21. Gabay, p. 39.
22. Quoted in Gabay, p. 39.
23. Quoted in Gabay, p. 154.
24. Gabay, pp. 183-84.
25. Ibid, p. 182.
26. Ibid, p. 90.
27. Quoted in Gabay, p. 77.
28. Quoted in La Nauze, p. 178.
29. Gabay, pp. 43-44, 47.
30. Stuart Macintyre, 'Alfred Deakin', in Grattan (ed.), *Australian Prime Ministers*, p. 39.
31. John Rickard, *A family Romance: The Deakins at Home*, Melbourne University Press (1996), p. 8.
32. Ibid, p. 6.
33. Gabay, p. 5.

34. Quoted in La Nauze, p. 67.
35. La Nauze, p. 67.
36. Rickard, *A Family Romance*, p. 9.
37. Gabay, p. 6.
38. H.B. Higgins, quoted in Rickard, *A Family Romance*, p. 30.
39. Ibid, pp. 9, 30.
40. Catherine Deakin, quoted in Rickard, *A Family Romance*, p. 30.
41. Quoted in Gabay, p. 6.
42. Rickard, *A Family Romance*, pp. 11ff, 33; Gabay, pp. 6-7.
43. Gabay, p. 8.
44. Quoted in La Nauze, p. 57
45. Gabay, p. 8.
46. Ibid, p. 7.
47. Rickard, *A Family Romance*, p. 33.
48. Ibid, p. 57.
49. Gabay, p. 109ff.
50. See Gabay, pp. 113ff, 182ff.
51. See Rickard, *A Family Romance*, pp. 90-91.
52. Gabay, pp. 11, 25.
53. Rickard, *A Family Romance*, p. 33.
54. Quoted in Gabay, p. 8.
55. Rickard, *A Family Romance*, p. 56; see also Gabay, p. 21 and La Nauze, p. 56.
56. Gabay, pp. 126ff, 138.
57. Ibid, p. 15. See also La Nauze, p. 71.
58. Gabay, p. 162.
59. Ibid, p. 23.
60. Quoted in Gabay, p. 23.
61. Gabay, p. 28.
62. Rickard, *A Family Romance*, pp. 50-51, 72-73.
63. Gabay, p. 26.
64. Quoted in La Nauze, p. 69; see also Rickard, *A Family Romance*, p. 81
65. Macintyre, p. 43; Rickard, *A Family Romance*, p. 86
66. Gabay, pp. 24, 82
67. Rickard, *A Family Romance*, p. 97; Gabay, p. 39, note 10
68. La Nauze, p. 72.
69. Ibid.
70. Gabay, p. 82.
71. Rickard, *A Family Romance*, p. 107; Gabay, pp. 157-58
72. Gabay, pp. 160-61.
73. Ibid, p. 161.
74. Quoted in Gabay, p. 167.
75. Manning Clark, *A History of Australia*, Volume V, p. 277.
76. Ibid, p. 267.
77. Gabay, p. 175.
78. Ibid, p. 177; see generally La Nauze, pp. 535-75.
79. Macintyre, p. 51.
80. Rickard, *A Family Romance*, p. 142.
81. Gabay, p. 177; La Nauze, pp. 604-05.
82. Gabay, p. 186.
83. Quoted in Rickard, *A Family Romance*, p. 147.

CHRIS WATSON

1. Bede Nairn, 'Watson, John Christian (Chris) (1867-1941), Australian Dictionary of Biography, National centre of Biography, Australian National University, http://adb.anu.edu.au/biography/watson-john-christian-chris-9003/text15849, accessed 21 December 2012, p. 3.
2. Malcolm Booker, *The Great Professional: A Study of Billy Hughes*, McGraw-Hill (1980), p. 150.
3. Nairn, p. 1.
4. Ibid, p. 6.
5. Ross McMullin, 'John Christian Watson' in Grattan (ed.), *Australian Prime Ministers*, p. 57.
6. Norman Makin, *Federal Labour Leaders*, Union Printing (1961), p. 18. See also Nairn, p. 7.
7. Al Grassby and Silvia Ordonez, *The Man Time Forgot: The life and times of John Christian Watson, Australia's first Labor Prime Minister*, Pluto Press (1999), pp. 7-13.
8. Fricke, *Profiles of Power*, p. 36.
9. Makin, p. 18.
10. Grassby and Ordonez, p. 19.
11. Ibid, p. 7.
12. Ibid, p. 24.
13. Makin, p. 21.
14. Manning Clark, *A History of Australia*, Volume V, p. 190.
15. Grassby and Ordonez, p. 5.
16. Manning Clark, *A History of Australia*, Volume V, p. 186.
17. Letter from George Walters to Watson dated 17 November 1904 regarding a speech given by Watson on Christian socialism. Item 25, MS 451, National Library of Australia Collection.

18. Grassby and Ordonez, pp. 95-98.
19. Ibid, p. 123.
20. Jeffrey B. Webb, *Guide to Christianity, Alpha* (2004), pp. 115-16.
21. Manning Clark, *A History of Australia*, Volume V, p. 186.
22. Grassby and Ordonez, pp. 179-80 (note 13).
23. Ibid, p. 157.

GEORGE REID

1. See Fricke, *Profiles of Power*, pp. 31-32.
2. W.G. McMinn, 'Reid, Sir George Houstoun (1845-1918)', Australian Dictionary of Biography, National Centre of Biography, Australian National University, http://adb.anu.edu.au/biography/reid-sir-george-houstoun-8173/text14289, accessed 30 January 2013, p. 6.
3. Sir George Houstoun Reid, *My Reminiscences*, first published by Cassell and Company, Ltd 1917, Hardpress Publishing Edition, p. 5.
4. Ibid, p. 2.
5. Fricke, *Profiles of Power*, p. 44.
6. Reid, p. 10.
7. McMinn, 'Reid, Sir George Houstoun', p. 1.
8. Reid, p. 12.
9. W.G. McMinn, *George Reid*, Melbourne University Press (1989), pp. 6-7.
10. Reid, p. 152.
11. Ibid, p. 4.
12. McMinn, 'Reid, Sir George Houstoun', p. 8.
13. Warhurst, 'The Faith of Australian Prime Ministers', p. 16.
14. Quoted in Colin Hughes, *Mr Prime Minister: Australian Prime Ministers 1901-1972*, Oxford University Press (1976), p. 39.
15. McMinn, *George Reid*, p. 71.
16. Manning Clark, *A History of Australia*, Volume V, p. 292.
17. Ibid, p. 149.
18. McMinn, *George Reid*, pp. 71, 276.
19. Reid, p. 144.
20. McMinn, *George Reid*, p. 5.
21. http://electionspeeches.moadoph.gov.au/speeches/1906-george-reid.

22. *The Sydney Morning Herald*, 24 February 1912, p. 17. The full text of Reid's paper is available in book form at the National Library in Canberra.
23. Reid, p. 351.
24. Manning Clark, *A Short History of Australia*, p. 198.
25. Ibid.
26. Quoted in McMinn, *George Reid*, p. 262.
27. Reid, p. 1.
28. Ibid, p. 22; but compare the passage at p. 228 on "conscience".
29. Ibid, p. 325.
30. Ibid, p. 154.

ANDREW FISHER

1. David Day, *Andrew Fisher: Prime Minister of Australia* (Fourth Estate, 2008), p. 416, my emphasis.
2. Makin, *Federal Labour Leaders*, p. 28 (see note 6 to the section on Chris Watson).
3. J.D. Bollen, *Protestantism and Social Reform in New South Wales 1890-1910*, Melbourne University Press (1972), p. 77.
4. Bollen, p. 78.
5. Quoted in Bollen, p. 123.
6. Manning Clark, *A History of Australia*, Volume V, p. 327.
7. Day, *Andrew Fisher*, p. 415-16. See also Peter Bastian, *Andrew Fisher: An Underestimated Man*, University of New South Wales Press (2009), p. 14.
8. Bastian, pp. 12 (Fisher's attendance at church on Sundays "varied in frequency over the years") and 14.
9. Grassby and Ordonez, *The Man That Time Forgot*, p. 114 (see note 7 to the section on Chris Watson).
10. Henry Boote, quoted in Day, *Andrew Fisher*, p. 412. But compare Bastian, p. 12 ("as an adult, [Fisher] showed little interest in church doctrine") and p. 367 (describing Boote's claim as "somewhat kind").
11. Quoted in Day, *Andrew Fisher*, p. 48. See also p. 104: three of Fisher's brothers died as young men, and Fisher was reminded by Rev. Wallace that death "is not far distant from any one of us".

12. D.J. Murphy, 'Fisher, Andrew (1862-1928)', Australian Dictionary of Biography, National Centre of Biography, Australian National University, http://adb.anu.edu.au/biography/fisher-andrew-378/text10613, accessed 2 February 2013, p. 1.
13. Bastian, p. 7.
14. Quoted in Day, *Andrew Fisher,* p. 10
15. Day, *Andrew Fisher,* pp. 20-21.
16. Murphy, p. 1.
17. Ibid.
18. Fricke, *Profiles of Power,* p. 52.
19. Bastian, p. 13.
20. Ibid, p. 367 (and note 26).
21. Day, *Andrew Fisher,* pp. 23-25. See also Makin, p. 29.
22. Beazley, *Father of the House,* p. 124.
23. Day, p. 148. A copy of the postcard is reproduced in Donald Horne, *In Search of Billy Hughes,* Macmillan (1979), p. 49.
24. Murphy, p. 2.
25. Ibid, p. 1.
26. Quoted in Day, *Andrew Fisher,* p. 63.
27. Day, *Andrew Fisher,* p. 47.
28. Bastian, p. 36.
29. Ibid.
30. Bastian, p. 93.
31. Murphy, p. 1.
32. Bastian, p. 13.
33. Ibid.
34. Murphy, p. 4.
35. Manning Clark, *A History of Australia,* Volume V, p. 384.
36. Murphy, p. 4. See also Bastian, p. 273.
37. Bastian, p. 305.
38. Day, *Andrew Fisher,* p. 344.
39. Murphy, p. 4; see also Day, *Andrew Fisher,* p. 374; Bastian, p. 316.
40. Day, *Andrew Fisher,* p. 342.
41. See Michael McKernan, *Australian Churches at War: Attitudes and Activities of the Major Churches 1914-1918,* Catholic Theological Faculty and Australian War Memorial (1980), pp. 117-18.
42. Ibid, p. 119.
43. Ibid, p. 153.
44. Bastian, p. 348.
45. Day, *Andrew Fisher,* pp. 410-11.
46. Bastian p. 367.

JOSEPH COOK

1. John Rickard, 'Sir Joseph Cook' in Grattan (ed.), *Australian Prime Ministers,* p. 97
2. F.K. Crowley, 'Cook, Sir Joseph (1860-1947)', Australian Dictionary of Biography, National Centre of Biography, Australian National University, http//abd.anu.edu.au/biography/cook-sir-joseph-5763/text9765, accessed 21 December 2012, p. 3.
3. John Murdoch, *Sir Joe: A Biographical Sketch of Sir Joseph Cook,* A Silverdale Historical Publication (1979), p. 2.
4. G. Bebbington, *Pit Boy to Prime Minister: the story of the Rt. Hon. Sir Joseph Cook, P.C., G.C.M.G.,* The University of Keele (1986), p. 3.
5. Murdoch, p. 1. See also Bebbington, pp. 8-10.
6. Crowley, p. 1.
7. Booker, *The Great Professional,* p. 206 (see note 2 to the section on Chris Watson).
8. Page, *The Prime Ministers of Australia,* p. 46 (see note 32 to the section on Edmund Barton).
9. Rickard, p. 90.
10. Crowley, p. 1.
11. See http://en.wikipedia.org/wiki/Primitive_Methodism.
12. Bebbington, p. 11.
13. Ibid, p. 12.
14. Murdoch, p. 2
15. Bebbington, p. 14.
16. Quoted in Bebbington, p. 15.
17. Bebbington, p. 25.
18. Crowley, p. 1.
19. Quoted in Murdoch, p. 6.
20. Quoted in Bebbington, p. 31.
21. Bollen, *Protestantism and Social Reform,* p. 92 (see note 3 to the section on Andrew Fisher).
22. Murdoch, p. 12
23. Crowley, p. 3
24. Quoted in Murdoch, p. 22
25. McKernan, *Australian Churches at War,* pp. 1, 25 (see note 41 to the section on Andrew Fisher.)
26. Ibid, pp. 27-28
27. Quoted in Murdoch, p. 22.
28. Quoted in Bebbington, p. 59.

29. Crowley, p. 4
30. Bollen, pp. 3, 115.
31. Quoted in Bebbington, p. 31.
32. The Rev. Dr. D.D. Rutledge, quoted in Bollen, p. 115.
33. See Bollen, pp. 115-17
34. The Rev. W.H. Beale, quoted in Bollen, p. 118.
35. Quoted in Bebbington, p. 35.
36. Fricke, *Profiles of Power,* p. 59.
37. Bebbington, p. 3.
38. Murdoch, p. 27.
39. Bebbington, p. 89.
40. The Rev. Wallace Deane, quoted in Bebbington, p. 89.
41. Grassby and Ordonez, *The Man That Time Forgot,* p. 163.

BILLY HUGHES

1. Geoffrey Bolton, 'William Morris Hughes', in Grattan (ed.), *Australian Prime Ministers,* p. 102.
2. Fred Daly, *From Curtin to Hawke,* Macmillan (1984), p. 32.
3. Donald Horne, *In Search of Billy Hughes,* Macmillan (1979), p. 51.
4. Ibid, p. 2.
5. Quoted in Fricke, *Profiles of Power,* p. 75.
6. Booker, *The Great Professional,* p. x.
7. Ibid, p. 67.
8. Bolton, 'William Morris Hughes', p. 103.
9. Manning Clark, *A History of Australia,* Volume V, p. 118; cf. Makin, *Federal Labour Leaders,* p. 53.
10. See Booker, pp. 2-3.
11. Manning Clark, *A History of Australia,* Volume VI, p. 5. See also p. 14 (Hughes "had no doubts about human beings usurping the divine prerogative of revenge").
12. Ibid, p. 96.
13. Ibid, p. 100.
14. Makin, p. 54.
15. Booker, p. 7.
16. L.F. Fitzhardinge, *The Little Digger 1914-1952: William Morris Hughes, A Political Biography,* Volume II, Angus & Robertson (1979), pp. xvi-xvii.
17. Ibid, p. xvii.
18. Manning Clark, *A History of Australia,* Volume V, p. 118.
19. L.F. Fitzhardinge, *That Fiery Particle 1862-1914: William Morris Hughes, A Political Biography, Volume I,* first published by Angus & Robertson 1964, Angus & Robertson Paperback Edition (1978), p. 1.
20. Ibid, p. 1; Horne, p. 6.
21. Fitzhardinge, *That Fiery Particle,* p. 2.
22. Quoted in Horne, p. 8.
23. Fitzhardinge, *That Fiery Particle,* p. 2.
24. Ibid.
25. Ibid, p. 3; Horne, p. 6.
26. Fitzhardinge, *That Fiery Particle,* p. 3, note 8.
27. Horne, p. 6, Fitzhardinge, *That Fiery Particle,* p. 4
28. Fitzhardinge, *That Fiery Particle,* p. 2
29. Ibid, p. 3. See also the website of the Llandudno Trinity Church.
30. Fitzhardinge, *That Fiery Particle,* p. 4.
31. Ibid, pp. 8-9.
32. Ibid, p. 9; Fitzhardinge, *The Little Digger,* p. xvi.
33. Fitzhardinge, *That Fiery Particle,* p. 8; Horne, p. 7.
34. Quoted in Fitzhardinge, *That Fiery Particle,* p. 11.
35. Sir Robert Gordon Menzies, *Afternoon Light: Some Memories of Men and Events,* Cassell (1967), p. 108.
36. Horne, p. 13.
37. Booker, p. 83. See also W.M. Hughes, *Policies and Potentates,* Angus & Robertson (1950), p. 99 (lamenting the fact that "with some, religion had become a mere byword; for God they had substituted what they called Reason.")
38. Quoted in Booker, p. 84.
39. Ibid, p. 85.
40. Quoted in Fitzhardinge, *That Fiery Particle,* p. 245. See also Hughes, *Policies and Potentates,* pp. 6-7.
41. W.M. Hughes, *Crusts and Crusades: Tales of bygone days,* Angus & Robertson (1948), p. 70.
42. Quoted in Booker, p. 203 (see also note 26 on p. 201).
43. Booker, p. 35.
44. Quoted in John Robertson, *J.H. Scullin: A Political Biography,* University of Western Australia Press (1974), p. 45.
45. Booker, p. 215.

46. Ibid, pp. 216-17.
47. Horne, p. 101.
48. Bolton, 'William Morris Hughes', p. 124.
49. Hughes, *Crusts and Crusades,* pp. 61-67.
50. Ibid, p. 93.
51. Manning Clark, *A History of Australia,* Volume V, p. 120.
52. Ibid, Volume VI, p. 51.
53. Available online at http://trove.nla.gov.au/ndp/del/article/45608571.

STANLEY MELBOURNE BRUCE

1. Quoted in Gerard Henderson, *Menzies' Child: The Liberal Party of Australia 1944-1994,* Allen & Unwin (1994), p. 41.
2. Manning Clark, *A History of Australia,* Volume VI, p. 310.
3. *The Age,* 10 January 1973.
4. Cumpston, *Lord Bruce of Melbourne,* p. 30 (see note 9 to the Introduction).
5. Heather Radi, 'Bruce, Stanley Melbourne (1883-1967)', Australian Dictionary of Biography, National Centre of Biography, Australian National University, http://adb.anu.edu.au/biography/bruce-stanley-melbourne-5400/text9147, accessed 21 December 2012, p. 6.
6. Judith Brett, 'Stanley Melbourne Bruce', in Grattan (ed.), *Australian Prime Ministers,* New Holland (2000), p. 146. And see generally Denning, *Caucus Crisis* (see note 19 to the section on James Scullin).
7. Dame Enid Lyons, *Among the Carrion Crows,* Rigby Seal (1977), p. 71.
8. Alfred Stirling, *Lord Bruce: The London Years,* The Hawthorn Press (1974), p. 19; see also Cumpston, pp. 103-06.
9. Cumpston, p. 106.
10. Quoted in Cecil Edwards, *Bruce of Melbourne: Man of Two Worlds,* Heinemann (1965), p. 239.
11. Radi, p. 6.
12. Alfred Stirling, quoted in Cumpston, p. 143.
13. Edwards, p. 407.
14. Fricke, *Profiles of Power,* p. 78.
15. Edwards, p. 12.
16. Cumpston, p. 1.
17. Edwards, p. 13.
18. Ibid, pp-11-12. See also Cumpston,

p. 2 (where the suggestion is made that Grammar's physical proximity to the Bruces' house may have been a factor).
19. Cumpston, p. 4.
20. Quoted in Cumpston, p. 5.
21. Edwards, p. 14.
22. Cumpston, p. 9.
23. Edwards, p. 16.
24. Cumpston, p. 102.
25. Edwards, p. 28.
26. Ibid, p. 46.
27. Quoted in Edwards, p. 56. See also Cumpston, pp. 18-19.
28. Christopher Waters, *Australia and Appeasement: Imperial Foreign Policy and the Origins of World War Two,* I.B. Taurus (2012), p. 265. See generally Cumpston, pp. 143-56.
29. Radi, p. 8. See generally Cumpston, pp. 175-211.
30. Edwards, p. 460.
31. Brett, p. 132.
32. Edwards, p. 120.
33. Manning Clark, *A History of Australia,* Volume VI, p. 248.
34. Brett, p. 137.
35. Edwards, p. 247.
36. Ibid, p. 340. For Bruce's testy relationship with Churchill, see generally Cumpston, pp. 201-222.
37. Edwards, p. 457.
38. Stirling, pp. 268, 485.
39. Ibid, p. 485.
40. Quoted in Cumpston, p. 143.
41. Quoted in Stirling, p. 486.
42. Cumpston, p. 101.
43. Stirling, p. 485.
44. Ibid, p. 492.
45. Edwards, pp. 407-08.

JAMES SCULLIN

1. John Molony, 'James Henry Scullin' in Grattan (ed.), *Australian Prime Ministers,* p. 142.
2. Robertson, *J.H. Scullin,* p. 4 (see note 44 to the section on Billy Hughes).
3. Molony, p. 143.
4. Ibid. See also Robertson, pp. 6-7
5. Robertson, p. 117.
6. Manning Clark, *A History of Australia,* Volume VI, p. 199.

7. Menzies, *Afternoon Light,* p. 119 (see note 35 to the section on Billy Hughes).
8. Molony, p. 146.
9. Ibid, p. 142. See also Robertson, pp. 380-81.
10. Quoted in Robertson, p. 303.
11. Quoted in Robertson, p. 395. See generally on the Premiers' Plan, Molony, pp. 148-49; Robertson, pp. 262-64.
12. Robertson, p. 187ff; Molony, p. 145.
13. Fred Daly, *From Curtin to Hawke,* Macmillan (1984), p. 34.
14. Menzies, *Afternoon Light,* p. 121.
15. Robertson, p. 16.
16. Ibid, p. 71.
17. Robertson, pp. 119, 210.
18. Manning Clark, *A History of Australia,* Volume VI, p. 287.
19. Warren Denning, *Caucus Crisis: The rise & fall of the Scullin government,* Hale & Ironmonger (1982), p. 37.
20. Ibid.
21. Robertson, p. 180.
22. Molony, p. 151.
23. Quoted in Robertson, p. 118.
24. Robertson, p. 40.
25. Ibid, p. 118.
26. Ibid, p. 210, note 21.
27. Molony, p. 143.
28. Robertson, pp. 119, 123.
29. Ibid, p. 479.
30. Fitzgerald, *The Pope's Battalions,* p. 31 (see note 14 to the Introduction).
31. Robertson, p. 123.
32. Molony, p. 150; Robertson, p. 123.
33. Robertson, p. 404.
34. Ibid, pp. 465-66.
35. Ibid, p. 37.
36. Ibid, pp. 54, 59.
37. Ibid, p. 82.
38. Ibid, p. 84.

JOSEPH LYONS

1. See Anne Henderson, *Joseph Lyons: The People's Prime Minister,* NewSouth (2011), pp. 245-56.
2. Manning Clark, *A History of Australia,* Volume VI, p. 371.
3. Ibid, p. 263.
4. Dame Enid Lyons, *So We Take Comfort,* Heinemann (1965), pp. 170-72.

5. Fitzgerald, *The Pope's Battalions,* passim.
6. Quoted in Kate White, *A Political Love Story: Joe and Enid Lyons,* Penguin Books (1987), p. 64.
7. Henderson, *Joseph Lyons,* p. 25.
8. Ibid, p. 37.
9. Ibid, p. 92.
10. Ibid, p. 94.
11. Ibid, p. 90.
12. Ibid, p. 93.
13. Quoted in White, pp. 55-56.
14. Henderson, *Joseph Lyons,* p. 94.
15. Quoted in White, p. 63.
16. Quoted in Anne Henderson, *Enid Lyons: Leading Lady to a Nation,* Pluto Press Australia (2008), p. 174. My emphasis.
17. Ibid, p. 3.
18. Ibid, p. 115.
19. Ibid, p. 207.
20. David Bird, *J.A. Lyons – The 'Tame Tasmanian',* Australian Scholarly Publishing (2008), p. xi.
21. Quoted in Henderson, *Enid Lyons,* pp. 242-43. See also Christopher Waters, *Australia and Appeasement,* pp. 141-2 (see note 28 to the section on S.M. Bruce); Bird, p. 210 (Enid was reading articles from the *Contemporary Review on Pacifism and the Peace Movement*).
22. Enid Lyons, quoted in Bird, p. 298.
23. Quoted in Bird, p. 105.
24. Bird, pp. 216, 271.
25. Quoted in Waters, p. 148.
26. White, p. 150; Henderson, *Enid Lyons,* p. 186.
27. Henderson, *Enid Lyons,* p. 206.
28. Henderson, *Joseph Lyons,* p. 125.
29. Bird, p. 335.
30. Manning Clark, *A History of Australia,* Volume VI, p. 263.
31. Quoted in Bird, p. 232.
32. Bird, p. 265.
33. Ibid, p. 216.
34. Henderson, *Joseph Lyons,* p. 74.
35. Dame Enid Lyons, *So We Take Comfort,* pp. 144-45.
36. Henderson, *Joseph Lyons,* p. 430. My emphasis. See also Bird, p. 233 (describing Lyons' call in September 1938 for a National Day of Prayer as "a further example of personal sentiment being translated into political principle, as Lyons was wont to do").

37. Fricke, *Profiles of Power*, p. 100.
38. W.J. Hudson, *Casey,* Oxford University Press (1986), p. 106.
39. Menzies, *Afternoon Light*, p. 125.
40. Anne Henderson, 'Joseph Aloysius Lyons', in Grattan (ed.) *Australian Prime Ministers,* p. 164.
41. Henderson, *Joseph Lyons,* p. 9.
42. Henderson, *Enid Lyons,* pp. 252-53.

JOHN CURTIN

1. See, for example, Sir Arthur Fadden, *They Called Me Artie,* Jacaranda Press (1969), p. 80 ("There was no greater figure in Australian public life in my lifetime than Curtin"). Fadden, it will be recalled, served as prime minister for five weeks in 1941, in the interim period between Menzies and Curtin.
2. J.D. (Jack) Lang, quoted in John Edwards, *Curtin's Gift: Reinterpreting Australia's greatest Prime Minister,* Allen & Unwin (2005), p. 21.
3. Edwards, *Curtin's Gift,* p. 20.
4. Manning Clark, *A Short History of Australia,* p. 261; cf. David Day, *John Curtin: A life,* HarperCollins (1999), p. 132; Edwards, *Curtin's Gift,* p. 20.
5. Day, *John Curtin,* p. 131.
6. Irene Dowsing, *Curtin of Australia,* Acacia Press (1969), p. 7.
7. Day, *John Curtin,* pp. 166-67, 202-03.
8. Geoffrey Serle, 'Curtin, John (1885–1945)', Australian Dictionary of Biography, National Centre of Biography, Australian National University, http://adb.anu.edu.au/biography/curtin-john-9885/text17495, accessed 31 January 2013, pp. 2, 6.
9. Day, *John Curtin,* p. 565.
10. David Day, 'John Joseph Curtin' in Grattan (ed.), *Australian Prime Ministers,* p. 218.
11. Day, *John Curtin,* p. 14.
12. Day, 'John Joseph Curtin', p. 218.
13. Day, *John Curtin,* p. 16.
14. Ibid, pp. 36-37.
15. Ibid, p. 36.
16. Day, 'John Joseph Curtin', p. 218; Day, *John Curtin,* p. 131 (note 6).
17. Patrick O'Farrell, *The Irish in Australia,* University of New South Wales Press (1993), pp. 132-33.
18. Serle, p. 1.
19. Day, *John Curtin,* p. 45.
20. Lloyd Ross, *John Curtin: A Biography,* first published by The Macmillan Company of Australia Pty Ltd 1977, Melbourne University Press Edition (1996), p. 10.
21. Day, *John Curtin,* p. 37; see also p. 131.
22. Ibid, p. 131.
23. Edwards, *Curtin's Gift,* p. 81.
24. Day, *John Curtin,* p. 52.
25. Ibid, pp. 20-21. See also Ross, p. 7.
26. Day, *John Curtin,* p. 43.
27. Ibid, p. 49.
28. Ibid, p. 131.
29. Ibid, pp. 163, 201.
30. Day, 'John Joseph Curtin', p. 221.
31. Day, *John Curtin,* p. 131.
32. Ross, p. 10; Day, *John Curtin,* pp. 53-56.
33. Day, *John Curtin,* pp. 130-31.
34. Ibid, pp. 131-32.
35. Ibid, p. 483.
36. Ibid, p. 65.
37. Day, 'John Joseph Curtin', p. 221.
38. Quoted in Day, *John Curtin,* p. 152.
39. Quoted in Day, 'John Joseph Curtin', p. 232; Day, *John Curtin,* pp. 414-15.
40. Serle, p. 6.
41. Edwards, *Curtin's Gift,* p. 90; Day, 'John Joseph Curtin', pp. 222, 225.
42. Day, 'John Joseph Curtin', p. 220.
43. Day, *John Curtin,* p. 89.
44. David Black, 'Biography of Elsie Curtin', John Curtin Prime Ministerial Library, available online at http://john.curtin.edu.au/resources/biography/ecurtin.html, note 5; see also Day, *John Curtin,* pp. 147-48.
45. Quoted in Ross, p. 33.
46. Ross, p. 85.
47. Dowsing, *Curtin of Australia,* p. 155.
48. Day, pp. 163, 242.
49. Black, 'Elsie Curtin', note 24.
50. Day, *John Curtin,* pp. 572-73.
51. Ibid, p. 571.
52. Edwards, *Curtin's Gift,* pp. 159-60; Day, *John Curtin,* p. 483 (photo); see also Fricke, *Profiles of Power,* p. 132.
53. Serle, p. 12.
54. Warhurst, 'The Faith of Australian Prime Ministers', p. 12
55. *The Argus,* 1 January 1943, p. 4.
56. Day, *John Curtin,* pp. 149-50.

57. Black, 'Elsie Curtin', note 2.
58. Ibid, note 49.
59. Day, *John Curtin*, p. 572; Black, 'Elsie Curtin'.
60. Day, *John Curtin*, p. 396.
61. Ibid, p. 445.
62. Ibid, p. 447.
63. Ibid, pp. 481, 572. See also Edwards, *Curtin's Gift*, p. 20.
64. Day, *John Curtin*, p. 468.
65. Ibid, p. 571.
66. Beazley, *Father of the House*, p. 73.
67. Day, *John Curtin*, p. 483.
68. Ibid, p. 567.
69. Ibid, pp. 571-72.
70. Ibid, p. 569.
71. Ibid, pp. 574-75.
72. Quoted in Day, *John Curtin*, p. 572; cf. Edwards, *Curtin's Gift*, p. 2.
73. Day, *John Curtin*, p. 572.

BEN CHIFLEY

1. Menzies, *Afternoon Light*, pp. 128-29.
2. Daly, *From Curtin to Hawke*, p. 21.
3. L.F. Crisp, *Ben Chifley: A Biography*, Longmans (1960), p. 420.
4. David Day, *Chifley*, HarperCollins (2001), pp. 358-59, 376-77.
5. Mike Steketee, 'The tough get going', *The Australian*, 1 November, 2008.
6. Crisp, p. 383.
7. Makin, *Federal Labour Leaders*, pp. 131-32.
8. Ibid, pp. 132-39.
9. Brian Carroll, *The Menzies Years*, Cassell Australia (1977), p. 167ff.
10. Ross McMullin, 'Joseph Benedict Chifley' in Grattan (ed.), *Australian Prime Ministers*, p. 248.
11. Day, pp. 16-17.
12. Crisp, p. 2.
13. Day, p. 19.
14. Ibid, pp. 18-19.
15. Ibid, p. 85.
16. Ibid, pp. 27-34.
17. Ibid, p.
18. Ibid, pp. 38-39.
19. Ibid, pp. 54-83.
20. McMullin, p. 249; Day, pp. 53-54.
21. Crisp, p. 7.
22. Ibid.
23. Day, p. 92.
24. Ibid, p. 264.
25. Ibid, p. 85.
26. Crisp, pp. 8-9; Day, p. 92.
27. Day, p. 93.
28. Quoted in McMullin, pp. 249-50; Crisp, p. 9.
29. Day, p. 94.
30. Crisp, pp. 112-13.
31. Crisp, p. 10; Day, p. 275 (note 32).
32. Day, p. 404; Makin, *Federal Labour Leaders*, p. 131; Beazley, *Father of the House*, p. 66. See also the website of the Archdiocese of Canberra and Goulbourn at http://www.cg.catholic.org.au/about/default.cfm?loadref=14
33. Paul Hasluck, *The Chance of Politics*, edited and introduced by Nicholas Hasluck, Text Publishing (1997), p. 29.
34. Quoted in Day, p. 380.
35. Ibid, p. 381.
36. Ibid, p. 422.
37. Quoted in Crisp, p. 383.
38. Quoted in Day, p. 495.
39. Quoted in Crisp, p. 383.
40. Beazley, *Father of the House*, pp. 50-51.
41. Crisp, p. 10 (note 5).
42. Day, pp. 212, 239 (note 18).
43. Ibid, pp. 155-56.
44. Ibid, p. 297.
45. Ibid, pp. 296-97.
46. Hasluck, p. 29.
47. Quoted in McMullin, p. 259.
48. Quoted in Crisp, p. 383.
49. Jenny Hocking, *Gough Whitlam: A Moment in History*, The Miegunyah Press (2008), p. 142.
50. Quoted in B.A. Santamaria, *A Memoir*, Oxford University Press (1997), p. 106.
51. Quoted in Day, p. 275.
52. Ibid, p. 479.
53. Fitzgerald, *The Pope's Battalions*, pp. 104-07.
54. Quoted in Crisp, pp. 382-83.
55. Ibid, p. 383.
56. Ibid, p. 384 (note 5).
57. Mungo MacCallum, *The Good, the Bad and the Unlikely: Australia's Prime Ministers*, Black Inc (2012), p. 122.
58. Daly, p. 106.
59. Day, p. 527.

ROBERT MENZIES

1. A.W. Martin, *Robert Menzies: A Life, Volume 1, 1894-1943*, Melbourne University Press (1993), p. 427.
2. Wallace Brown, *Ten Prime Ministers: Life Among the Politicians*, Longueville Books (2002), p. 21.
3. Daly, *From Curtin to Hawke*, p. 95; MacCallum, *The Good, the Bad and the Unlikely*, p. 89.
4. Cameron Hazelhurst, *Menzies Observed*, George Allen & Unwin (1979), p. 303.
5. Menzies, *Afternoon Light*, p. 12.
6. Martin, *A Life, Volume 1*, p. 9.
7. Maisie McKenzie, *Outback Achiever: Fred McKay, Successor to Flynn of the Inland*, Boolarong Press (1990), pp. 177-78.
8. Menzies, *Afternoon Light*, p. 10.
9. Martin, *A Life, Volume 1*, p. 9.
10. Hazelhurst, p. 13.
11. Martin, *A Life, Volume 1*, p. 10.
12. Menzies, *Afternoon Light*, p. 9.
13. Hazelhurst, p. 11.
14. Menzies, *Afternoon Light*, p. 10.
15. Martin, *A Life, Volume 1*, p. 14.
16. Menzies, *Afternoon Light*, p. 9.
17. Hazelhurst, p. 33.
18. Martin, *A Life, Volume 1*, pp. 22-23; MacCallum, *The Good, the Bad and the Unlikely*, p. 87.
19. Quoted in Hazelhurst, p. 27.
20. Quoted in Manning Clark, *A History of Australia*, Volume VI, p. 8.
21. Martin, *A Life, Volume 1*, pp. 22-23.
22. Ibid, p. 42; Hazelhurst, p. 34.
23. Quoted in Hazelhurst, p. 43.
24. Martin, *A Life, Volume 1*, p. 44.
25. Ibid, p. 70.
26. Quoted in Hazelhurst, p. 74.
27. Quoted in Martin, *A Life, Volume 1*, p. 80.
28. Martin, *A Life, Volume 1*, p. 113.
29. See Hazelhurst, p. 109.
30. Ibid, p. 140ff.
31. Quoted in Martin, *A Life, Volume 1*, p. 155.
32. Ibid, p. 156.
33. See note 28 to the section on S.M. Bruce.
34. Quoted in Waters, *Australia and Appeasement*, p. 66.
35. Quoted in Hazelhurst, p. 138.
36. Ibid, p. 140.
37. Kate White, quoted in Hazelhurst, p. 152 (re Lyons).
38. Quoted in Hazelhurst, p. 196. My emphasis.
39. Quoted in Waters, p. 132.
40. Ibid, p. 189.
41. Ibid, p. 201.
42. Ibid, p. 195.
43. Menzies, *Afternoon Light*, p. 16.
44. Quoted in Hazelhurst, p. 182; see also Waters, p. 54.
45. Quoted in Hazelhurst, p. 184.
46. Allan Martin, 'Sir Robert Gordon Menzies', in Grattan (ed.), *Australian Prime Ministers*, pp. 186-87; see also Hazelhurst, p. 237.
47. Menzies, *Afternoon Light*, p. 126.
48. Quoted in Hazelhurst, p. 266.
49. Quoted in Waters, p. 265.
50. Menzies, *Afternoon Light*, pp. 19-20.
51. Ibid, p. 22.
52. Quoted in Hazelhurst, pp. 224-26.
53. Quoted in Martin, *A Life, Volume 1*, p. 372.
54. Quoted in Hazelhurst, p. 283. For a somewhat different perspective, see Ian Hancock, *The Liberals: The NSW Division 1945-2000*, The Federation Press (2007), passim. Hancock describes as a "myth" the notion that Menzies was "the founder" of the Liberal Party.
55. Henderson, *Menzies' Child*, p. 67 (see note 1 to the section on S.M. Bruce).
56. Ibid, p.77.
57. A.W. Martin, *Robert Menzies: A Life, Volume 2, 1944-1978*, Melbourne University Press (1999), pp. 57-58.
58. Wallace Brown, *Ten Prime Ministers*, p. 17.
59. Sir Robert Menzies, *The Measure of the Years*, Cassell Australia Ltd (1970), p. 91.
60. Ibid, p. 92.
61. Henderson, *Menzies' Child*, p. 106.
62. Quoted in Fitzgerald, *The Pope's Battalions*, p. 44.
63. Quoted in Henderson, *Menzies' Child*, p. 107.
64. Ibid.
65. Heather Henderson (ed.), *Letters to My Daughter: Robert Menzies, letters, 1955-75*, Pier 9 (2011), p. 43.
66. Wallace Brown, p. 34.
67. Menzies, *Afternoon Light*, p. 38.
68. Judith Brett, *The Forgotten People*, first published by Melbourne University Press 1993 (2007 edition), p. 121.
69. *The Canberra Times*, 15 March 1954, p. 2.

My emphasis. See also Martin, *A Life, Volume 2*, pp. 470-71, 476-78, 507.
70. McKenzie, pp. 108-09, 113.
71. Text accessible on line at http://www.menziesvirtualmuseum.org.au/transcripts/Speech_is_of_Time/501_ModSci_Civilization.html.
72. Henderson, *Letters to My Daughter*, p. 272.
73. See Martin, *A Life, Volume 2*, pp. 28-29 (Martin quotes from Menzies' hilarious account of a wedding ceremony at St Stephen's Presbyterian Church in Macquarie Street, Sydney, conducted by the Rev. George Cowie).
74. Henderson, *Letters to My Daughter*, p. 65.
75. Ibid, p. 153.
76. Ibid, p. 163.
77. McKenzie, p. 175; see also Martin, *A Life, Volume 2*, p. 560.
78. McKenzie, p. 176.
79. Ibid, p. 179.
80. Menzies, *Afternoon Light*, p. 12.
81. McKenzie, pp. 180-81.

HAROLD HOLT

1. MacCallum, *The Good, the Bad and the Unlikely*, p. 127; Ian Hancock, 'Harold Edward Holt' in Grattan (ed.), *Australian Prime Ministers*, p. 274.
2. Tom Frame, *The Life and Death of Harold Holt*, Allen & Unwin (2005), p. 31.
3. John Murphy, quoted in Frame, p. 63.
4. Simon Warrender, *Score of Years*, Wren Publishing (1973), p. 147.
5. Ibid.
6. Quoted in Frame, p. 270.
7. Quoted in Frame, p. xii.
8. Frame, p. 303.
9. Hancock, p. 273; Frame, pp. 6-7.
10. Frame, p. 11.
11. Hancock, p. 275; Frame, pp. 7-8.
12. I.R. Hancock, 'Holt, Harold Edward (1908-1967)', Australian Dictionary of Biography, National Centre of Biography, Australian National University, http://adb.anu.edu.au/biography/holt-harold-edward-10530/text18693, accessed 29 January 2013, p. 2.
13. Dame Zara Holt, *My Life and Harry*, Herald & Weekly Times (1968), p. 26.
14. Hancock, 'Harold Edward Holt', p. 275;

MacCallum, *The Good, the Bad and the Unlikely*, p. 127.
15. Hancock, 'Harold Edward Holt', p. 283; Hancock, 'Holt, Harold Edward', p. 7.
16. Quoted in Hancock, 'Harold Edward Holt', p. 283.
17. MacCallum, *The Good, the Bad and the Unlikely*, p. 128.
18. Hancock, 'Harold Edward Holt', p. 276.
19. Frame, p. 157.
20. Warhurst, 'The Faith of Australia's Prime Ministers', p. 5. See also Judith Brett, *Australian Liberals and the Moral Middle Class: From Alfred Deakin to John Howard*, Cambridge University Press (2003), p. 131ff.
21. Hancock, 'Holt, Harold Edward', p. 4.
22. Quoted in Frame, p. 135.
23. Hasluck, *The Chance of Politics*, p. 142.
24. Hocking, *Gough Whitlam*, pp. 300-01.
25. Hancock, 'Harold Edward Holt', p. 279.
26. Ibid, p. 281.
27. Alan Reid, *The Power Struggle*, Shakespeare Head Press (1969), pp. 13, 90; Henderson, *Menzies' Child*, pp. 193, 197-98.
28. Zara Holt, p. 256.
29. E.g., MacCallum, *The Good, the Bad and the Unlikely*, p. 130.
30. Quoted in Frame, p. 277.
31. Reid, *The Power Struggle*, p. 80.
32. Wallace Brown, *Twelve Prime Ministers*, p. 52.
33. Frame, p. 273-74.
34. Sir Alec Downer, quoted in Frame, p. 277.
35. See *The Canberra Times*, 23 December 1967.
36. Hancock, 'Holt, Harold Edward', p. 6.
37. Quoted in Frame, p. 271.

JOHN GORTON

1. Alan Trengove, *John Grey Gorton: An Informal Biography*, Cassell Australia, (1969), p. 163.
2. K.C. Masterman, Gorton's housemaster at Geelong Grammar. Quoted in Ian Hancock, *John Gorton: He Did It His Way*, Hodder (2002), pp. 12-18.
3. Trengove, p. 127.
4. Ibid, p. 248.
5. Fitzgerald, *The Pope's Battalions*, p. 200.
6. Quoted in Hancock, p. 367.
7. Ibid, pp. 368-70.

8. Alan Reid, *The Gorton Experiment: The Fall of John Grey Gorton*, Shakespeare Head Press (1971), p. 12.
9. See Edward St John, *A Time to Speak*, Sun Books (1969), pp. 164ff; cf. Hancock, pp. 213-23.
10. *The Age*, 10 January, 1969.
11. St John, *A Time to Speak*, p. 3.
12. Ibid, p. 32.
13. Reid, *The Gorton Experiment*, p. 9.
14. Hancock, p. 6.
15. Ibid, p. 1.
16. Quoted in Hancock, p. 86.
17. Quoted in Trengove, p. 150.
18. C.S. Lewis, *Mere Christianity*, first published by William Collins 1952, thirty-seventh impression, Fount Paperbacks (1983), p. 92.
19. Hancock, pp. 179-80.
20. Ibid, pp. 390-91.
21. Trengove, p. 31.
22. Hancock, p. 12.
23. Ibid, p. 13.
24. Trengove, pp. 37-38.
25. Hancock, p. 15.
26. Ibid, p. 63. My emphasis.
27. Quoted in Hancock, pp. 32, 40.
28. Ibid, pp. 404-06 (for the full text of Gorton's speech).
29. Trengove, p. 158.
30. Quoted in Trengove, pp. 164-65.
31. Hancock, p. 106. It should be noted that the reference to Matthew 5:48 was originally Gorton's own.
32. Ibid, pp. 106-07.

BILLY MCMAHON

1. S.R. Davis (ed.), *The Australian Political Party System*, Angus & Robertson (1954). McMahon's paper, entitled 'The Liberal Party', was reproduced at pp. 29-51 of the book.
2. McMahon, 'The Liberal Party', p. 31.
3. Ibid, pp. 29-31.
4. Ibid, p. 31.
5. Peter Sekuless, 'Sir William McMahon', in Grattan (ed.), *Australian Prime Ministers*, p. 315.
6. Peter Coleman, 'Bill McMahon: From "Christus Veritas" to the Department of Labor', *The Bulletin*, August 10, 1963, p. 17.

7. Ibid.
8. Robbie Swan, 'McMahon never made the pages of Penthouse', *The Canberra Times*, April 10, 1988, p. 4.
9. Coleman, p. 17
10. Swan, p. 4.
11. John Edwards, 'Inside Billy McMahon', *The Australian Financial Review*, 31 May 1972, p. 3.
12. Coleman, p. 17
13. Swan, p. 4
14. Ibid.
15. Coleman, p. 17
16. Ibid.
17. Ibid.
18. Ibid.
19. Edwards, p. 3.
20. Coleman, p. 18
21. See, e.g., Reid, *The Gorton Experiment*, pp. 392-444 (see note 8 to the section on John Gorton).
22. Quoted in Brian Carroll, *Australia's Prime Ministers: From Barton to Howard*, Rosenberg (2004), p. 225.
23. Quoted in Sekuless, p. 321.
24. Heather Henderson, *Letters to My Daughter*, p. 224.
25. Ian Hancock, *John Gorton*, p. 345. See generally Alan Reid, *The Power Struggle*, passim (note 27 to the section on Harold Holt); Hasluck, *The Chance of Politics*, edited and introduced by Nicholas Hasluck, Text Publishing (1997), pp. 146-164, 184-196.
26. Julian Leeser, 'McMahon, Sir William (Billy) (1908-1988)', Australian Dictionary of Biography, National Centre of Biography, Australian National University, http//abd.anu.edu.au/biography/mcmahon-sir-william-billy-15043/text26240, accessed 21 December 2012, p. 1.
27. 'Sir William McMahon: A long road to the top in Australia', Obituary, *The Times* (London), 1 April 1988, p. 1.
28. Deane Wells, *The Wit of Whitlam*, Outback Press (1976), p. 68; Daly, p. 192.
29. Various Catholic and Protestant clergymen ran full-page newspaper ads in the last weeks of the campaign. One K.J. Parker of Seaforth in Sydney took out an ad on 1 December 1972

charging that "freedom of worship" itself was under threat. These sorts of views were prominently reported. See, for example, 'Labor under attack on moral attitudes', *The Sydney Morning Herald,* 27 November 1972, p. 1; 'Morality issue divides churchmen', *The Sydney Morning Herald,* 28 November 1972, pp. 1, 8; 'PM warns of racial danger in ALP policy', *The Sydney Morning Herald,* 1 December 1972, p. 1. For Whitlam's response to this campaign see his interview with Graham Perkin of *The Age,* reproduced in *The Sydney Morning Herald* on 28 November 1972, p. 8.

30. See, e.g., Susan Mitchell, *Stand By Your Man,* Random House (2007), pp. 6-9, 37-38.
31. Wells, p. 72.
32. MacCallum, *The Good, the Bad and the Unlikely,* p. 148.
33. See Larry Writer, 'Sonia McMahon: the truth about my marriage', *The Australian Women's Weekly,* November 2007, pp.50-54. Lady McMahon was responding to the chapter about her late husband in Susan Mitchell's book *Stand By Your Man.*
34. John Edwards, 'Inside Billy McMahon', p. 3.
35. Mitchell, p. 57.

GOUGH WHITLAM

1. MacCallum, *The Good, the Bad and the Unlikely,* p. 160.
2. See Susan Mitchell, *Margaret Whitlam: A Biography,* Random House Australia (2006), p. 381.
3. Gough Whitlam, *Abiding Interests,* University of Queensland Press (1997), p. 306.
4. Ibid, p. 82
5. Quoted in Barry Cohen, *Life With Gough,* Allen & Unwin (1996), p. 40.
6. Whitlam, *Abiding Interests,* p. 317.
7. See Mitchell, *Margaret Whitlam,* pp. 21-24.
8. Jenny Hocking, *Gough Whitlam: A Moment in History,* The Miegunyah Press (2008), p. xvii.
9. Ibid, p. 16.
10. Ibid, p. 22.

11. Ibid, p. 45; see also Clem Lloyd, 'Edward Gough Whitlam' in Grattan (ed.), *Australian Prime Ministers,* pp. 328-29.
12. Hocking, *A Moment in History,* pp. 22-23.
13. Carroll, *Australia's Prime Ministers,* p. 230; Hocking, *A Moment in History,* p. 25.
14. Lloyd, p. 329.
15. Hocking, *A Moment in History,* p. 47.
16. Quoted in Hocking, *A Moment in History,* p. 30.
17. Cohen, p. 40.
18. Hocking, *A Moment in History,* p. 39.
19. Ibid, p. 71.
20. Mitchell, *Margaret Whitlam,* pp. 54-55.
21. Quoted in Hocking, *A Moment in History,* pp. 27-28.
22. Hocking, *A Moment in History,* p. 46.
23. Ellen McIntosh, 'A Whitlam not to be Goughed-at', *Penrith Press,* 25 May 2009, available online at http://penrith-press. whereilive.com.au/news/story/yes-she-is-related-to-that-whitlam-she-even-has-the-same-facial-expressions/. See also Cohen, p. 37.
24. Brian Carroll, *Whitlam,* Rosenberg (2011), p. 13.
25. Hocking, *A Moment in History,* p. 47.
26. Ibid.
27. Mitchell, *Margaret Whitlam,* p. 56. My emphasis.
28. Ibid, p. 56.
29. Carroll, *Whitlam,* p. 16.
30. Cohen, p. 39.
31. Carroll, *Whitlam,* p. 17.
32. Cohen, p. 39.
33. Hocking, *A Moment in History,* p. 55.
34. Quoted in Wells, *The Wit of Whitlam,* pp. 46-47 (see note 28 to the section on Bill McMahon).
35. Hocking, *A Moment in History,* p. 59.
36. Ibid.
37. Ibid, p. 63.
38. Carroll, *Whitlam,* p. 17; Hocking, *A Moment in History,* p. 63.
39. Hocking, *A Moment in History,* pp. 100-01.
40. Whitlam, *Abiding Interests,* p. 85; see also pp. 91-93.
41. See Graham Freudenberg, *A Certain Grandeur: Gough Whitlam in Politics,* first published by Macmillan 1977, Sun Books edition (1978), pp. 24-38.

42. Fitzgerald, *The Pope's Battalions*, p. 212.
43. Beazley, *Father of the House*, p. 7. See generally pp. 177-83, 192ff.
44. Carroll, *Australia's Prime Ministers*, pp. 105-6.
45. Whitlam, *Abiding Interests*, p. 209.
46. Quoted in Wells, p. 81.
47. Mitchell, *Margaret Whitlam*, pp. 277-80.
48. Carroll, *Australia's Prime Ministers*, p. 242.
49. Quoted in Cohen, p. 206.
50. Whitlam, *Abiding Interests*, p. 169.
51. Ibid, p. 81.
52. Cohen, p. 48.

MALCOLM FRASER

1. Brown, *Twelve Prime Ministers*, p. 146.
2. Quoted in Henderson, *Menzies' Child*, p. 243.
3. See, for example, Grattan (ed.), *Australian Prime Ministers*, p. 470; cf. Warhurst, 'The Faith of Australian Prime Ministers', p. 10 (Anglican).
4. Philip Ayres, *Malcolm Fraser*, Mandarin Australia (1979), p. 6.
5. John Edwards, *Life wasn't meant to be easy: a political profile of Malcolm Fraser,* Mayhem (1977), p. 22.
6. Malcolm Fraser and Margaret Simons, *Malcolm Fraser: The Political Memoirs,* The Miegunyah Press (2010), p. 18.
7. Edwards, *Life wasn't meant to be easy,* pp. 10, 14.
8. Ayres, p. 11.
9. Ibid, pp. 13-19.
10. Ibid, p. 22.
11. Quoted in Edwards, *Life wasn't meant to be easy,* p. 17.
12. Ayres, p. 29.
13. Ibid, p. 28.
14. Ibid, p. 31.
15. Fraser and Simons, p. 24.
16. Ayres, p. 35.
17. Fraser and Simons, pp. 45-46.
18. Ibid, p. 45.
19. Quoted in Hugh Trevor-Roper, *The Wartime Diaries*, edited by Richard Davenport-Hines, I.B. Tauris (2012), p. 42.
20. Quoted in Fraser and Simons, p. 48.
21. Ibid.
22. Quoted in Ayres, p. 53. My emphasis.
23. Fraser and Simons, pp. 7, 235-37; Ayres, pp. 193-96. For the full text of the introductory section of the lecture, see Sally Warhaft (ed.), *Well May We Say The Speeches That Made Australia,* Black Inc. (2004), pp. 463-65.
24. See D.M. White and D.A. Kemp (eds.), *Malcolm Fraser on Australia*, Hill of Content (1986), pp. 110-111.
25. Quoted in Ayres, p. 40.
26. See Ayres, p. 193.
27. Fraser and Simons, pp. 234-35, Ayres, pp. 190-91.
28. Edwards, *Life wasn't meant to be easy*, p. 27.
29. Fraser and Simons, p. 271.
30. Edwards, *Life wasn't meant to be easy,* p. 27.
31. Quoted in White and Kemp, p. 170.
32. Quoted in Gough Whitlam, *The Truth of the Matter,* Penguin Books Australia, second edition (1983), p. 60.
33. As to Menzies' attitude in 1974, when Bill Snedden was the Liberal leader, see Henderson, *Letters to My Daughter,* p. 260 ("This is something that shocks me. The House of Representatives is the House that is in charge of the finances of the country ... for the Senate to deny supply to the Government of the country is a matter without precedent"). Menzies changed his tune in 1975, giving fulsome support to Fraser and Kerr in private: see Martin, *A Life, Volume 2,* p. 563.
34. As to Gorton, see Gerard Henderson, 'John Grey Gorton' in Grattan (ed.), *Australian Prime Ministers,* p. 300 (Gorton voted ALP at the December 1975 election in protest). As to McMahon, see Robbie Swan, 'McMahon never made it to the pages of Penthouse', *The Canberra Times*, p. 4 ("totally wrong").
35. Fraser and Simons, p. 19.
36. Ayres, p. 142.
37. Fraser and Simons, pp. 175-76.
38. Ayres, p. 145.
39. Quoted in Edwards, *Life wasn't meant to be easy,* p. 49.
40. Quoted in Ayres, p. 129. See also White and Kemp, p. 110, quoting Fraser's speech on 3 October 1979 at the National

Youth Conference in Canberra ("For an individual and for a nation, the way that they walk through life I think is infinitely more important than the position they ultimately achieve.")

41. Fraser and Simons, p. 13.
42. Quoted in White and Kemp, p. 65.
43. Fitzgerald, *The Pope's Battalions*, p. 238.
44. Quoted in White and Kemp, p. 126.
45. Ibid, p. 43.
46. Quoted in Ayres, p. 53.
47. Ibid, p. 54.
48. Quoted in Fraser and Simons, p. 7.
49. Fraser and Simons, p. 7.
50. Warwick Fairfax, *The Triple Abyss: Towards a Modern Synthesis*, Geoffrey Bles (1965), p. 410.

BOB HAWKE

1. James Cunningham, 'Clem Hawke, thoughtful man of humour, integrity', *The Age*, 26 December 1989, p. 15.
2. Stan Anson, *Bob Hawke: An emotional life*, McPhee Gribble (1991), pp. 17, 19.
3. Bob Hawke, *The Hawke Memoirs*, William Heinemann Australia (1994), pp. 22-23.
4. Sue Pieters-Hawke, *Hazel: My Mother's Story*, Pan Macmillan (2011), p. 53
5. Ibid.
6. See Hazel Hawke, *My Own Life: An Autobiography*, The Text Publishing Company (1992), pp. 77-78, 99-100, 116-19, 134
7. Neal Blewett, 'Robert James Lee Hawke' in Grattan (ed.), *Australian Prime Ministers*, p. 386.
8. See generally John Potts, *A History of Charisma*, Palgrave Macmillan, (2009).
9. Robert Pullan, *Bob Hawke: A Portrait*, Methuen of Australia (1980), p. 22.
10. Bob Hawke, p. 3.
11. Ibid, p. 8. See also Hazel Hawke, p. 28.
12. Blewett, p. 382.
13. Bob Hawke, p. 5.
14. Pullan, p. 23.
15. Bob Hawke, p. 3.
16. Ibid, p. 4.
17. Pullan, pp. 22-23.
18. Bob Hawke, p. 4.
19. Anson, p. 25.
20. Pullan, p. 22.
21. Bob Hawke, p. 4.
22. See generally Phillip Pendal, 'Hawke, Albert Redvers George (Bert) (1900–1986)', *Australian Dictionary of Biography*, National Centre of Biography, Australian National University, http://adb.anu.edu.au/biography/hawke-albert-redvers-george-bert-12608/text22711, accessed 31 January 2013.
23. Bob Hawke, p. 13; cf. Pullan, pp. 37-38.
24. Bob Hawke, p. 14.
25. Ibid, p. 20.
26. Hazel Hawke, p. 26.
27. Ibid, pp. 34-35.
28. Bob Hawke, p. 17; Hazel Hawke, p. 34.
29. Hazel Hawke, pp. 35, 37.
30. Ibid, p. 37.
31. Ibid, p. 39.
32. Pieters-Hawke, pp. 50-52; see also Bob Hawke, p. 18.
33. Pullan, pp. 52-53.
34. Bob Hawke, p. 21.
35. Quoted in Pieters-Hawke, p. 53.
36. Pullan, pp. 52-54.
37. D'Alpuget, Blanche, *Robert J Hawke, Prime Minister: A biography*, Melbourne University Press (2010), p. 11.
38. Bob Hawke, pp. 20-21.
39. See Roy Williams, *God, Actually: Why God probably exists, Why Jesus was probably divine, and Why the 'rational' objections to religion are unconvincing*, Lion (2009), pp. 300-04, 319-24.
40. Hazel Hawke, p. 39.
41. John Hurst, *Hawke: The definitive biography*, Angus & Robertson (1979), pp. 18-19.
42. Anson, p. 111.
43. Antonio Buti, *Sir Ronald Wilson: A Matter of Conscience*, UWA Press (2007), p. 37.
44. Pullan, p. 54.
45. Hazel Hawke, p. 83.
46. Ibid, p. 47.
47. Bob Hawke, p. 25.
48. Ibid, p. 27.
49. Hazel Hawke, p. 54.
50. D'Alpuget, p. 11. See also Pullan, p. 54 ("I just didn't know").
51. D'Alpuget, p. 11.
52. Blewett, p. 383.
53. Ibid.
54. Bob Hawke, p. 34.
55. Ibid.

56. Hazel Hawke, p. 83.
57. Blewett, p. 383.
58. Ibid, p. 384.
59. Quoted in Hurst, p. 141.
60. Hazel Hawke, pp. 109-10.
61. Blewett, p. 384.
62. Quoted in Carroll, *Australia's Prime Ministers*, p. 262.
63. Craig McGregor, *Time of Testing: The Bob Hawke Victory*, Penguin Books (1983), p. 151.
64. Anson, p. 112.
65. Blewett, p. 389.
66. Megalogenis, *The Australian Moment*, p. 231.
67. A transcript of the segment is reproduced in Pullan, p. 137.
68. Bob Hawke, p. 509.

PAUL KEATING

1. Anne Henderson, *Mary MacKillop's Sisters: A Life Unveiled*, HarperCollins (1997), p. 305.
2. Edna Carew, *Keating: A Biography*, Allen & Unwin (1988), p. 7
3. Kim Beazley, quoted in Carew, p. 194; see also Don Watson, *Recollections of a Bleeding Heart: A Portrait of Paul Keating PM*, Knopf (2002), pp. 59-60.
4. Watson, p. 3.
5. Carew, p. 54.
6. Fitzgerald, *The Pope's Battalions*, pp. 287-88.
7. Anne Henderson, *Mary MacKillop's Sisters*, p. 307.
8. Jonathan Sacks, *The Dignity of Difference: How to Avoid the Clash of Civilizations*, Continuum (2002), p. 60.
9. David Day, 'Paul John Keating' in Grattan (ed.), *Australia's Prime Ministers*, pp. 414, 435.
10. John Edwards, *Keating: The Inside Story*, Viking (1996), p. 35.
11. Paul Keating, "Australia and Asia and the New Order after the Financial Crisis", 11th Anniversary Lecture, marking the 64th anniversary of John Curtin's death, 2 July, 2009, available online at http://john.curtin.edu.au/events/speeches/keating2009.html
12. Michael Gordon, *A True Believer: Paul Keating*, University of Quensland Press (1996), p. 32.
13. Carew, p. 183.
14. Watson, p. 3.
15. Father Michael McCarthy, quoted in Carew, p. 7.
16. Ibid.
17. Gordon, p. 33; see also Edwards, pp. 36, 39.
18. Carew, p. 7.
19. Watson, p. 4.
20. Anne Henderson, *Mary MacKillop's Sisters*, p. 305.
21. Ibid, p. 307.
22. Ibid, pp. 305-06.
23. Quoted in Edwards, p. 43.
24. Anne Henderson, *Mary MacKillop's Sisters*, p. 305.
25. Ibid, p. 309.
26. Ibid.
27. Quoted in Edwards, p. 43.
28. Watson, pp. 4-5.
29. Carroll, *Australia's Prime Ministers*, pp. 276-77; Watson, p. 13.
30. Watson, p. 11.
31. Anne Henderson, *Mary MacKillop's Sisters*, p. 313.
32. Fitzgerald, p. 260.
33. Edwards, pp. 34-35.
34. Day, 'Paul John Keating', pp. 410-11.
35. Ibid, p. 412. See also Edwards, pp. 72-79, esp at p. 77 (re Whitlam); Carew, pp. 22-27.
36. Quoted in Megalogenis, *The Australian Moment*, p. 29.
37. Edwards, p. 106; Carew, p. 28.
38. Quoted in Watson, p. 143.
39. Edwards, p. 123.
40. *The Sydney Morning Herald*, 20 April 2004.
41. *Gaudium et Spes* (1965), 51.
42. Gordon, p. 57.
43. Quoted in Watson, p. 143.
44. Quoted in Gordon, p. 58.
45. Ibid.
46. Gordon, p. 33.
47. Watson, p. 76.
48. Ibid, p. 535.
49. Quoted in Watson, p. 4.
50. Ibid, pp. 76, 422.
51. Ibid, pp. 533-34.
52. Parliamentary Hansard, 2 February, 1995,

p. 357. See Rosa Inserra, *Mary MacKillop: Holy Mother to the poor,* Cardigan Street Publishers (1995).
53. Watson, p. 650.
54. Paul Kelly, *The March of Patriots: The Struggle for Modern Australia,* Melbourne University Press (2009), p. 201.
55. Watson, p. 444.
56. Ibid, p. 454.
57. Kelly, p. 20.
58. The text of His Holiness's address can be read online at http://www.vatican.va/holy_father/john_paul_ii/speeches/1986/november/documents/hf_jp-ii_spe_19861129_aborigeni-alice-springs-australia_en.html; see also Mark Brett, 'Making Space for justice after Mabo: Theological critiques of sovereignty', *ABC Religion and Ethics,* 3 July 2012, available online at www.abc.net.au/religion/articles.
59. Mark Brett, "Making Space for justice after Mabo: Theological critiques of sovereignty", *ABC Religion and Ethics,* 3 July 2012, available online at http://www.abc.net.au/religion/articles/2012/07/03/3538034.htm.
60. Carew, p. 151.
61. Edwards, p. 36; Carew, p. 46-47.
62. Edwards, p. 303.
63. Ibid, p. 237.
64. Watson, p. 689.
65. Edwards, p. 25; Carew, pp. 94, 192.
66. Watson, p. 63.
67. Greg Barns, *What's Wrong with the Liberal Party?* Cambridge University Press (2003), pp. 29-31.
68. Watson, p. 281.

JOHN HOWARD

1. Marion Maddox, *God Under Howard: The Rise of the Religious Right in Australian Politics,* Allen & Unwin (2005), p. 293 (describing Howard's faith as "amorphous and malleable"). See also Maddox's article 'Best of 2011: God under Gillard', *ABC Religion and Ethics,* 16 January 2012, available online at www.abc.net.au.
2. Paul Kelly, *The March of Patriots,* p. 330 (see note 54 to the section on Paul Keating).

3. Wayne Errington and Peter van Onselen, *John Winston Howard: The Biography,* MUP (2007), pp. 349-50.
4. Maddox, *God Under Howard,* p. 224.
5. See John Howard, *Lazarus Rising: A Personal and Political Autobiography,* HarperCollins (2010), p. 419.
6. Ibid, p. 421.
7. Maddox, *God Under Howard,* pp. 38, 282.
8. Quoted in Kelly, p. 290.
9. Warhurst, 'The Faith of Australian Prime Ministers', p. 11.
10. Howard, p. 227.
11. Ibid, p. 15
12. Ibid.
13. Errington and van Onselen, p. 16.
14. Howard, p. 15.
15. Errington and van Onselen, p. 15.
16. Ibid, p. 4; Howard, p. 8.
17. Errington and van Onselen, p. 15.
18. Maddox, *God Under Howard,* p. 3.
19. Howard, p. 132.
20. Maddox, *God Under Howard,* p. 2.
21. Errington and van Onselen, pp. 11, 16-17.
22. Ibid, p. 79.
23. Maddox, *God Under Howard,* pp. 6-7.
24. Ibid, p. 7.
25. Michelle Grattan, 'John Winston Howard' in Grattan (ed.), *Australian Prime Ministers,* p. 442
26. See generally Don Wright, *Alan Walker: Conscience of the Nation,* Open Book Publishers (2003).
27. Errington and van Onselen, p. 11.
28. Maddox, *God Under Howard,* p. 19.
29. Craig McGregor, 'What John Howard wants', *The Sydney Morning Herald,* 20 June 1987.
30. Errington and van Onselen, p. 26.
31. Maddox, *God Under Howard,* pp. 149-50.
32. Ibid, pp. 243-44.
33. Ibid, p. 251ff.
34. Quoted in Frank Brennan, *Acting On Conscience: How can we responsibly mix law, religion and politics?* University of Queensland Press (2007), pp. 119-20; see also Howard, p. 43
35. Howard, p. 243.
36. Ibid; see also Maddox, *God Under Howard,* p. 189.
37. Graham Freudenberg, *A Figure of Speech: A political memoir,* John Wiley (2005), p. 112.

38. See Howard, p. 489 (on drugs); David Barnett and Pru Goward, *John Howard, Prime Minister*, Viking (1997), p. 754 and Maddox, *God Under Howard*, p. 52 (on euthanasia); Brennan, p. 182 and Maddox, p. 96 (on gay marriage).
39. Maddox, *God Under Howard*, pp. 78-80.
40. Ibid, p. 75.
41. Howard, pp. 73-75.
42. Grattan, p. 456.
43. Errington and van Onselen, p. 70.
44. Ibid, p. 224.
45. Maddox, *God Under Howard*, pp. 42-45.
46. Quoted in Waleed Aly, 'What's Right? The future of conservatism in Australia', *Quarterly Essay* 37, 2010, p. 77
47. Ibid, pp. 76-78. See generally Anne Manne, 'Love and Money', *Quarterly Essay* 29, Black Inc (2008).
48. See generally Jim Wallis, *God's Politics: Why the American Right Gets It Wrong and the Left Doesn't Get It*, Lion (2005), pp. 87-205.
49. Howard, p. 441.
50. See, for example, Frank Rich, *The Greatest Story Ever Sold: The Decline and Fall of Truth – The Real History of the Bush Administration*, Viking (2006).
51. Brennan, p. 101; Carroll, *Australia's Prime Ministers*, pp. 307-08.
52. Statement Against Military Action in Iraq, World Council of Churches Executive Committee, Geneva, 18-21 February, 2003.
53. Quoted in Brennan, p. 110.
54. Ibid, p. 11.
55. Ibid, p. 109.
56. Ibid, pp. 110-11.
57. See, for example, Maddox, *God Under Howard*, p. 130 (as to the churches' views on Hindmarsh Island) and pp. 143-45 (on the Howard Government's response to Wik).
58. See generally David Marr and Marion Wilkinson, *Dark Victory*, Allen & Unwin (2003); Margot O'Neill, *Blind Conscience*, New South (2008). Some of the authors' opinions may be open to question, but as far as I am aware the facts as they stated them have never been challenged in any significant way.
59. Marr and Wilkinson, pp. 258-59.

60. Address by John Howard at the National Press Club, 8 November 2001.
61. Quoted in Marr and Wilkinson, p. 262.
62. Ibid, p. 47.
63. Robert Manne with David Corlett, "Sending Them Home: Refugees and the New Politics of Indifference", *Quarterly Essay* 13 (2004), pp. 31-32.
64. Quoted in O'Neill, p. 12.
65. Ibid, p. 186.
66. Ibid, p. 16.
67. Quoted in Peter Hartcher, *To the Bitter End: The dramatic story behind the fall of John Howard and the rise of Kevin Rudd*, Allen & Unwin (2009), p. 239; Kelly, p. 356.
68. See Aly, 'What's Right?', p. 66.
69. Alister McGrath, *Christian Theology*, Blackwell Publishing (2007), p. 361.
70. See Greg Clarke, 'Do Christians need a Christian prime minister?' *The Drum*, 29 July 2010, available online at http://www.abc.net.au/unleashed/35572.html.
71. Peter van Onselen (ed.), *Liberals and Power: The Road Ahead*, Melbourne University Press (2008), p. 37.
72. See Paul Gallagher, *Faith and Duty: The John Anderson Story*, Random House Australia (2006), p. 151; Peter Costello with Peter Coleman, *The Costello Memoirs: The Age of Prosperity*, Melbourne University Press (2008), pp. 160-63.
73. Grattan, p. 458.
74. Interview with Tony Jones, 'Lateline', ABC Television, 8 November 2001.
75. Errington and van Onselen, p. 188.
76. *The Sydney Morning Herald*, 12 December 2005.

KEVIN RUDD

1. John Harrison, 'The Bonhoeffer Effect', *ABC Religion and Ethics*, 31 August 2010, available online at www.abc.net.au.
2. Barrie Cassidy, *The Party Thieves: The Real Story of the 2010 Election*, Melbourne University Press (2010), p. 7.
3. E.g., Roland Boer, 'Our Christian Prime Minister', *New Matilda*, 2 June 2009, available online at http://newmatilda.com.
4. Nicholas Stuart, *Kevin Rudd: an unauthorised political biography*, Scribe

(2007), p. 146; Macklin, *Kevin Rudd*, pp. 134, 168, 209 (see note 15 to the Introduction).

5. Stuart, p. 100.
6. See, for example, Christopher Pearson, 'Rudd a cafeteria Christian', *The Australian*, 10 February 2007, available online at www.theaustralian.com.au/news/opinion; Andrew Bolt, 'Who is the real "Kevin Rudd"?', *Herald Sun*, 5 October 2007, available online at http://blogs.news.com.au/heraldsun; Janet Albrechtsen, 'PM proves a convert to the politics of faith', *The Australian*, 14 July 2009, available online at http://blogs.theaustralian.news.com.au.
7. See generally Peter van Onselen, 'Rudd more sinned against than sinning', *The Weekend Australian*, March 23-24, 2013, p. 20; Nicholas Stuart, *Rudd's Way: November 2007-June 2010*, Scribe (2010), passim, esp. pp. 165, 170; Lindsay Tanner, *Politics With Purpose: occasional observations on public and private life*, Scribe (2012); Maxine McKew, *Tales From the Political Trenches*, Melbourne University Publishing (2012); Troy Bramston, *Looking for the Light on the Hill: Modern Labor's Challenges*, Scribe (2011); Phillip Adams, interview with Kevin Rudd, Late Night Live, ABC Radio National, 4 August 2010, full transcript available online at www.abc.net.au/radionational; Ranya Alkadamani, 'Rudd was a demanding boss but not a difficult one', *The Australian*, 18 September 2012, p. 14.
8. Cassidy, pp. 38-41.
9. See generally Jim Wallis, *Seven Ways to Change the World: Reviving Faith and Politics*, Lion (2008), pp. 111-28.
10. Matt Prater, Pastor of New Hope Church in Brisbane, interview with Kevin Rudd in 2006; available online at www.historymakersradio.com; transcript of interview available online at www.rodbenson.com [incorrectly dated as 2009] ('Matt Prater interview').
11. John Howard, 'Why we took on Saddam's Iraq', *The Australian*, 25 October 2010.
12. Stuart, pp. 136-38.
13. Mark Latham, *The Latham Diaries*, Melbourne University Press (2005), p. 213.
14. Tony Jones, interview with Kevin Rudd,

'Lateline', ABC Television, 2 October 2006, transcript available online at www.abc.net.au/lateline/content/2006.
15. Kevin Rudd, 'Faith in Politics', *The Monthly*, October 2006, available online at www.themonthly.com.au.
16. See David Marr, 'Power Trip: The Political Journey of Kevin Rudd', *Quarterly Essay* 38, 2010, p. 57, Maddox, *God Under Howard*, p. 283; Stuart, pp. 120-24, 209.
17. Stuart, pp. 122-23.
18. Marr, 'Power Trip', p. 85.
19. Stuart, p. 21.
20. See Kevin Rudd's maiden speech to the House of Representatives, 11 November 1998, available online at http://parlinfo.aph.gov.au/parlInfo/search/display/display.w3p;query=Id%3A%22chamber%2Fhansardr%2F1998-11-11%2F0134%22.
21. Macklin, p. 39.
22. Marr, 'Power Trip', p. 10.
23. Macklin, p. 39.
24. Marr, 'Power Trip', pp. 8-9; see also Kevin Rudd's maiden speech to the House of Representatives, 11 November 1998 (see note 20 above).
25. Macklin, p. 30.
26. Matt Prater interview.
27. Marr, 'Power Trip', p. 10.
28. Stuart, pp. 27-28.
29. Marr, p. 7. Cf. Stuart, pp. 27-29; Macklin pp. 42-51.
30. See Marr, pp. 11-13; Stuart, pp. 29-34; Macklin, pp. 52-54.
31. Marr, pp. 13-15; Stuart, p. 35; Macklin, pp. 54-56.
32. 'The God Factor', 8 May 2005, *Compass*, ABC Television, transcript available online at www.abc.net.au/compass ('The God Factor').
33. Marr, p. 13.
34. Macklin, p. 67.
35. Stuart, p. 36
36. Quoted in Marr, p. 14.
37. Ibid, p. 8.
38. Macklin, p. 59.
39. Quoted in Marr, p. 18.
40. See MacCallum, *The Good, the Bad and the Unlikely*, p. 200.
41. Marr, p. 20.
42. Marr, pp. 20-21.

43. Stuart, p. 46; Marr, pp. 20-21; Kevin Rudd interview with the author.
44. Macklin, p. 67.
45. Stuart, p. 47.
46. Ibid, pp. 58-59.
47. Ibid, p. 54.
48. Marr, p. 23.
49. Macklin, p. 163.
50. Stuart, p. 52; Marr, p. 22.
51. Kevin Rudd, quoted in Macklin, p. 70.
52. Stuart, p. 52.
53. Ibid, p. 54.
54. Macklin, p. 83.
55. Stuart, p. 68; Macklin, p. 82.
56. Quoted in 'New Australian prime minister has Catholic roots", *Catholic Review*, December 2007, available online at http://catholicreview.org/article/work/working-families/new-australian-prime-minister-has-catholic-roots.
57. Macklin, pp. 163-65.
58. Marr, pp. 56-57.
59. Matt Prater interview.
60. Marr, pp. 64-65.
61. Stuart, pp. 244-45.
62. Warhurst, 'The Faith of Australian Prime Ministers', p. 6.
63. Ibid. See also Margot Saville, *The Battle for Bennelong: The adventures of Maxine McKew, aged 50something*, Melbourne University Press (2007), p. 81.
64. See generally Lenore Taylor and David Uren, *Shitstorm: Inside Labor's Darkest Days*, Melbourne University Press (2010).
65. Ian Macfarlane, Governor of the Reserve Bank of Australia (1996-2006), quoted in Kevin Rudd's maiden speech to the House of Representatives, 11 November 1998 (see note 20 above).
66. See Cassidy, pp. 36-39.
67. Marr, pp. 66-67.
68. Marr, p. 79; see also Macklin, pp. 151-55.
69. Marr, p. 49.
70. Caroline Overingham, *Inside the Australian Wheat Board Scandal*, Allen & Unwin (2007); Stephen Bartos, *Against the Grain – the AWB Scandal and Why It Happened*, UNSW Press (2007).
71. The God Factor (see note 32 above).

JULIA GILLARD
1. Transcript of Interview with Jon Faine, ABC Radio 774, 29 June 2010, available online at http://www.pm.gov.au/press-office/transcript-interview-jon-faine ("Jon Faine interview").
2. Jacqueline Kent, *The Making of Julia Gillard*, Penguin (2010), p. 104.
3. See Warhurst, 'The religious beliefs of Australia's prime ministers' (note 1 to the section on Alfred Deakin).
4. See, e.g., John Warhurst, 'Reflections on Gillard's atheism', *Eureka Street*, 16 October 2011, available online at www.eurekastreet.com.au/article.aspx?aeid=24159 ("the first unequivocally atheist PM").
5. See http://conservativeweasel.blogspot.com.au/2013/01/wikipedia-editors-argue-over-calling.html.
6. Kent, pp. 12-13.
7. Ibid, pp. 22-23.
8. Ibid, pp. 10-11.
9. Jon Faine interview.
10. Quoted in Kent, p. 16.
11. Jon Faine interview.
12. See, for example, the website of the Coral Coast Christian Church, http://www.coralcoastchurch.org/july10.htm.
13. Kent, pp. 29-30.
14. Ibid, p. 33ff.
15. Ibid, p. 39.
16. Ibid, p. 84ff.
17. Ibid, p. 279.
18. Ibid, p. 17.
19. Ibid, p. 71.
20. Interview with Tony Jones, 'Lateline', ABC Television, 12 September 2006, transcript available online at http://www.abc.net.au/lateline/content/2006/s1739520.htm
21. The God Factor (see note 32 to the section on Kevin Rudd).
22. Kent, p. 238ff.
23. Quoted in Kent, p. 263.
24. See ACL website.
25. Warhurst, 'Reflections on Gillard's atheism' (see note 4 above).
26. Kent, p. 273.
27. Ibid, pp. 3, 243.
28. Ibid, p. 279.
29. See Kent, pp. 275 ("I think that one of the problems for women ...").

30. See, for example, Malcolm Farr, 'What Peter Slipper's sexist text messages actually said', 9 October, 2012, available online at http://www.news.com.au/national-news/revealed-what-peter-slippers-sexist-text-messages-actually-said/story-fndo4eg9-1226492172640.

31. For a full transcript of the speech see http://www.smh.com.au/opinion/political-news/transcript-of-julia-gillards-speech-20121010-27c36.html.

32. Kent, p. 101. See also Warhurst, 'Reflections on Gillard's atheism' (note 4).

33. Quoted in Kent, p. 212.

CONCLUSIONS

1. Gordon, *A True Believer*, p. 264.

2. See Edwards, *Curtin's Gift*, pp. 23-25; Day, *John Curtin*, pp. 294-95, 517-18.

3. See Hal G.P. Colebatch, "The Left Rewrites Its History on Refugees", *Quadrant*, October 2010; Robert Manne, "Tragedy of Errors", *The Monthly*, March 2013, pp. 18-25.

4. Manning Clark, *A History of Australia*, Volume VI, p. 498.